MEATH

towards a history

Dit wish to Loveen

Ham O'Conn hide
G Mean McCing (Pshren)

MEATH

towards a history

Margaret Conway

First published 2010

The History Press Ireland
119 Lower Baggot Street
Dublin 2, Ireland
www.thehistorypress.ie

British Library Cataloguing in Publication Data.
A catalogue record for this book is available from the British Library.

ISBN 978 1 84588 978 4

Typesetting and origination by The History Press
Printed in Great Britain

CONTENTS

FOREWORD

PLAIN LIVING AND HIGH THINKING

My mother was an extraordinary woman. Although she would make no claims to be a historian or a skilled researcher, these were the pursuits she engaged in all of her life. In sorting her papers, I have been astounded at the depth and breadth of her work, and by her respect for the knowledge stored in the living tradition. There is correspondence with Máirtín Ó Cadhain, author of *Cré na Cille*, with Séamus Ó Duilearga and Seán Ó Súileabháin of the Irish Folklore Commission, with Alan Bliss, of University College Dublin whose field was Hiberno-English, and with sources in the United States in pursuit of her interest in the life and deeds of John Boyle O'Reilly, among others.

She was *ildánach* – gifted – in many ways. She made a perfect pen-and-ink drawing of Bective Abbey when she brought us as children to see it, and some of her paintings are in the collection of Meath County Council. In her younger years, she made all our clothes: I remember in particular my first Communion in 1936, when she made the outfit, and embroidered a Celtic motif on the dress, cloak and headband. She produced plays with the Ballivor Amateur Dramatic Society – one of which was *The Rising of the Moon* by Lady Gregory. In later years she was often invited to take part in discussions on social and religious themes in the new Irish television service Telefís Éireann.

Maighréad Uí Chonmhidhe was a native of County Louth, the youngest of eight children of John Callan and Annie (*née* Durnin) of Colga in the parish of Reaghstown, who bought out their small holding under the Wyndham Act of 1903. Both the Callans and the Durnins had a tradition of learning. Her paternal grandfather was literate in Irish and could read

Margaret Conway.

English, and her mother's family believed themselves to be connected by blood to the eighteenth-century Gaelic poet Peadar Ó Doirnín (Peter Durnin).

The unwritten motto of the household she was reared in would have been 'plain living and high thinking'. Of her four brothers who emigrated to the United States, James published poems in *Ireland's Own*, and another, Bernie, played the violin in the orchestra of the Waldorf Astoria in New York. The youngest Philip wrote plays published by Gills (now Gill & Macmillan) popular with drama societies, scripted a radio series *Round the Fire*, broadcast on Radio Éireann in the forties, and another series of sketches entitled *According to Cocker*. Her only sister, Annie Kelly taught at the national school in Stormanstown, County Louth. She had a great repertoire of traditional songs which were recorded by Seán Corcoran, a folk-song collector.

The Callan children attended the local national school in Aclint. Maighréad was a much-loved child, and when she reached the age of fourteen and the end of her primary education, the master advised her family to send her to a secondary school for a year, as there were no vacancies for a national school monitor at that time. 'This entailed,' as she wrote in 'Child of the Century', an autobiographical fragment, 'considerable pinching and straining for, in homes like ours, the economic side of the household was constantly discussed and children realised almost from the cradle that it was hard to make ends meet and keep out of debt.'

She spent a year at the Sacred Heart Convent secondary school in Armagh, where pupils were introduced to finding sources of information for themselves, and completed her term as monitor in the Mercy Convent in Dundalk during the years 1916-18. It was during her final year there that she attended Irish courses in Omeath, where an Irish College was founded around 1917 and where Irish was still spoken well into the twentieth century. With W.P. Ryan, she was awarded her qualification as a teacher of Irish in 1918.

She gained first place in the King's Scholarship for entrance into Carysfort Teacher Training College in Blackrock County Dublin. After leaving Carysfort in 1920, her first teaching post was at King's Inns primary school in Dublin's north inner city, run by the Sisters of Charity, and she lodged in Berkeley Street, near Parnell Square and O'Connell Street. These were the heady years of the War of Independence, extraordinary and exhilarating times to be young and taking part in the National Movement.

Margaret Conway's parents, John and Annie Conway *c.* 1919.

Maighréad was an active member of Craobh an Chéitinnigh (Keating Branch) of the Gaelic League in Parnell Square, through which chance meetings with the likes of Michael Collins and many others who had distinguished careers in the public service afterwards were not uncommon. She also knew Seán T. O'Ceallaigh who was later President of Ireland (1945–1959). The League seemed to create an unspoken bond between people of various strands of nationalism. No one who lived through these years could fail to devote themselves to the betterment of the new nation they were committed to bring about.

9

The post-Treaty split ushered in a time of great personal sadness for her. Some acquaintances were no longer willing to greet her on the street – something she found hard to understand – and some of her closest friends were interned by the leaders of the fledgling state. Worst of all, from her perspective, the New Establishment turned its back on the common people and everything that the revolution had meant to her. The Military Ball held at the Metropole Ballroom on New Year's Eve 1922 was indicative of this disregard, the full dress uniforms re-enacting the symbolism of the former colonial masters. Even the release of some of the internees could not recreate the youthful company that had had such a formative influence on her.

The loss of her father in June of 1923 prompted her to make a clean break with the city, and in 1923 Maighréad came to teach in Coolronan in the parish of Ballivor in County Meath. She met my father, Thomas F. Conway, also a teacher and one of a long-established Meath family who shared her

King's Inns primary school *c.* 1922.

Coolronan school pupils *c.* 1932.

patriotism and love of the cultural heritage of the Irish language. Her marriage to him in 1924 was the beginning of her enchantment with Meath's
history, people and landscape.

My mother was soon active in public life and, after the local elections
of 1934, she was appointed as one of two teacher representatives on the
Vocational Education Committee; the other was Pádraig Ó Luasaigh,
a native of Baile Mhúirne in West Cork. Together they were willing to
respond to the demand for evening classes in Irish. She served on the Library
Committee, and was a strong supporter of the county library service. She
also served on voluntary committees: Conradh na Gaeilge, naturally, and the
Committee for the Restoration of Stella's Cottage spring to mind.

Margaret Callan (later Conway) and monitor colleagues, Mercy Convent, Dundalk
c. 1918.

Throughout her working life she felt called upon to put her wisdom and experience at the service of whatever new movement was being put in train. It was almost inevitable that she would be appointed Secretary of Meath Archaeological and Historical Society, which was launched in 1937, and that she should hold that position until 1962. She was competent and efficient in the basic administrative tasks, maintained the records of the society, convened meetings, and wrote detailed reports of council meetings. The annual reports she wrote were comprehensive and showed her awareness of their usefulness as future material for the society's history.

At crucial moments she summarised the story of the society to date, incorporating those parts from the earlier days as she learned of them. I have some of these reports in their original form, in her strong, legible hand, with few if any corrections. She was a clear thinker and expressed what she thought cogently, an ability which stood her in good stead in her role as editor of *Ríocht na Midhe*, the society's learned journal. She could give context and form to an article with a simple phrase or sentence, and could iron out an awkward expression with a minimum of alteration.

In a letter to my mother, Helen Roe, a distinguished scholar and the first woman president of the *Royal Society of Antiquaries of Ireland*, describes a newly formed historical society in the Irish Midlands as being 'full of aimless and formless good will', and goes on to pay tribute to my mother, 'I do not think it will long survive unless the willing horse is discovered somewhere … as you full well know you're it [for Meath] and the grey mare too!'

She delivered lectures at the society's outings, one on Oliver Goldsmith in 1939 at the society's outing to Lissoy and Ballymahon, and on Tlachtgha in 1957 at their outing to that famed hill. (Both these lectures have been published in *Seanchas na Midhe*, a selection of lectures (Sligo 2009)). She was the first editor of *Ríocht na Midhe* from 1955 until 1967. She wrote fluently, with style and a sense of history, and had the capacity to draw together ideas from various sources and convey them with clarity, intelligence and imagination.

In addition to her many practical gifts was her generosity of spirit. She was modest, devoid of vanity, serene and comfortable in her personality and so seemed to have all the time in the world for whatever was happening at a particular moment. My parents' household was a welcoming one, and the atmosphere they fostered was one free of constraint: we had warmth, comfort, laughter, endless conversation and a sense of joy in living. We also all had our jobs to do, indoors and out. I loved keeping her company on the evenings when she opened the library cupboard in the national school next door, to help placing the returned books back on the shelves. Among the people who received hospitality through the years were Peadar O'Donnell, James Plunkett and Benedict Kiely, Professor McBride of University College Dublin, Dr Lucas of the National Museum, hitchhikers from the continent, and traveller women sheltering in harsh weather.

Her work with the society, to which she brought all her gifts and commitment, was done in her spare time from her teaching. As a primary school teacher, she saw her role as that of a wise godparent to the children who, without disturbing the instinctive respect they had for their parents, awakened in their hearts a sense of wonder at the beauty and riches of the world and a desire to use to the full their gifts of mind and body. I spent four years as her pupil, from the age of eight to twelve, and I recall how she appreciated the children's knowledge of ballads brought from home; the beautiful hand-stitching on the dress of one of the children as an illustration of back-stitching; her sharing of her love of particular poems with the class. We delved into the greats – Tennyson's *Morte D'Arthur* and Shakespeare's *Julius Caesar*, as well as classics of Irish literature in English and in Irish.

Her participation in the School Folklore project in 1937, initiated by the Folklore Commission, was an opportunity for her to tell the children how valuable their home culture and traditions were. Her offer of articles to *The Meath Chronicle* was a natural continuation of her educational philosophy and her respect for the beliefs and traditions of the home culture.

In the issue of 15 December 1956, *The Meath Chronicle* introduced *The Parish History Of Meath* with these words:

> Mrs Maighréad Uí Chonmhidhe N.T., Moattown, Kildalkey (secretary of the Meath Archaeological and Historical Society) has very kindly prepared a series of articles on Meath history which will appear week by week in 'The Meath Chronicle' on this page and in this place. She is a very modest lady, and we claim for her what she deprecates – the scholarship and the assiduity which goes with it, on this subject, wide as it is ...

My mother offered the articles to the county newspaper because she, in common with others whose names regularly appeared in printed reports of historical activities, was often asked questions about the history of particular places in the county. She refers to Dean Cogan's scholarly work *Ecclesiastical History of Meath*, and writes that:

> ... much of the local history has yet to be written, and it can only be written from information collected on the spot ... If local history is to be compiled we must do it ourselves – we ordinary plain people of Meath, who love our own homes and farms and villages, and feel the charm which haunts them like perfume from a vanishing Eden.
>
> I propose therefore during this winter by courtesy of The Meath Chronicle to give in all humility, the benefit of my limited experience in this field to those interested.

So began the series of articles *The Parish History of Meath*, to be followed by a longer series *Towards a History of Meath*, both collected in this volume. In a letter to the editor of *The Meath Chronicle*, offering to write the second series, she outlined her plans, 'Since I finished the last series I have been thinking of doing something not quite so haphazard – not indeed a real history, but a kind of chatty series – partly chronological, partly topographical.' And she concludes, 'I would like to use the long or the short term of life left to me doing something useful for our own county.'

My mother was retired from teaching by then and it was her custom to work for a few hours every morning in her study from about eleven o'clock after she had had her morning cup of coffee. Among her books was a rare copy of Dean Cogan. She had Revd John Brady's booklets on the history of the parishes of County Meath, William Wilde's *The Beauties of the Boyne and its tributary the Blackwater*, P.W. Joyce's *Irish Names of Places*, and Justin McCarthy's *History of Ireland*. There was also *Royal Meath* by Revd Donnchadh O'Meachair OMI and various other works.

She had rescued account books from bonfires when a 'big house' was being vacated. She had notes of the material collected in Coolronan for the Schools Folklore Collection in 1937, and copies of *Béaloideas*. She also had access to the Meath County Library copies of Thompson's *Statistical Survey of County Meath*, Books of Survey and Distribution, and Archdeacon John Healy's works. Her memory was prodigious and she referred to the notes she made from her reading on index cards only to check references. The articles were written on lined foolscap paper which came in folded pages of about eight double pages. The deadline she worked to was probably a week in advance and sometimes she sent her copy by post but more often she drove into An Uaimh and submitted it by hand.

A measure of the success of the articles and the chord they struck with readers of the newspaper was the size of her weekly postbag. It grew quickly during the first series, and most weeks, during the second series, replies to her appeals for information from her readers numbered in the hundreds and came from as far afield as the United States. Again and again in her writing she is appealing to her audience to fill in gaps in our knowledge as much as she is trying to convey to the current generation the value of what they have inherited.

Méadhbh Piskorska

ONE

ANTIQUITY

NEWGRANGE
A CHALLENGE TO MODERN ENGINEERS

The estuary of the Boyne, the *Inver Colpa* of the legends, separates the modern county of Meath from Louth, and six miles up the river, where the flat coastal land gives place to high sloping banks, stands the ancient and beautiful town of Drogheda. It is the gateway to the central plain, and it has a dignity in its old grey walls, and turrets and spires that makes it the worthy entrance to any kingdom.

The name, *Droicead Átha*, means the bridge of the ford; the first bridge, no doubt of wood, may date from the seventh or eighth century, for we know there was then an abbot who is recorded in the Annals as 'the bridge-maker'. But long before there was a bridge, the ford was of great importance, because it carried the great North Road across the river, and before there was a road, it must have been an important crossing place for the very earliest inhabitants of the Boyne Valley.

A few miles further inland, the river gives a sweep around a stretch of land in which today we may see many great mounds and standing stones. If one takes the road from Drogheda to Slane, signposts will show the way to Dowth, Knowth and Newgrange.

There are three outstanding mounds in the great Bronze Age cemetery of Brúgh na Bóinne, which the late Professor MacAlister describes as 'one of the most important prehistoric monuments in the world'. From the outside, it is hard to realise that the Newgrange mound is an acre in extent and over forty feet high. Entering the mound by its narrow door-way the visitor passes down a more or less straight corridor over sixty feet in length, constructed of stones some fifteen feet long, supporting huge roof slabs.

The great central chamber is about twenty feet in diameter and twenty in height. It has three recesses, one of which contains a large stone hol-lowed like a saucer. The great stones of which the whole is formed are so arranged as to support one another in the form of a dome, on which is piled the twenty-feet layer of stones which form the mound. It would tax the powers of a modern engineer to produce another Newgrange, even if he were given unlimited material and manpower, and all the resources of present-day machinery to aid him. What manner of men, then, produced this structure, which has stood there by the river through the storms and stresses of thirty-five centuries?

They were the Bronze Age people, known in legend as the *Tuatha de Danann* the clan of the god Dana. We know that the first men on earth used tools of wood and stone, and their one great discovery was fire. Then somewhere, sometime, and most probably by accident, it was found that there was a kind of stone that could be melted and moulded into shape; that could be hammered hard; that would take an edge sharper than stone. The age of research had begun. Men searched for metals, experimented with them, and, in a comparatively short time had learned to mix copper and tin into the hard, durable compound we call bronze. Men with bronze tools and weapons are believed to have invaded Ireland about 2,000 years before the birth of Christ. The stone-using natives had no chance against what legend calls 'The Sword of Light' which the strangers flashed aloft. The Tuatha made themselves masters of the Boyne Valley; they lived on the hill-tops of Meath, and buried their dead in palaces more lasting than the homes they occupied in life. The remains they left at Tara, at Brugh na Bóinne, at Loughcrew, at Four Knocks and elsewhere, are all cemeteries.

These tombs were rediscovered during the past century and a half, and most of them had been rifled, at a much earlier period, for the gold which they were believed to contain. In some there were remains of cremated burials, with pottery vessels and beads of amber and other objects. A study of these remains and a comparison with finds in Europe have led antiquar-ians to believe that the Bronze Age people came from the Middle East, had a connection with the civilisations of Egypt, Greece and Crete, and reached Ireland via the Baltics and Scandinavia.

The weight of evidence for these conclusions has filled many learned volumes and to go into any detail about it here would not be possible. I mention one clue to illustrate the kind of evidence the scientific investigator concerns himself with: the ornamentation on the stones. The most remarkable stone at Newgrange is the huge slab that guards the entrance. It has a beautiful pattern of spirals inscribed almost all over it, except at the ends where there is a filling-in of lozenge patterns.

To a lay observer it would seem natural enough that such a pattern might be invented independently in every country of the world; the experts can prove a European connection. More obvious is the similarity between our burial mounds and the pyramids of Egypt. Both point to a belief in a future life and perhaps a worship of the great dead or a faith in their power to help the living. One old name of the Brúgh is the Brúgh (or Palace) of Aongus, the son of the good God, and our legends are full of incidents in which this Aongus came out from his palace to help human warriors when they were hard pressed in battle.

The gigantic burial mounds of the Newgrange type seem to be the work of a special group of people who entered Ireland from the east, somewhere along the coast between Dundalk and Bray. They were aristocrats among builders. Their period is thought by some authorities to have been relatively short, but to be of an earlier date than that of the smaller burial remains found all over the country.

It is believed by some that the beautifully ornamented stones may have been inscribed by an earlier people long before they were used as tombs, and that their art derived from Iberia. But these are questions for the expert, and the ordinary visitor will be satisfied that Newgrange and its sister sites, as well as Fourknocks and Loughcrew, date from, at the latest, 1500BC, and that they are unrivalled in size among megalithic structures.

What is more interesting is the legendary lore relating to them. In our oldest existing manuscripts we have a whole cycle of tales relating to the Tuatha De Danann; stories of Taillte and Lugh; Cian and Balor; Brigid the poetess and Dian Cecht, the great healer; stories of wars and journeys of loves and rivalries; of feats of skill and trials of wit; which make these early shadowy people come alive to us as vividly as the Trojan warriors or the half-human gods of high Olympus.

According to one story, when the Tuatha De Danann came to Ireland, they found before them a people called the Fir Bolg. These they defeated and banished to Connacht, while they themselves lived in the rich lands of Meath. In the final battle the King of the Fir Bolg was slain, and his beautiful wife, Taillte, became the wife of one of the new rulers, and the foster-mother of the boy hero Lugh. She chose her own burial place and asked her husband to cut down the woods all around it so that there should be a great open space around her *leácht* (tomb) where her funeral games could be celebrated. This was done and when she died at the time we now call the first of August, the funeral games were organised by Lugh, and were held every year at the same time. The day became known as *Lugh Nosad*, the funeral games of Lugh, and to this day Lughnasa is the Gaelic name for August. The Book of Lecan dates the death of Taillte as 3500BC, and says that the Aonach of Taillte was celebrated by every king who reigned in Tara from then to the coming of Patrick and for 400 years after.

After that it was held less regularly, owing perhaps to the Danish wars. But we know that as late as 1168 the Annals record that Rory O'Connor celebrated Aonach Tailtean, and so many of the people of Meath, Connacht, and Ulster attended it in that year that their horses were quartered from Mullach Tailltean to Mullach Aidi (the modern hill of Lloyd).

These bare bones of the story show that there is a historical founda-tion for the mythological tales of Ireland. In passing, we might note how many famous women there were in ancient Ireland. Besides this Taillte, who gives her name to Teltown and is the patroness of our county Gaelic sports grounds, there were the three queens of the De Danann: Éire, Fodla, and Banba, whose names came to be given to Ireland, the first being still the official name, and the others now only poetic ones.

Then there was Macha, the warrior queen, whose palace was on the height *of Ard Macha* or Armagh and, at a later time, the famous Maeve of Connacht. Another De Danann woman, Tlachtgha, brought the Lia Fail to Tara. Her *dún* is now known by the rather prosaic name of Hill of Ward. Part of the Loughcrew hills is called Sliabh na Caillighe, the old woman's mountain, and a great stone there is known as the Hag's Chair. There is what seems to be a modern tale of how this old woman dropped the stones on the hills, but she is more aptly regarded by Pearse as the symbol of ageless Ireland:

Mise Eire;
Sine me na an Cailleach Beara.
Mor mo gloir;
Mise a rug Cu Culainn croga.
Mor mo nair;
Mo chlann fein a threig a mathair.
Mise Eire;
Sine me na an Cailleach Beara.

(I am Ireland;
Older I am than the old woman of Beare.
Great my glory;
I bore the valiant Cu Culainn.
Great my shame;
My own children to forsake their mother.
I am Ireland.
Older I am than the Old Woman of Beare.)

The art of storytelling was very highly developed in ancient Ireland, long before any of the tales were written down, and there were many grades of storytellers in the houses of kings, the highest being the *file*. He had to narrate in learned poetic form the *seanchas* and the *dinn-seanchas* (the history and place lore) and the chief stories of Ireland to the lords and nobles assembled at *feis* (feast) or *aonach* (fair).

The telling would be dramatic and might be, in part at least, accompanied by music. It was the counterpart of the theatre of other times, and the audience was no less critical than the modern lovers of, for example, Shakespearean drama, who know in advance every turn of speech and gesture, and compare the manner and interpretation of the actor with others they have seen in the same role. It was long before the tales were written in the form in which they are now extant, and Gerard Murphy, Professor of Celtic Literature at University College Dublin, points out how far the manuscript falls short of the oral narration. It would seem, he says:

... to be related to living story-telling much as the museum today is related to living material culture. For it is the law of oral narration that the story improves as the appreciation of the audience begins to affect the narrator.

Up to the Middle Ages, these wonder tales of Ireland were popular, and they were carried to the continent of Europe by missionaries and other travellers, both orally and in written versions. Some of them became the source of great works of literature in other languages, even down to the travels of Gulliver. The tragedy is that they did not develop unhampered in Ireland itself. The first Norman invaders appreciated Gaelic literature, but as the English language spread, the respect for native culture diminished. Manuscripts were lost or destroyed and oral narrators, without the patronage of the great, lost the classical tradition and told rather simple folk tales to amuse ordinary listeners. There was no printing press to record the old or encourage the new, so we have no Decameron and no Ring Cycle in modern Irish.

But at least we have enough stories left to give life to our ancient monuments, and every native should have at least one good tale to tell to the stranger. At Brúgh na Bóinne what could be more appropriate than *The Wooing of Etain*? You will find it in many children's books and Micheál MacLiammoir used the legend in his play *Where Stars Walk*.

The townland of Colp, not far from the mouth of the Boyne, introduces one of the first of our Gaelic ancestors, for it is named from *Colpa* the swordsman of Milead, who came to Ireland some 700 years before the birth of Christ.

At the time, Greece was the great power in south-eastern Europe, the centre of a wonderfully developed culture whose influence is felt all through the subsequent history of Europe. Materially, it was soon destined to fall before the new military state which had its origins on the day that Romulus and Remus quarrelled over the foundations of their new home on the banks of the Tiber. There was, at the same time, in central Europe, in the highlands where the Danube has its source, another people known to history as the Celts, a fair-skinned, blue-eyed, dark-haired people who had already begun spreading their empire in all directions for centuries.

Wave after wave of Celtic peoples occupied France and Spain and Britain, and spread northwards to intermingle with the Teutonic races of the north. Finally, they reached Ireland, tradition says, by way of Spain. Tradition says too, that their leader, Milead, never came to Ireland, but his father, Brogan, came accompanied by his grandsons, and Scotia, the mother of the boys, was also of the party. As might be expected, the first part of Ireland they sighted was the coast of Kerry.

As they were about to land, the De Danann magicians raised a magic mist which scattered their ships all round the coast. One reached the mouth of the Boyne, but in landing it became submerged in the tide, and Colpa, its captain, was drowned. Ever afterwards the harbour was called *Inbher Colpa*, the river-mouth of Colpa, though since the loss of the Irish language that name has been forgotten by the local people and the townland of Colp is the only Milesian memory that remains.

Serious readers may not be impressed by this legend, but the best antiquarians, basing their conclusions on actual material remains, confirm the Spanish connection. They say that there were several waves of Iron Age people, some from Spain, and others from Northern Europe. These latter were fair-haired and may have been Teutons who had adopted the Celtic language and culture.

It is convenient to call the whole of the Iron Age invaders 'Gaels', as their particular Celtic language is Gaelic. Kindred with Gaelic were the languages of all Western Europe, and traces of them remain in the Anglo-Saxon of England, and the Latin-based languages of France and the Iberian Peninsula. Welsh, Manx, and Breton still survive as separate languages. Many place names on the Continent are of Celtic origin, as well as the vast majority of our own Irish place names. We do not know with any great certainty what names of other words were absorbed into the Gaelic language from the Bronze Age De Danann.

What we do know is that the Milesian invaders, with their bright iron swords, soon conquered them in the physical sense. But it would appear that they were much less civilised, for they adopted many of their customs, like the holding of the funeral games of Tailltean, and respected their places of burial with superstitious awe. It is of interest to us in Meath that the last battle for the mastery of Ireland was fought at Tailltean, for it shows that even then the plain of Meath was the most important part of the country, and that to rule Meath was to rule Ireland.

Legend has it that the De Dannan, when defeated in battle, retired to their dwellings under the hills or *sidheans*, and that they are the *aos sidhe*, the people of the fairy hills, transmuted in popular tradition into the tiny spirits who guard the crocks of gold, steal away human children, and wreak misfortune on men who interfere with their mounds and lone bushes.

Some authorities hold that the De Danann were not people at all, but rather the pagan gods of the Milesians. Be this as it may, the fear of the fairy people, men or gods, has preserved Bronze Age sites from destruction for 2,000 years. Not every *rath* or ring has a tradition of fairies attached to it, and thereby we may get a valuable clue to the antiquity of a particular site. In recent years, even children have ceased to believe these stories, and the bulldozers know no fear. Increasingly, we need an enlightened public spirit to save our ancient monuments from destruction.

The tradition of the crock of gold may, and very probably does, refer to the grave goods buried with distinguished people in the Bronze Age cemeteries like Brúgh na Bóinne.

The belief that these included gold caused many of the burial mounds to be rifled as far back as Danish times. In actual fact, excavations to date have revealed very little of intrinsic value in burial mounds, but here and there all over the country, gold objects from the Bronze Age have been found, which show that these De Danann, whoever they were, were the world's greatest craftsmen. The gold collection in the National Museum surpasses anything in Europe.

There are necklets, rings, torques, and ornaments of beautiful workmanship, and though comparatively few of them come from Meath, we are represented by a sizeable collection, if we include bronze weapons. There is a whole hoard from the Doon, Athlone, and a most remarkable gold sundisc from Ballyjamesduff; both these places are roughly in the former Meath. There are countless small objects from almost every parish, and when we come to a later period we find ourselves associated with one of Ireland's most precious relics, the Tara Brooch from Bettystown.

TARA'S PERIOD OF GREATEST MAGNIFICENCE

It is shortly after the beginning of the Christian era that Meath emerges as a great power in Irish history. Ulster, the most important of the earlier kingdoms, had been subdued, or at least greatly weakened, in the wars with Queen Maeve of Connacht. Now it appears that there were many clans of Ulster descent living in what is now called Meath, subject to the local rulers. These revolted and sought to set themselves up as a free kingdom, with the aid of the King of Ulster. But, from across the Shannon, came Tuathal Teachtmhar, and defeated them in a great battle at Skreen. (It was not called Skreen in those days, but Aicill. Its modern name *Scrín* means 'a shrine' and derives from early Christian times when relics of St Columcille were preserved in the monastery there.)

Tuathal decided to form a new central kingdom which would be in a commanding position between the Ulstermen on the North and the Leinster and Munster kingdoms on the south. He took in a portion of Ulster, including the Hill of Taillte, which had been, perhaps, the frontier stronghold of that kingdom; a portion of Munster including the Hill of Tlachtha (Hill of Ward) near Athboy; a portion of Connacht including Uisneach, and most of north Leinster including Tara.

These four hills had been famous sanctuaries, and the habitations of the ruling chiefs from time immemorial; now they were all in the new kingdom of Meath. Tara became the chief royal seat, but Tuathal appears to have had palaces on all of them, for we are told he celebrated the feast of Samhain with great solemnity on the Hill of Tlachtha, and the Feast of Bealtaine on the Hill of Uisneacht.

Thus, for the time being at least, there were once again five provinces in Ireland. Legend has it that the division into five parts is of much greater antiquity, but legend is not at all clear as to what the original five provinces were. What is certain is that the modern Irish word for province is *cúige* which means 'a fifth part'.

It was not to be expected that the ruling families of Leinster and Munster would submit to their new arrangement without a struggle, and though Tuathal's successor, Conn of the Hundred Battles, defeated both of them, they never quite became willing vassals of the High Kings who ruled at Tara. The descendants of Conn were more successful in other directions. They established themselves as kings of Connacht and all the north of Ireland except the districts from the Bann to the Sea of Moyle.

These kindred kings and their descendants are known as the *Síol Cuinn* or the Seed of Conn, and the most famous of them all is Cormac Mac Airt, Conn's grandson, who ruled at Tara as High King of Ireland from 227 to 266. He exacted allegiance from every chief of every tribe in the whole island, and Tara in its time came to its great magnificence. Kingly residences had no doubt crowned the hill for hundreds of years before his time, but he built and rebuilt on a scale hitherto unknown.

The *Teach Miodh Cuarta* (the House of the Mead-Circling), the great banqueting hall is described in glowing terms in early Irish literature, and the track of its foundations, still to be seen quite clearly on the hill, show that the writers did not exaggerate, with regard to its size at any rate. The hall was 700 feet long and 45 wide, and, according to the plan given in the Book of Leinster, the roof was supported by two rows of pillars running lengthways which divided the huge room into a wide central portion and two narrow side aisles. The late Professor O'Riordáin says that, 'the ancient builder would have found no insurmountable difficulty in constructing the building' but adds that 'only excavation will give us an exact picture of the methods used'.

The ancient plans show great alcoves allocated to the various groups of guests; kings and chiefs; poets and historians; healers and champions, in a strict order of precedence. Feis Teamhrach was held here every three years, and, the manuscript says, 'as many men would fit in it as would form the choice part of the men of Ireland'. It is further stated that in regard to magnificence of materials, nothing like it had been seen on earth since the temple of Solomon.

If we remember that these accounts, though based on earlier manuscripts, were not copied in their present form till the tenth century, when Christian pilgrims from Ireland were familiar with the glory of Rome itself, we must come to the conclusion that Tara in its glory was one of the most remarkable royal seats of the western world.

It would be tedious to go further with descriptions of Tara here, for it is the subject of many books, and there are guidebooks available which give accounts of every aspect of the history, literature, and topography of Ireland's greatest monument.

Corman Mac Airt was not only a great warrior and builder but a great man of letters. He established colleges of law and history and wrote, among other things, the celebrated *Teagasc Ríogh* or *Instruction of a King*, in which he lays down the principles of good government. We have, of course, no actual copy of this work or any other writing actually dating from pre-Christian Ireland, but in later writings they are referred to as being in existence in the eleventh and twelfth centuries. Two or three historical tracts written before the coming of Patrick are even said to have been in existence in the seventeenth century. It is quite believable that the art of writing was known in Ireland centuries before the coming of Patrick. We can hardly imagine, for instance, that Cormac, who had such close associations with the continent, who built his banqueting hall in the style of a Roman Basilica, and was familiar with the Christian faith, could have failed to adopt the Roman

26

learning also. It is equally impossible to imagine that an insular people, undisturbed for so many centuries, could have developed the highly polished literary forms in their language by oral usage alone.

There are many references in historical tales to the knowledge of the Christian faith in Ireland in the third century. One is that Art, the father of Cormac, asked to be buried in a certain place where he predicted that a Christian church would one day be built. When he was dead, his people attempted to carry his body to Brúgh na Bóinne, where all the former kings of Ireland were buried, but 'if all the men of Erin were drawing it thence, they could not'. So he was interred at the spot he had designated and three sods were cut in honour of the Blessed Trinity and so the place is called *Tré-foit* (three sods) to the present day, with the slight variation in English to Trevet.

The similar story of the burial of Cormac in Rosnaree is better known. Both are evidence of communication with Roman Britain and lend credibility to the strange life story of St Patrick's boyhood in the following century.

THE ORIGIN OF THE GREAT TRIBUTE

What was life like outside the monasteries in the 350 years from the coming of St Patrick to the beginning of the Danish invasions? The early chronicles are so concerned with the religious history of the period that their accounts of purely secular affairs are rather meagre. When we remember that the writers of most of our chronicles were monks of the tenth and later centuries, we can understand that the emphasis is on the ecclesiastical side of whatever clashes occurred between what we would now call Church and State.

There were High Kings of Tara, all of them the Uí Neill families in unbroken succession through the early centuries of Christianity down to the later days of the Danish wars, though they ceased to live at Tara in 565 – that is a century after the new faith was firmly established. They still had, nominally, the allegiance of the whole of Ireland, but it was only the northern half of the country that was united under kings of the same royal family. In particular, Leinster was still refractory, and for an understanding of the later history of Meath it is necessary to go into this centuries-old rivalry.

It began in the almost legendary times of King Tuathal Teachtmhar (the Lawful) who first established the strong central kingdom of Meath in AD76. Tuathal had two daughters, and after he had secured the fealty of all the provincial kings he wisely cemented the alliance with Leinster by giving the elder girl in marriage to the king of that province. After some time, however, rumour reached the King of Leinster that the younger daughter was by far the more beautiful.

The King of Leinster may have seen her on the occasion of a *feis* at Tara, or have heard her praises sung by some visiting minstrel. He determined to have her for his wife, so he hid the elder daughter away in one of his palaces and came to Tara with the news that she was dead. Tuathal willingly gave him the hand of the younger girl and he brought her home to Leinster. Inevitably, after a time, the sisters met and the deception was discovered. The story has it that both girls died of grief and shame. When the news reached Tara, Tuathal was understandably enraged.

Gathering his armies he marched against Leinster, slew the king and, as was the custom of the time, exacted the honour price for the death of his daughters and the insult to his name and race. The tribute is known as the Boraimhe (Boru), possibly because cows formed a great part of it. I quote from Elizabeth Hickey's *The Legend of Tara*, the whole tribute exacted:

> 15,000 cows, 15,000 swine, 15,000 wethers; the same number of mantles, silver chains and copper cauldrons, one great cauldron to be set up in Tara in which would fit 12 pigs and 12 kine; 30 red-eared cows with their calves, with halters and spancels of bronze and bosses of gold.

Making allowances for the exaggeration of legend, the tribute was a crushing one. Every High King at Tara for centuries afterwards felt honour bound to exact the tribute at the beginning of his reign and it is said that:

> It is beyond the testimony of angels,
> It is beyond the testimony of recording saints,
> All the kings of the Gaels
> That made attack upon Leinster.

During Patrick's lifetime, Laoghaire waged constant war against the Leinstermen. In 598, the Ard Rí, Aodh MacAinmire, was defeated and slain while trying to exact the tribute; one of his successors was badly defeated at the Hill of Allen in 722, but a little later the High King, Aodh Allen, won a decisive victory at Ath Seannaigh in the present County Kildare.

Beyond these forays into Leinster, we may read some traditional antipathy, perhaps, even a difference of race. Whatever the root of the trouble, it had profound effects on the history of Ireland, for it was the basis for the alliance formed by a later Leinster King (Diarmuid) with the Norman invaders. Douglas Hyde stresses this in a reference to King Tuathal:

> Under evil auspices, and in an evil hour, he extorted from Leinster the first of the Boru tributes which contributed so largely to mould upon lines of division and misery our unhappy country, from that day until the present, by estranging the province of Leinster, throwing it into the arms of foreigners, and causing it to put itself into opposition with the rest of Ireland.

In the absence of central government with a national civil service and national army, each little *tuatha* (of which there were seventeen in the ancient Kingdom of Meath) was largely self-contained, and the ordinary man probably never left its boundaries except when he went in the train of his chief to take part in wars such as those against the Leinstermen.

But in every tuatha there was a class of men who were nor ordinary farmers or labourers, the *aes dana*: poets, historians, healers, and artists. These people travelled from kingdom to kingdom and so kept a unity of culture over the whole island. In the old stories, passages describing the arrival of a stranger at a king's court occur repeatedly. To the question, 'Where have you come from?' his answer runs something like this, 'In the Grianan of Ailech I slept last night; with O'Connor of Sligo the night before; to Tara of the Kings I go tomorrow.'

This is the concept of nationhood we must try to understand. A common literature, close contacts in matters of learning and art, news of one kingdom circulating to all the others; but in the material things of life everything very decentralised, and each little state rather like one big family.

When the monasteries were founded, they seem to have gradually replaced the *aes dana* of the pagan world. It may even be that their establishments were on the sites of the druid temples, but we know very little with certainty on that point. We do know that the early monks went about from place to place, from one school to another, all over the country, just as the *aes dana* did. Braccan from Ardbraccan went to the Aran Islands; Breandan from the school of Finian returned to his native Munster; Columcille left Derry to found monasteries at Durrow and Kells. St Scire of Kilskyre is also commemorated in Tyrone; Dympna of Kildalkey gives her name to Tydavnet in Monaghan; Fechin of Fore has associations with the west and has left his name in Termonfechin in County Louth.

Hardly is there a saint in the early history of the Irish Church who is not associated with more than one site, and the 'poor scholar' closer to our own time met with a welcome and respect that is surely an inheritance from the days of the Brehons.

THE ANTIQUITY OF AN UAIMH
INTERESTING SPECULATION ON ITS ORIGIN

The town officially known as *An Uaimh* (Navan), the largest in the present county of Meath, is sometimes said to be less ancient than Trim or Ceanannus Mór, and to the visitor it certainly looks like a modern town. But its position at the confluence of the Boyne and Blackwater would lead one to suspect that, in spite of appearances, it must have been important from very early times. The one striking monument that bears this out, the moat or mound standing enormously high over the town and looking across it to the two rivers.

Nobody calls this mound by any name now that would suggest its origin, but the Annals call it the Mound of Odhbra (pronounced in modern Irish 'owra') and thereby introduce the controversy about the correct name of what, for some centuries, has been known to English speakers as 'Navan'. In the early days of the Gaelic League, the local pioneers of the language movement called the town Nua Chongbhail ('Nua-con-vawl'), on the unquestionable proof given by O'Donovan that the Nua Chongbhail fre-quently mentioned in ancient records stood where the modern Navan now stands. O'Donovan was the first and greatest of modern topographers. He was attached to the team of workers who made the Ordnance Survey of Ireland in the 1830s.

Everywhere he went he tried to collect local information about place names from both Irish and English speakers, and then compared his findings with any references to be found in manuscript or printed sources. He worked under great duress; there were no rapid means of travel in those days, and no telephones; there were no local libraries where reference books might be consulted. So he was obliged to write to his colleagues in Dublin asking them to search for the information he required in such collections as were available.

In O'Donovan's time, the extant material was scattered and not indexed or catalogued, as much of it is today. These circumstances made it understandable that he may have overlooked sources with which the modern topographer is familiar.

In the case of Navan, O'Donovan did note that the local Irish speakers called the town *An Uaimh* and understood that as meaning 'the cave'. Joyce, writing in 1869, says that 'the present colloquial name of Navan is An Uaimh (the cave); this name is still remembered by the old people and we find it also in some of our more modern Irish annals'. (This quotation shows that Irish was still spoken in Navan at the time.)

Joyce is satisfied that 'the cave' referred to the cave underneath the great mound of Odhbhra. He says that when people forgot who Odhbhra was, they began to call the place *An Uaimh*, either because it had formerly been called *Uaimh Odhbhran* or because the two words sounded rather similar. 'The town of the cave' might be in an earlier grammatical form *Baile na h-Uamhan* (pronounced 'Uvan') while the town or grave or other site name, prefixed to the name *Odhbhra* might give the form *n-Odhbhran*, which would sound 'nowran' or 'novran'. Either of these would give 'The Novane' in English, which is the form found in early English documents. This seems more likely than that *Nua Chongbhail* could have been corrupted into either *An Uaimh* or Navan.

Who was this Odhbhra? As might be expected from the legends of Tailltean and other great sites, Odhbhra was a woman, a Spanish lady. Heremon, the Milesian chief and law-giver, had a wife named Odhbhra who did not accompany the expedition to Ireland. They had three sons who were too young for warfare at the time, but later they and their mother followed the father to the new colony, expecting to find him ready to welcome them with open arms.

Instead, they found Heremon married to another woman, the Princess Tea, presumably a De Danann lady who was not averse to a dalliance with the conquering chief. This Tea is said in many accounts to have had her *rath* at Tara, and the great wall around it gave the hill its name – *Tea-mur* or 'Tara's wall'. This derivation is probably fanciful, for there are many other Taras in

31

Ireland, all said to be so-called because they are high places for watching or outlook. Nevertheless, there was certainly a Princess Tea, and I have heard that the name (pronounced 'Tay') survived among Gaelic families until it became anglicised as Theresa.

The forsaken Spanish princess died of grief and her three sons buried her with funeral rites befitting her rank. They raised a great cairn over her and the place became known as the Place of the Tomb of Owra, which would easily be called *Tuaim* or *Grave of n-Owran*, corrupted to the Novan. This great mound probably has an inner chamber like Brúgh na Bóinne, and, though the tradition of its existence is now lost, its presence would have at one time led people to call it 'An Uaimh' or 'the Cave'. Thus we have two parallel explanations, both connected with the mound or moat.

The Nuachongbhail would be a new town or holding or habitation established nearer the river at some later period, just as the town of Athboy is in the valley below the hill site of Tlachtgha (Hill of Ward) or the modern town of Drogheda below the Mill Mound. There are dozens of places in Ireland called New Town which bear out the theory that the original settlement in Navan was at Moatlands and the later town nearer the rivers.

Against all this, it is only fair to quote Sir William Wilde:

> The moat of Navan, which forms such a conspicuous object from all sides, is of the military class, and well worthy of inspection, from its size and its appearing to have been in part formed out of the natural hill.

But remembering the many Bronze Age burial mounds which were afterwards used as fortified dwellings places, and even as the sites of early Christian churches, Wilde's remarks do not necessarily contradict the romantic story of the Princess Odhbhra.

Not far distant, on the western bank of the Boyne at Athlumney, a great souterrrain or burial chamber was discovered during the cutting of the railway in 1849. There was a passage of over fifty feet in length, with a cruciform chamber at the end constructed of huge slabs similar to Newgrange. At the time, only some animal bones were found there, and I have never heard that any further excavations were made or that the site is even accessible at present.

On the other side of the river a quantity of iron, bronze, and silver objects was found at the same time; they were mainly harness buckles, head-stalls, bridle-bits, and clasps; there were also quantities of bones, both human and animal. These are in the National Museum, and the experts date them to the ninth century. That was the period of the Danish invasions, and it would appear to be the burial of a warrior with his horses and chariots, and perhaps some of his soldiers who perished in the same battle.

Two almost identical finds have been made in Norway. It seems that, though the Danes came as raiders, they imitated the Irish style of decoration and that the Irish craftsmen in turn were influenced by Danish ideas. Irish objects of the ninth century have been found in 120 graves in Norway, and in the Viking cemetery near Islandbridge, Danish and Irish objects have been found, together with some of mixed Irish and Norse styles.

So rested the remains of Milesian and Viking, separated in time by a mere thousand years, until the march of progress, with even-handed indifference, disrupted their rest.

THE LORE OF ROADS

In the days when the High Kings reigned in Tara, there were fine great roads leading from the royal fortress, so that the king and his company could travel with speed and comfort to every *cuige* or province to collect his due tribute, and so that the vassal kings and nobles could visit Tara for the great *feis*, when laws were promulgated, disputes settled and festivities celebrated.

It is a far cry from those days to ours, more than 1,600 years, and there has been a correspondingly great change in methods of road making. Yet antiquarians are able to trace, in part, the course of some of these ancient highways. One, for instance went through Ratoath, crossed the Liffey by a ford made of interwoven branches, the *Ath Cliath* destined to give a name to the city which grew up around it, and went on to the coast of *Cuala* (Wicklow), much as the Bray road of today. This route was the *Slighe Cualann*, for *slighe* was the term used for a great road.

The more familiar *bóthar* is defined in the ancient record as a road for cattle, its breadth to be such that, 'two cows fit upon it, one lengthwise. the other athwart, and their calves and yearlings fit on it along with them'. There were plenty of such roads all through the country, and it is recorded as early as the second century that there were laws governing their care and maintenance. It is quite probable that, in spite of the changes of the centuries, many of these roads are in use today.

New roads would be built as necessity for them arose; a powerful man, Irish chief, Norman marauder, or Cromwellian planter, builds himself a new fortress or mansion, on a site far from the public highway, chosen for security or beauty or both. He must build a road to it. The growth of towns and the changes in agricultural economy naturally made new roads necessary and led to the abandonment of others, and the process continues today. It would be, therefore, very difficult to determine with certainty the age of every road, and I do not know that anyone has made a comprehensive study of the subject.

In Meath we have many clues to the location of ancient roads in actual material remains, in oral tradition, and in place names. *Bohermeen* is, of course, 'the fine or smooth road', and the *Bóthar Alainn*, near An Uaimh, is almost certainly 'the beautiful road'. Where the name of a road was written down in English at an early period, the 't' in the written Irish form came to be sounded and the word became 'bother', later 'batter'. There is one village and four townlands called Batterstown, the town of the road.

There must be many more Batterstowns not recorded and the parish collector should note them, giving their exact location. Then there is Yellowbatter, Greenbatter and Batterjohn, 'John's Road'. I know of two places called Butterstream and my own conjecture is half translation like Batterjohn, the original name being *Bóthar an tSrutha*. I do not know if there is a Stonybatter in this county, but the Dublin one is so well known to farmers going to the market that it is worth mentioning, particularly as it is a part of the great *Slighe Cualann*, which is identified with certainty. Its meaning, 'stony road', is an indication of the fact that ancient roads were paved like the Roman ones.

If you are collecting road names note that in North Meath, *bóthar* is softened to a sound like English 'bore' or 'bawr' and that the common word *boreen* may also enter into place names, e.g. Boreen-na-hatha, where the last word should be spelled *haitinne*, 'the little road of the furze'. How much nicer it sounds when you know what it means. Another word for road is *Bealach*, and Moyvalley, on the Kildare border, means 'the plain of the road', and not 'of the valley'. Then there is *conair*, a road wide enough to bring dogs on, presumably wolfhounds on leash, and *cosán*, 'a footpath'. I cannot recall places in Meath named from these, but I am sure some readers will.

A special kind of road is a *tóchar*, pronounced 'tohar' in the north. In early times, before drainage was done extensively, marshes and land subject to flooding made road construction difficult. The road might have to wind and wind to keep on the high ground, but sometimes the low strip could be made passable by a causeway of branches, earth, and stones, well tramped down. Such a causeway is called a *tóchar* in Irish, and I know many roads bearing this name still. But there must be dozens of *tóchars* that I do not know, and they should all be recorded, as they may be forgotten where roads are widened, and turns taken out; and they are valuable clues in tracing old roads.

Coming nearer to our own time, Thompson in 1802 says there were then only turnpike roads running through the county, one from Dublin to Drogheda, and the other from Dublin to Navan, both remarkably well kept. The one to Navan had only just been completed in 1802. It is the present road through Dunshaughlin. The taxes paid at the pike gates by vehicles passing through paid for these roads, but the others were kept by the cess raised by the Grand Jury and the yearly cost was over £30,000, an enormous sum if we consider labour at 1 *d* a day. It seems, however, that there was a good deal of corruption and not very efficient overseeing. Thompson calls it 'public robbery'. Later, road-making was undertaken during the Famine as relief work, and new straight roads, called new line roads, were built and are well known to all by that name.

Space does not permit me to talk about our beautiful bridges, so admired by foreigners and so little appreciated by ourselves that we deface them with all manner of signs and notices. Some of them date from the time of Grattan's Parliament, some are much older. According to Wilde, the oldest was the bridge below Donaghmore, of which but one arch remained in his time. It was called Babe's Bridge, and in the Annals it is stated that in 1330 a great flood of the Boyne swept away all the bridges from Trim to Drogheda, except Babe's.

STORY OF MAEL SECHNAILL THE GREAT

The poet Thomas Moore, writing during the days of depression that followed 1798, saw 'through the waves of time, the long-faded glories they cover' and to him the last and greatest of Ireland's days of glory were:

> … the days of old
> Ere her faithless sons betrayed her;
> When Malachy wore the collar of gold
> Which he won from her proud invader.

The Malachy of Moore's poem is the Ard Rí, more properly named Mael Sechnaill, the second monarch of Ireland to bear that name. The first defeated and slew the great Danish chief Turgeis. The second was the great soldier, patriot, and statesman whose name is linked with that of Brian Boru in the final defeat of the Danes at Clontarf.

Mael Sechnaill was King of Meath in the latter half of the tenth century. He lived, as his predecessors for many years had done, at Dun na Sgiath on the shore of Lough Ennel in the present Co. Westmeath. The surrounding district was then the Royal Tuath or private family possession of the O Mael Sechnaills. But he was active all during his reign in the struggle against the Danes of Dublin. In the year 979, he won a decisive victory over them at Tara, and followed it up by an attack on Dublin itself, the result of which was that the Danish King of Dublin had to pay a heavy tribute and release all his Irish prisoners.

The fact that Tara was the scene of this and other battles during the Danish wars goes to show that though long abandoned as a royal residence, it was still the symbolic centre of the Kingdom of Meath. It extended then from the Shannon to the sea and was the symbolic centre of Ireland.

Shortly after this, the High King of Ireland, Domhnall O'Neill died, and in accordance with law and custom, the choice of his successor fell on Mael Sechnaill, the chief of the Meath branch of the royal family. He did not, however, receive the universal acknowledgement due to a High King. For many years, the Danes of Limerick had been harassing Munster and, after a long struggle, the tide of victory had turned in favour of a brave Irish leader, Brian of Dal Cais, who later made himself King of Cashel. Brian was a great soldier and a man of ambition, and he was not disposed to acknowledge for Cashel any over-lordship of a High King of Tara. He forced the chiefs of Ossory and Leinster to pay homage to him rather than to Mael Sechnaill.

So the High King had not only the struggle with the Danes on his hands, but the struggle to assert the principle of law and tradition against a powerful rival. This double warfare went on for seven or eight years, and though Brian ravaged Meath and Connacht, he was frequently defeated in battle. The High King had the first stone bridge constructed across the Shannon at Athlone, which made a concerted action against Brian easier. A kind of peace was made in 998 when it was decided that Brian was to be independent king of the southern half of the country.

The late Professor Mac Neill, in his *Phases of Irish History*, writes that from early Christian days there was a theory all over western Europe that, while in the world there were many kingdoms, there was an overall King of the World. First the Roman Emperor was so regarded, and in later centuries Charlemagne and his successors who took his place as Emperors of the Holy Roman Empire. This concept continued down to Napoleon and was only finally broken down by the rise of the modern European nation states just over a century ago. MacNeill gives a translation of a poem written under Brian's rule on the rights of Cashel:

> Cashel overheads every head,
> Except Patrick and the King of the Stars,
> The high-king of the world and the Son of God,
> To these alone is due its homage.

The Danes of Dublin naturally availed of the internal strife to extend their own kingdom, but Mael Sechnaill was powerful enough to keep them in check. During the period that he was at war with Brian, he twice besieged them in Dublin, and it was on the second occasion that he carried off the most precious of the Danish treasures: the gold collar of Tomar and the sword of Carlus. It is said that he engaged in single-handed combat with two Danish princes and slew both of them, 'taking from the neck of one his massive gold collar and from the dying grasp of the other his jewel-hilted sword, which he himself ever afterwards wore as trophies'.

But it is not for his achievements as a soldier that Mael Sechnaill chiefly deserves the title of 'the Great', which the annalists have accorded him. It is rather for the way in which he sacrificed his personal dignity of rank for the good of his country. Brian of Munster's power was growing yearly, and having inflicted a crushing defeat on the Danes and their allies the Leinstermen, he made peace with them all, and with their aid, demanded that Mael Sechnaill should surrender the High Kingship to him.

This violation of the former treaty between the two Irish kings could have led to further civil war, and no matter which of them might get the upper hand, the ultimate victors would be the Danes. It is easy for us to see this now, but it took a very great man to see it at the time. Mael Sechnaill was such a man. He surrendered to Brian, and in the years that followed, served him and his country with the greatest loyalty.

Brian was of the stuff of which dictators are made. He was a wily statesman and had hopes of establishing himself as monarch over Danes and Irish alike, and even of founding an empire overseas. He made marriage alliances with his former enemies, and for a while all went well, but it is said that it was through his own marriage with the mother of the Danish king of Dublin that the final conflict broke out. This ambitious Irish woman, Gormlaith, was sister of the King of Leinster and had been affianced to Mael Sechnaill in her youth. While bride of the ageing Brian, she was plotting a great invasion of Ireland by new Norse forces, so that her son Sitric should be High King and the whole country united as part of the Norse empire.

Shortly before the great invasion in 1014, Sitric, with his Leinster allies, met and defeated Mael Sechnaill's forces at Swords, which was an important place in the south of the Meath Kingdom, being the seat of one of the great Columban monasteries. Mael Sechnaill appealed for help to Brian but help was not forthcoming. On the great day at Clontarf, the Meath and Connacht men fought side by side with those from Munster, but the Ulster O'Neills held aloof. On the other side were the Norse from England, Scotland and the Isle of Man, from Normandy and Flanders as well as from the mainland of Scandinavia. It is estimated that there were 20,000 on each side.

The Norse forces included contingents in heavy armour, who initially inflicted great slaughter on Brian's men, but, as the day wore on, the weight of their equipment wearied the men out and the more lightly clad Irish, exchanging swords for battle axes, cut them down. The Meath men, who had been held in reserve in the morning, entered the fray in the evening to deliver the decisive blow. Victory for the Irish and the ignominious rout of the Danes ended Danish hopes of establishing a great empire, and of securing the sovereignty of Ireland.

But Brian's hopes of establishing a hereditary monarchy for his family vanished on the field of Clontarf. His son the Righ-Dannaidh (the heir apparent) was killed, with many more of his kinsmen, so the valiant Mael Sechnaill returned to the High Kingship without opposition and reigned till his death eight years later.

FIRST INCURSIONS
ISOLATED RAID STARTS ERA OF TERROR

In the year 795, a party of sea-robbers swooped on the island of Racra (Lambay, off the coast of Dublin), plundering and burning the church there.

This date is usually given as the beginning of the Danish period in Irish history, and the date of the battle of Clontarf, 1014, as marking its close. But the raid of 795 was an isolated incident, and though it must have been what we would nowadays call a 'sensation', it was not followed up for twelve years.

Similar raids on the west coast were followed by another lull. The whole thing must have seemed as remote from the everyday lives of the people of Meath as a great storm or earthquake in a far-off country. The next generation was to find that an era of terror had begun. In retrospect, we see in these first raids the end of Ireland's Golden Age and the beginning of the Age of Conquest.

Who were these Danes? They were the peoples of Norway, Sweden, and Denmark, and they called themselves a name meaning Northmen (Norsemen) – that is, the northern branch of the Germanic race. In Ireland they were called by various names – Genti (heathens), Gaill (foreigners), and Lochlannaigh (the peoples of the land of Lochlann, said to be an old division of Scandinavia). The name 'Viking' is from the Old Norse word meaning 'one who cruises around bays or creeks', and as understood in Ireland and other countries at the time, meant simply 'pirate'.

These northern pagan peoples, by whatever name we call them, existed on the borders of the great new Christian empire being built up by Charlemagne, crowned Holy Roman Emperor in the year 800. In the border warfare they seem to have learned that Christian rulers do not always apply the charity of the Gospel to the vanquished, and many writers give this as the cause of the ruthless destruction of monasteries and churches which is so characteristic of the Danish invasions. We must not forget, however, that the monasteries were almost the only equivalent of towns in Ireland at the time, and that they were the storehouses of many valuable treasures.

At this period, the Northmen seemed to have developed the art of ship-building to a very high degree. They built long, light, undecked vessels in which, in a sea fight, every man could take a hand. In these they ravaged, and eventually settled on, the coasts of Europe, from Ireland to the Caspian Sea in southern Russia. They occupied England in spite of the resistance of King Alfred; they sailed up all the rivers of western France and for some years had a settlement as far inland as Paris. They later occupied Sicily and other outposts on the Mediterranean. They had much earlier conquered the Hebrides and other Scottish islands. It is well to bear all this in mind when judging the resistance of the Irish and their final victory.

After the first sporadic raids, the foreigners managed to establish settlements on the coasts, the first being Dublin and Annagassan, 18 miles north of Drogheda. These settlements consisted of a semi-circle of earth to protect their ships which were pulled up on the strand. The Irish annals apply the name *longphort* to such a settlement, that is, a defence for ships, but the term afterwards came to mean any kind of fortified camp. *Port* means a harbour or gateway into the country, and *long*, of course, means 'a ship'.

In the year 832, that is thirty-seven years after the raid on Lambay, a strong leader of the invaders united the raiding parties and succeeded in getting up the rivers and making permanent longphorts on the inland lakes. They were beginning to know the geography of the country and, when necessary could take a short-cut by carrying their light vessels overland from one waterway to another. This strong leader was Turgeis (written in some chronicles in latinised form as Turgesius) and it was in his time that Meath became the chief scene of conflict. Turgeis's forces had come down Lough Neagh to occupy Armagh, the Chief See of Ireland, and at the same time navigated the Shannon to Lough Ree and raided the great school of Clonmacnoise, as well as establishing the settlements at Dublin and Annagassan already referred to.

In Clonmacnois, Turgeis's wife Ota, we are told, mounted the high altar of the church and from it delivered her *precartha*, which means some kind of pagan speech or prophecy. From here the Kingdom of Meath was plundered. But at the same time another fleet sailed up the Boyne, and the Four Masters tell us that they took prisoner Dubhlitir Odhar of Tara, and put him in fetters in their ships. It is thought that the ocean-going ships were able to come up the Boyne as far as Rossnaree, and that lighter boats, which were carried or towed from home, served for transport farther up the river and its tributaries. The annals mention sixty ships on the Boyne and sixty on the Liffey. The former fleet plundered Bregia (East Meath).

The Irish were quite unprepared for this kind of warfare. They had no means of attacking an enemy whose base was on water, and even for land warfare they had no standing army to cope with such numerous and well-trained forces as Turgeis had mustered. But the King of Meath was astute enough to see that if the strong leader were gone, the power of the Danes would be greatly diminished, and so he resorted to a piece of strategy. This King of Meath was named Maelsechnaill (sometimes given in textbooks as Malachy) and he lived near Lough Owell, Mullingar.

The Danes were very anxious, apparently, to marry Irish ladies, and Maelsechnaill let it be understood that he was willing to give his daughter in marriage to Turgeis himself. Presumably the fact that he had already one wife (at least) did not count. If the legend is true, a meeting place was arranged and the Irish princess, with fifteen ladies in waiting, advanced to meet Turgeis with his fifteen attendants. But when they came near, the ladies cast aside their veils and revealed themselves as sixteen strong, young fighting men. In the hand-to-hand combat which followed, the Irish got the best of it and took Turgeis himself, alive, into the presence of Maelsechnaill. We are not told anything about the interview, or trial, but that Maelsechnaill drowned Turgeis in Lough Owell with his own hand. Whatever we may think of the morality of this method, it was effective at least, for after nine years of success the tide of battle now began to turn in favour of the Irish.

Very Revd Dr Moran of Tullamore has made a study of the details of the warfare in East Meath during the next five years (845–850), and has published it in a paper in *Ríocht na Midhe* in 1956. In the next article I shall try to summarise his scholarly account.

TWO

VIKINGS IN MEATH

DANISH DEPREDATIONS CONTINUE
GREAT BATTLE AT SCURLOGSTOWN

After the drowning of Turgeis in the year 845, the tide of battle turned very much in favour of the Irish. During the next three or four years there was much fighting in Meath because the Vikings were still firmly entrenched in Dublin, and from there, could make raids on the plain north of the city. Then there was the fleet on the Boyne, and between the two fronts, the district of Bregia (East Meath) was severely harassed. Its chief, Tighernach, lived on the crannog at Lagore.

There is now only a marsh where once there was a lake, and on an island in this lake was the King of Bregia's fortified dwelling. For the year 846, the Four Masters give the following record, 'A victory was gained by Tighernach, lord of Lough Gabhor, over the foreigners at Dairedisirt-Dachonna, when twelve score of them were slain.' The exact location of this battlefield is not known but it may be somewhere between Trim and Lagore.

The Vikings, having moored their ocean-going vessels at Rosnaree, sailed upstream in their smaller boats as far as Scurlogstown, the point on the river nearest to Dunshaughlin. From there they started off, either for an attack on Lagore or for purposes of collecting cattle and other spoils from the surrounding countryside. Tighernach and his forces swooped and defeated them, as the entry in the Annals shows. He may not have pursued them further for they were tough fighters, and he may have avoided another engagement near the river where the intervention of the guards left behind to mind the boats might turn the tables.

We must also consider the possibility that the Vikings, having lost some important person in the battle, were anxious to break off the engagement and retire when they were still capable of conducting an orderly retreat. It would be reasonable to suppose, from what we know of the Vikings, that they would have carried their dead with them for burial to the safety of their headquarters.

This reconstruction of the battle is prompted by observation of a curious burial mound at Scurlogstown. It is situated near a stream that crosses the main Trim–Dublin road, between Laracor and Kilmessan junctions and enters the Boyne a short distance further on. The shape of the mound bears a close resemblance to the shape of an upturned boat, some thirty feet in length and sloping to a height of nine feet. It is known from excavations made in other countries, that when a great Viking leader died his boat was often buried with him, but though Viking cemeteries have been excavated at Islandbridge (Dublin) no ship burial has yet been found in this country.

The fighting in Meath at this period was made more complicated by an alliance between the Vikings and Cinaedh, the chief of Duleek. Such an alliance may appear treacherous to us, but against the background of the times there was nothing unusual about it. The first raiders had carried off captives whenever they could, and the girls among these were often married, willingly or unwillingly, to Scandinavians. The boys probably found wives too, so in a generation there was a new factor in the situation, the Gaill-Gaedhil, who could speak two languages and whose religion was more likely to be pagan than Christian.

Such was much of the population of the Scottish coasts and islands, and in the subsequent wars in Ireland the Gaill-Gaedhil may have been the link between the foreigners and the native population. As early as the days of Turgeis, the references in the Annals suggest that the invaders mingled with the Irish, helped Irish chiefs in raids against their neighbours, and stirred them up to rebellion against the Ard Rí. This was the case in Duleek. Cinaedh revolted against Maelsechnaill, King of Meath (who, it will be remembered, lived in the Royal Tuath in the present Westmeath) and with the aid of a party of foreigners, presumably from the Boyne fleet, laid waste the plains of Meath from the Shannon to the sea. With the help of Cinnaedh, the Viking succeeded in plundering Lagore a few years after their defeat by Tighernach.

Some fifteen years later it is recorded in the Annals that Lorcan, King of Meath, accompanied the brothers Olaf and Ivarr, who ruled as joint kings of Dublin, when they broke into the burial mounds at Newgrange, Knowth, and Dowth and carried off whatever burial treasures there may have been there. Similar plundering occurred in other parts of Ireland. It is said 'they left not a cave they did not explore.' These places were, of course, very ancient, and it was probably forgotten by the Irish themselves that they were more than ordinary mounds of earth, for one record says that it was by means of their pagan magic that the Vikings knew of the existence of the buried treasure.

The Vikings' excitement at these discoveries is evident in the many references to the raiders' stories in Scandinavian literature. Here is one quotation:

> Leifer went on a Viking raid to the west. He plundered Ireland and found there was a large underground house. It was dark within until he made his way to a palace where he saw a light shining from a sword which a man held in his hand. Leifer slew the man and took the sword and much treasure besides.

Still the successive High Kings fought against the Vikings. In the years that followed this plundering, the country was fairly peaceful and the Danish power became so weak that Dublin itself was wrested from them at one point and they were driven across the sea. One cause of their weakness was that new parties of foreigners who came made war on the ones already settled in the country, and there are many records of sea battles between the two tribes. Carlingford Lough was frequently the scene of conflict, possibly because it was the kind of anchorage each side wished to possess, being so like their native fjords.

From this time on, we hear the original Norsemen referred to as the *Finn Gaill* (fair foreigners) and the newcomers as the *Dubh Gaill* (dark foreigners). Many writers think these latter were from Denmark itself, and that the *Dubh* can hardly refer to the colour of their hair but rather to their dark-coloured ships or sails. From the name of the first foreigners we get the word *Fingal*, applied to the district north of Dublin, and from the latecomers we get the surname 'Doyle', now so long in the language that those who bear it may consider themselves pure Irish.

The names *Olaf* and *Ivarr* were very common in Scandinavia and soon appeared in Irish form as *Amhlaoib* and *Iomhair*. The former is still a common Christian name in Munster, and has been strangely anglicised to Humphrey.

As a surname, its English form is MacAuliffe. From *Ivarr* we have, with the adoption of the Irish *Mac*, the surnames MacIvor, MacKeever, and other variants; in some cases the *Mac* was dropped during the penal days and the name became Eivers, Keevers, Ivory, etc. The village of Ballivor in Meath derives evidently from some *Ivarr*, but which one I have been unable to find out.

There are other very interesting linguistic relics of the Norse period to which I shall return later. There is one point that must be made before continuing the sequence of events and that is the gradual adoption of the Christian faith by the settled Norsemen in Ireland and the Scottish islands. As early as the time of Cineadh and Tighernach there is a record of the Danes and Norsemen having a naval encounter in Carlingford Lough, and we are told that one of the leaders prayed fervently to St Patrick for victory, and that his men promised to donate all of the spoils of battle to the Church. At the same time they asked the help of their own fierce gods, Thor and Woden, to give them their ruthless courage. In England, Scotland, and the Isle of Man the remains of memorial crosses erected by the Danes over their dead are still standing, but instead of Christian subjects these monuments bear illustrations from their own pagan mythology.

Christianity prevailed eventually, and within the next hundred years the records tell us of Danish princes going on pilgrimage to Iona, which they had so often plundered, and of Danish children bearing such names as *Maelmuire* (servant of Mary). In the meantime, the conquests continued unabated in Britain and on the Continent, and sometimes we read of Danish kings of Dublin taking their forces over to fight in Britain and ruling over the large Danish provinces there. So strong was the Danish power in England that later on, when there were Danish Bishops in Dublin, they gave allegiance, not to the Archbishop of Armagh, but to the Primatial See of Canterbury (they called themselves Primates of Ireland, meaning of the Danish colonies in Ireland).

It would be tedious to recall all the battles fought between the Irish and the foreigners during the century following the conflicts we have mentioned. In general, it may be said that the tide of victory in the northern half of Ireland was with the natives, while the foreigners became very strong in the south and had separate independent kingdoms at Limerick and Waterford, as well as at Dublin. The success of the Irish in the northern half was due largely to the energy of successive High Kings, who, it will be remembered, were drawn alternately from the Aileach (northern) and Meath branches of the O'Neills.

The most famous of the former was Aedh Finnliath, who died in 879, and was succeeded by an equally famous king, Flann Sinna. Before his time, Meath had been repeatedly raided by the kings of Cashel who were evidently trying to establish themselves as High Kings. One of them got so far as to encamp at Tara, and, though he was a bishop, burned Clonmacnoise and Durrow. In the end, the last High King, Cormac of Cashel, was defeated and slain by Flann Sinna on the banks of the Barrow and the Cashel dynasty was no longer a force in the land. (This Cormac was also a bishop and is now remembered as the compiler of the Book of Rights and other important records.)

During these troubled years, the Annals record that the great Aonach of Taillte (Teltown) was abandoned, but it was restored when peace, or comparative peace, was established by Flann's successor, Niall Glundubh, in the year 916. Most of his campaigns and those of his immediate successors were outside the boundaries of Meath. Some were even naval encounters off the Hebrides and others were attacks on Dublin itself.

NATIVE AND FOREIGN RAIDERS
WHY ROUND TOWERS WERE BUILT

I have tried to show that the popular idea of the Norsemen, or Danes, as barbaric, pagan robbers is only true for the early period of the invasions. Afterwards, the permanent Danish settlements on the coasts became trading centres whose intercourse with the rest of the Danish dominions brought a new prosperity to Ireland. The native Irish princes soon took part in this commerce, building ships on the Danish pattern, and manning them with professional Danish sailors. We read of trade in wine, silks, jewels, and valuables of all kinds. We read, too, of tributes of wine being exacted by various kings from the Danish cities in their dominions, and the princes and chieftains of Meath must often have savoured the heady produce of France imported through Dublin or Drogheda. It was not all warfare.

In the monasteries there was much activity during periods of peace, the evidence being in the number of our historical records written or copied during the tenth and eleventh centuries. Add to this the intermarriage of Gael and Gall, and the alliances made by native chiefs with the foreigners in their various internal wars.

It is difficult to build up a picture of life in Meath in these centuries; even the best historians treat the period rather cursorily, and do not always agree. A.M. Sullivan writes:

> During the Danish struggle the Irish nation was undergoing disintegration and demoralisation. Towards the middle of the period the Danes became converted to Christianity; but their coarse and fierce barbarism remained long after, and it is evident that contact with such elements, and increasing political disruption among themselves, had a fatal effect on the Irish ... we find professedly Christian Irish kings themselves as ruthless destroyers of churches and schools as the pagan Danes of a few years previously.

The ancient Irish Annals show that the Irish played their part in plundering the wealthy monasteries. Here are a few examples.

Trevet (*Trí Fóid*, three sods) was a very ancient church on the site of the burial place (in pre-Christian times) of King Art, father of the great Cormac. It is not far distant from Tara. There are records in the Annals of the Four Masters of its various saintly abbots from the year 700 onwards. Then:

848:    Cineadh, with the Danes, burned the oratory of Trevet, within which were 260 persons.

917:    The abbot of Trevet was slain in his own house by the Danes.

1145:   Trevet was burned by Donnchadh, and sixty persons were killed therein

1152:   Trevet was plundered by Hy-Bruin. (The Hy-Bruin were Connacht people, who had extended their power into the present Cavan.)

In the references to the Abbey of Kildalkey we find that in 837 the Gailenga (a Meath clan) killed Egnech, the abbot (who was a bishop and a noted scribe as well) with his people. The Danes killed a later abbot in 885.

The abbots of Kilbrew, on the other hand, all seem to have died peacefully, but then they were near the protecting stronghold of Lagore. The Kells, Dulane and Ardbraccan districts seem to have suffered most from both native and foreign raiders, and Donaghmore was plundered six times.

Most people nowadays accept the view put forward by Petrie, in the last century, that it was as a protection against these attacks that the round towers were built. Before discussing them, however, and before coming to the greatest of all the personalities of the period, Maelsechnaill Mór, there are some interesting little footnotes on the era which I would like to add. They are all taken from a little book called *Scandinavian relations with Ireland during the Viking Period* by A. Walsh, published in 1922.

In reference to the commerce introduced by the Danes, the book refers to the Norse word *mangari*, a trader, which came into Irish as *mangaire* and was until very recently used in Meath English as *mangar*, meaning hay manager, corn manager, etc. The Irish word *margradh* and the English word *market* derive from the Norse, as does the word *penny*.

There is a long list of Irish words relating to ships and their equipment (keel, anchor, oar-lock, etc.) and of technical terms for such operations as slackening a sail, and making ready to embark, all derived from Norse. Other derived words relate to armour, house-building, fishing, etc. Many are now obsolete but a few familiar ones are *bád* in Irish and 'boat' in English, *boga* and 'bow', *fuinog* and 'window', *stol* and 'stool', *iarla* and 'earl', *sraid* and 'street'.

In the Norse language there are words borrowed from Irish like *cros* (cross), which is natural, and less likely ones such as the Irish for girl, madman, shoes, and oats. The sagas or long stories, for which Iceland in particular is famous, are thought to derive from Norse contacts with Irish bards. This reminds us that during all the troubled period we are discussing, there were poets to describe the Irish victories while chieftains in battle sent back glowing accounts of adventure to the waiting ladies. Fragments of these compositions survive but unfortunately very few have been put in a sufficiently modern form for ordinary readers.

The great Maelsechnaill of Meath, High King till the usurpation by Brian, had a poet named MacCoisse. On one occasion, the O'Neills of Ulster plundered the poet's castle at Clara (in Westmeath). The poet set out for the northern palace at Aileach to lodge a complaint. On arrival he was received with the honour due to his rank, and during the course of the evening was asked to tell a story. He gave a list of all the stories he knew, and the King of Aileach found that there was one of among them whose title was unfamiliar, so he asked MacCoisse to tell that one.

In it he described, with assumed names, the plunder of his castle at Clara. The king enjoyed the wonderful language and the graphic presentation so much that the poet felt emboldened at the end to reveal the truth and beg for the restoration of his property. It was granted in full, and MacCoisse there and then composed and recited a long poem in praise of the O'Neill king and his family.

Such incidents, and there are many of them in medieval stories, help us to realise that during the Danish wars, as during all wars, life went on in the traditional way, violence and horror alternating with kindliness, heroism and romance.

We might consider what special relics of Danish times remain in Meath. Some place names have already been referred to, namely the 'Sta' prefixes in Stamullen, Stameen, Stackallen, which Joyce believes to be the Norse word for a house substituted for the Irish *teac*. Thus *Stameen* was in Irish *Teac mín*, the fine or gentle homestead. Most people know that Howth and Leixlip are purely Danish names, but in the list of Meath townlands I can find none that are obviously Danish except the second half of the name Ratoath, to which reference has already been made. Swainstown and Elgarstown seem to be named from two Norsemen, but it is not known who they were.

There must be other remains of graves and fortified encampments near the Boyne. The fact that local tradition attributes many earthworks to the Danes is said to be the result of the very first anti-Irish 'journalist' who came among us, Gerald of Wales, one of the first Normans. He tried to prove that the native Irish were savages, incapable of producing anything artistic or architectural. Anything, therefore, that existed before the Normans must have been built by the Danes. In time, even the Irish themselves accepted this reasoning.

ORIGIN OF THE ROUND TOWERS
PETRIE'S GREAT ELUCIDATION

Of all our ancient monuments, the most impressive are the round towers. Foreign visitors may indeed be interested in our ruined churches and castles, but they have seen similar remains in other countries. Even our burial mounds are not unique. But the round towers are our own peculiar memorial; an expression, we like to think, of the spirituality of our people and of their perfection as architects, craftsmen, and artists.

In Meath, we have two beautiful specimens. One is on the banks of the Boyne at Donaghmore, in a quiet pastoral setting. The other crowns the height of Ceannanus Mór, dominating the town of crosses and churches that straggles down to the winding Blackwater.

It may seem strange to contemporary readers that, up to the last century, the wildest theories were propounded as to the origin of the round towers. Some maintained that they were of pagan origin and built by sun-worshippers from the east; others, going to the opposite extreme, held that the Danes built them. The authors of these theories were men who were neither able to read original Irish manuscripts nor to collect and understand the traditions surviving in the spoken language of the country. They were influenced by the long-standing assumption that the native Irish Christians were in a state of barbarism and quite incapable of producing anything until the Normans came to civilise, instruct and re-Christianise them.

In the year 1833, George Petrie, a brilliant Irish scholar, presented to the Royal Irish Academy *An Essay on the Origin and Uses of the Round Towers of Ireland*. Every statement made by him was backed by references to original documents in Latin and Irish, as well as by a scientific study of each of the hundred-odd remaining towers and the local legends attached to them. The essay was awarded a gold medal and a prize of fifty pounds and the author was thereby encouraged to continue his studies into all kinds of early Christian architecture in Ireland. After twelve years, he published the whole in a work published by M.H. Gill and available to view in Meath County Library Local Studies Department.

Petrie's conclusions on round towers may be summarised as follows:

1. From the time of St Patrick there were *cloigtheachs* (literally 'bell-houses') separate from the churches, built of stone and cylindrical in shape. There is no proof that the earliest belfries were, or were not, as high as the surviving towers.

2. The celebrated *Gobhán Saor*, who is known to have lived in the early seventh century, is remembered in connection with certain towers (not the Meath two) where the adjacent remains of early churches can, with comparative certainty, be dated to the year AD620.

3. Towers continued to be built up to the time of the Norman invasion, but less frequently.

4.   The top (or bell) storey may have been also used to house a beacon-light to guide travellers, or as a watchtower in time of war.

5.   The majority of the towers were built during the period of the Danish invasions, and were planned as places of safety for people and valuables. Petrie is inclined to date Donaghmore at about the year 900, but with no great certainty, and suggests a similar date for that of Ceannanus Mór, but they may be much earlier.

There were many towers in Meath as elsewhere, of which no trace now remains. The *cloigtheach* of Slane was burned by the Danes in 950. Long after the Danes were defeated there is this entry in the Annals, 'A.D. 1127. A great hosting by Connor Mac Farrell O'Loghlinn, together with the northern people of Ireland to Meath; they burned the steeple (cloigtheach) and church of Trim, and both full of people.' A little later there is this record, 'A.D. 1171. The Cloigtheach of Teach Ard [Tiltyard, near Trim] was burned by Teheran O Runic, with it full of people in it.' There are frequent similar records for towers outside Meath.

Though most people have seen a round tower, it may not be out of place to quote the following general description from Petrie, with some abridgement:

These towers are rotund, cylindrical structures, usually tapering upwards, and varying in height from fifty to perhaps one hundred and fifty feet; and in external circumference, at the base, from forty to sixty feet, or somewhat more. They have usually a circular projecting base, consisting of one, two or three steps or plinths, and are finished at the top with a conical roof of stone, which, frequently, as there is every reason to believe, terminated with a cross formed of a single stone. The wall, towards the base, is never less than three feet in thickness, but is usually more and occasionally five feet, but always in accordance with the general proportions of the building. In the interior they are divided into storeys, varying in number from four to eight, and each about twelve feet in height. These storeys are marked either by projecting belts of stone, set-offs or ledges, or holes in the walls to receive joists, on which rested the floors. In the uppermost of these storeys the wall is perforated by two to eight apertures, most usually four, which sometimes face the cardinal points. The lowest storey is sometimes composed of solid masonry, and when not so it has never any aperture to light it. The entrance doorway is in the second storey, eight to thirty feet from the ground, and only large enough to admit a single person at a time. The intermediate storeys are each lighted by a single aperture, placed variously, and usually of very small size. In their Masonic construction they present a considerable variety, but the generality of them are built in that kind of careful masonry called sprawled rubble, in which small stones, shaped by the hammer, if necessary, are placed in every interstice of the larger stones so that very little mortar appears, and the outside presents an almost uninterrupted surface of stone.

Petrie notes that the upper portions of some towers show signs of having been rebuilt, and we hardly need the Annals to tell us that slender buildings of such great height must have sometimes suffered from storms and lightning strikes.

The position of the doorway so high above the ground, and the fact that the doorway faces the sacristy of the adjoining church, is fair evidence that the tower was a place to which the clergy could speedily convey the precious altar-goods when under attack. In the second storey, the aperture was placed directly over the door so that if the attackers arrived before the scaling ladder was pulled up, or if they improvised any other means of reaching the entrance, the people above could beat them off by dropping stones on their heads. They may have used other weapons or missiles but if their store of ammunition became exhausted, and the enemy succeeded in setting fire to the woodwork inside, there would indeed be a holocaust. This must be the grim story behind each entry quoted above.

The tower at Donaghmore is built of undressed limestone, except for the finely cut stones around the door and other openings. There are but two lights in the top storey and they face east and west. The doorway is twelve feet above ground and is finished with a perfect semicircular arch. Above the keystone is another large dressed stone, closely joined to it, and the two together are the background on which a figure of Christ is carved.

At Donaghmore and Kells there are carved human heads on each side of the architrave, and in both towers the upper windows exhibit a variety of finish, some having a flat, stone lintel, some an angular head, and others a semicircular arch.

THREE

SAINTS AND HOLY WELLS

LEGEND OF THE ORIGIN OF THE BOYNE

Six wells in all baptise the infant Boyne.

Readers from the Carberry-Clonard country who can name all six wells
may award themselves six marks. Legend had it that Nuada-Neacht, a poet-
king of Leinster in the first century, had a secret well in his garden from
which no one but himself and his cup bearers was allowed to draw water.
If any other dared to approach, the well would burst up and blind him. But
Boan, the queen, defied the curse, even to the point of walking round the
well three times from right to left. The well rose and burst over her, breaking one of her eyes. She fled in terror that any one would see how her
beauty had been destroyed, but the waters followed her till she rushed into
the sea at Inver Colpa and was drowned. The waters that so pursued her
were forever called by her name; and so began the River Boyne.

This story is but one of many which are known to us in relation to the
wells of Ireland. It is easy to understand that miraculous powers were attributed to wells in the early ages of the world. Water, one of man's primal
needs, gushing from the earth in a pure and unfailing stream, inspired worship of the god who must surely dwell therein. Where water was scarce, or
of poor quality, the owner of a really good well naturally guarded it jeal-
ously, and so arose the many stories like the one quoted above.

The coming of Christianity did nothing to diminish the honour paid
to the ancient springs. On the contrary, they acquired a new dignity. Water

used in baptism took on the symbolism of grace and Christian purity. The Bible narrative of the blind man, who recovered his sight, when on the word of Our Lord, he washed his eyes in the pool of Siloe, was something readily understood by the Irish who had been accustomed to look for healing qualities in water. So the early saints, in their wisdom, blessed the sources, and the fairy well of Boan became the well of the Blessed Trinity.

The other five wells which baptised the infant Boyne are Tobarcro (*Tobar Croiche Naoimh*, the well of the holy cross), Tobar Aluinn near Ballyboggan, Lady Well at Glyn, Carbury Well, and Tobar na Cille.

There is scarcely a parish in Ireland without its holy well. According to Joyce, nearly 150 townlands have names beginning with Tobar. In this diocese there is a parish of Tubber. Many of the holy wells in Meath, however, are called by the English name of the patron saint: St Patrick's Well at Castletown, St Brigid's Well at Ardsallagh, Kieran's Well at Carnaross and St Ultan's Well at Ardbraccan. These latter two are, of course, known to everyone as places of pilgrimage, as are the wells at Slane and Killyon.

It would appear that in former times there were pilgrimages to very many others whose names are now forgotten. There was a specially prescribed station to be made on a special day, the Patron Day, and afterwards there would be a 'Pattern' or 'Fair' (in the older sense of a day of rejoicing as well as a day of buying and selling). Many wells had the cure of a particular disease, and grateful pilgrims left votive offerings behind them on the tree – for no holy well was without its ancient ash or thorn. Near Meath there is a well called in English 'Toheravilla', which means 'the well of the great tree' (*tobar an bhile*).

The Well of St Aedh (who gives his name to Ralugh in Westmeath) is still well known to cure headaches; the saint once met a man suffering from a severe headache and on being asked to perform a miracle he took the pain on himself and so relieved the man. Near Ceanannus Mór is a place called Toberboyoga, *tobar buidh-eoige*, the well of the jaundice. The Well of St Nicholas in Tullaghanogue has a cure for, I think, sore throats, but I am subject to correction, and will be glad to hear from readers who can name the healing properties ascribed to other wells.

There is material for a whole volume in the history of the Bride wells alone, not to mention all the St John's wells, the St Patrick's wells, and the rarer ones dedicated to St Laurence and St Nicholas. Devotion to St Brigid produced the name St Brigid's Well as far away as London. That well later gave its name to a prison in the locality and so Bridewell has come to be a common name for prisons.

More pleasant it is to recall that in 1687, a few years after the martyrdom of Blessed Oliver Plunket, Robert Barnewall, Baron of Trimblestown, had the courage to enclose and repair St Brigid's Well at Iskaroon (Dunderry) and inscribe the fact on a stone, asking pilgrims to pray for his soul.

PATRICK'S FIRST IRISH DISCIPLES
ROYAL COUNTY MEN IN PLACE OF HONOUR

One of the best-known dates in Irish history is 432, the year that St Patrick was sent to our island by Pope Celestine. We picture him coming to the Hill of Slane to light his Pascal fire as a sign that the fires of paganism were soon to be extinguished forever, and I think most of us, in childhood, had the impression that till Laoire on Tara saw the sky reddening over Slane, neither he nor anybody else had ever heard the name of Christ.

This over-simplified account is typical of how tradition focuses on the highlights of a story, as an artist picks out the highlights of a landscape, omitting the confusion of details so as to give a picture that is satisfying, and, in the spiritual sense, more true than the reality.

But as Meath was the scene of Patrick's first great missionary triumph, there is a special interest for us in the real details of his coming, in so far as they are known, against the background of the state of western Europe at that time.

At the time of the birth of Christ, Rome was the centre of the known world. From a small settlement on the banks of the Tiber, she had, during 700 years, extended her influence throughout Italy, had conquered the great civilisation of Greece and been civilised by it in return; had crossed the Mediterranean into North Africa, and spread westward into Spain, France, and Britain, and northward to the Rhine. It was to Rome that Peter and Paul came in obedience to the Divine command to teach all nations.

For 300 years their successors worked in secret and in the face of persecution against a strong and highly materially civilised paganism. The new faith permeated all levels of society by degrees, and the final triumph came when the Emperor Constantine publicly made Christianity the approved religion of all his dominions in the year 312. Therefore, officially at least, Roman Britain became a Christian country.

The Latin language, laws, and customs had long been introduced; Roman roads had been built and Roman towns housed the soldiers and civil servants. Now Christian churches took the place of the former temples of the gods, and even if the vast bulk of the native people remained pagan – worshipping Roman or Celtic deities – the upper classes, the provincials, already Latinised, must have followed the example of the Emperor with the alacrity of their type in all ages and places.

It is probable that Patrick's family were provincialised Celts, but it is a matter of dispute among scholars where exactly they lived. All we can say with certainty is that it was in a Roman town on the western coast of either Britain or Gaul (France).

During the fourth century, the vast empire was being harassed by the 'barbarian' peoples all round their frontiers. The natives of Wales and Scotland in the mountain regions on the edge of Roman Britain began raiding that territory, and the Irish kings often assisted them, and occasionally did a bit of raiding on their own account.

The famous Niall of the Nine Hostages, High King of Ireland, is known to have carried his arms as far as the Loire, and his successor, Daithí, was killed by lightning in the Alps during a foray into the very heart of the empire. It was soon after the death of Niall that the Roman legions were withdrawn from Britain (411), in the hundredth year after Constantine. At least one reason for the withdrawal was the strength of the attacks from across the Irish Sea.

The boy Patrick, therefore, was a captive from the Christian Roman Empire, but by the time he returned to Ireland as a missionary, Britain was no longer subject to Roman rule. Christianity was, however, well established, and it appears that many of the priests who accompanied him were from Wales. If we bear in mind that for the Irish kings who had been helping the Welsh against the Roman power in Britain for a century, we can readily believe that there was considerable Christian contact. Many Irish chiefs had Welsh or British wives; many of these must have known Christianity and some may have been Christians.

Yet one would expect the attitude of the raiding Irish to be hostile to the religion of the Romans. When Patrick and his companions attempted to land on the Wicklow coast they found such hostility that they were obliged to sail northwards to the shores of Brega, in East Meath. This fact is recorded in a life of St Patrick by Tireachán, who was a disciple of St Ultan of Ardbraccan, and though it was not compiled until about the year 700 it was based on earlier books and naturally on the living tradition on Meath.

This is how Fr Brady quotes from Tireachán:

> He went up from the sea to the plain of Brega at sunrise ... Then at prime he came to Glenn Sescnan, and there he built his first church, and he brought away a boy, Sescnen, afterwards a bishop, with him, and he left there two boy foreigners.

Fr Brady adds that Glenn Sescnen has been identified by the late Fr Paul Walsh as the valley of the Delvin River which enters the sea at Gormanston, and that it is probable that this first church was at Tullock. The quotation from Tireachán continues:

> At vespers he came to the estuary of the Delvin unto a certain good man, and he baptised him; and he found with him a boy whom he liked, and he named him Benignus, because he grasped between his arms and his breast the feet of Patrick; and he willed not to remain with his father and mother, but wept for fear he might not abide with Patrick.

Thus Patrick's first Irish disciples, Sescnen and Benignus, were both Meath men, and the very first church in Ireland was in Meath. It was after this that Patrick sailed northwards to Down and founded his church at Sabhal (Saul), at which site there are celebrations and monuments in modern times which suggest that it has the honour of being our first Christian church. It was not until the following spring, 433, that Patrick returned to Meath to face the High King at Tara. In the meantime, he had visited Antrim, where, as a slave, he had tended his master's sheep on the slopes of Sliábh Mis. Tradition says that he failed to convert old Milcho.

According to Fr Brady (and I am quoting or condensing from his articles in *Ríocht na Midhe*) , the Book of Armagh gives in Latin a list of the churches founded by Patrick in Brega, beginning *Primum in Culmine*. Culmen means a hill and would, therefore, be the Latin equivalent of 'tullock'. There was a church at Tullock dedicated to St Patrick down to the Middle Ages, and some traces of it still remain. It is near the site of an ancient moat or rath, the dwelling place of the local chief, maybe the father of the boy Sescnen.

Perhaps the two foreign boys left behind were aspirants to the priesthood;

perhaps they were left as hostages for the safety of the young prince who was departing with the strangers; we can only speculate. Why did Patrick not go at once to Tara? Did he hear from these good people that their king would be hostile? It seems likely enough.

We have forgotten the masters of Glen Sescnen and Tullock who, to their eternal credit, welcomed him, and we pay no pilgrim's tribute to Patrick's first church.

PATRICK'S CHALLENGE TO THE DRUIDS
THE FIRES AT SLANE AND TARA

When St Patrick was being considered in Rome as Apostle to Ireland, some of the learned men there objected to him on the grounds of his 'rusticity'. Later in his life, he himself recorded in his *Confessions* that he was 'a rude and untaught sinner'. But he adds that, by the grace of God who called him directly to his mission, he is, 'on the top of the wall … exalted above measure in this world'.

The story of his dramatic encounter with the High King of Ireland shows that, whatever his academic shortcomings, he had the courage and imagination that were needed to attack and capture the cultured pagan citadel, with one bold stroke of inspired genius.

After his first visit to the Brega coast, he had gone north and spent the winter in Ulster, the province where he had spent his boyhood as a slave. We can imagine that during his absence, the news of his visit had spread inland to Tara, and that the Druids were perturbed at this direct approach of the new culture which had already been filtering in. It is possible that Patrick intended that first foundation at Tullock as a challenge to them to marshal their forces.

Whether he did or not, it is certain that when spring came he returned by boat to the mouth of the Boyne with his missionary companions, and, as the Book of Armagh tells us, 'he left holy Loman at the mouth of the Boyne to guard the ship forty days and forty nights', while he and the others travelled by land to the Hill of Slane, then known as *Ferta Fer Feice*, the grave of the men of Fiac. It was the eve of Easter, 25 March 433. When night fell, he kindled the Pascal fire, the symbol of the new life of grace brought by the risen Christ.

But on Tara, tradition tells us, another feast was being celebrated. Part of the ceremony of that feast was that the Ard-Rí should light an enormous fire on the top of the hill. What exactly that feast was we do not know. Some think it was the *Baal-tine*; others hold that the Baal-tine would not have been so early. Certainly in later times it gave its name and traditions to May Day. But 25 March, the turn of the year, the vernal equinox, may very likely have had its own special Fire of Spring too.

Whatever the feast, the whole court of Laoire was assembled, and we can imagine that there was a vast concourse of people ready for a night of feasting, music and dancing. When the sky reddened over Slane there must have been consternation. To the majority it was frightening, because it was unnatural, sacrilegious, and ominous. The Druids and learned men around the king, however, were in no doubt at all. They knew it was the foreigner who had appeared on their shores the previous year. They appreciated the boldness of his challenge, and counselled the King that if the fire was not quenched that night it would never be quenched in Ireland.

Chariots were yoked in haste, and the Ard-Rí and his retinue drove the High Road to the Hill Sanctuary of Slane. That famous meeting of Laoire with Patrick deserves to be the subject of a great painting or a great drama. As the story has come down to us, we only know that by the power of Patrick, the Druids were unable to quench the fire, and that Laoire was fair minded enough to ask the stranger to appear at Tara on the morrow to argue his case. We may presume that the royal company returned to the palace, whether or not they carried on their own delayed celebration there. I think they did, with the heightened excitement of a Dance of Death.

The Druids, however, were not vanquished yet. They determined to kill Patrick and his followers before they should reach Tara on the morrow. So a company of armed men stole out from the royal *dún* and waited in ambush by the roadside for the saint and his followers. It would be an easy victory: the strangers had no weapons. Soon they heard in the distance the chanting of the approaching procession. The words have come down to us through the ages under the title of *Lúireach Pádraig* (the Breastplate of Patrick). It was the shield that no human weapon could pierce:

> I bind unto myself today
> The strong name of the Trinity
> In the Unity of God of the Elements.

It is a long hymn of singular beauty, a version of which in modern Irish is to be found in many prayer books, while there are various English translations in school books and anthologies:

> Christ before me
> Christ behind me
> Christ on my right hand
> Christ between me and every man
> That meditates evil to me.

We should hear the whole magnificent hymn sung in our churches in Patrick's language, the language the waiting soldiers heard it in; though as yet from their hiding place they could see nothing. The sound grew louder, the voices were close at hand – the singers should be in sight, but all that the men saw in the roadway was a flock of deer.

They were too surprised to move, and before they realised what was happening, the saintly company had passed them by in their miraculous disguise, and the chant faded in the distance towards Tara. When they told their story, *The Deer's Cry* is the name they gave that strange hymn, and *The Deer's Cry* has remained the name for the Easter Song of Patrick to this day.

In one account of the life of St Patrick there is a long description of the dispute that took place on Tara between the saint and the wise men of Loire. The incidents recorded may not all be literally true, but they show us at least what the tradition was a couple of centuries after Patrick's time. The Book of Armagh dates from about 800; the more fanciful stories are in later books, founded no doubt on manuscripts now lost. The best known story is that of the burning hut. I quote it in the translation used in *The Legend of Tara*:

> The dispute waxed high, and the people varied from one side to the other … Then with the agreement of all … in a new manner a new house is built, whereof the one half is made of wood which was dry and eaten of worms; and the boy Benin and the Magician, each being bound hand and foot, are placed over against each other; the boy arrayed in the Magician's garment is placed in the dry part of the building, and the Magician, clothed in the robe of St Patrick, is placed in the green part, and the fire is put thereto. And behold an event marvellous and much unwonted! The fire, furiously raging, consumed the Magician even to ashes, with the green part of the building

wherein he stood, and the robe of the Saint wherewith he was clad was neither scorched or soiled; but the blessed youth, Benin, standing in the dry
part thereof, the fire touched not, yet reduced to a cinder the garment of the
Magician that wrapped him round ...

Fr Callary quotes authorities to prove that the scene of this incident of the
trial by fire was a little to the east of the Mound of the Hostages. Not far
away, under the sod of deserted Tara, sleeps Loire, the last pagan King of
Ireland, who, miracles notwithstanding, died as he had lived, worshipping
the elements.

THE GLORY THAT WAS TRIM
CHRISTIANITY BROUGHT UPRIVER

While Patrick was disputing with the Druids on the Hill of Tara on Easter
Sunday 433, the boy Loman was guarding his ship at the mouth of the
Boyne. The Book of Armagh tells us that he had been ordered to wait there
for forty days and forty nights, but that he remained another forty, before
'under the pilotage of the Lord, he went in his boat against the flow of the
river as far as the Ford of Trim'.

This account might suggest that St Patrick parted from his young disciple at the beginning of Lent, and perhaps spent the holy season in prayer
and preparation for the public celebration of Easter on the Hill of Slane. If
so, it would have been almost midsummer when Loman, travelling against
the current, came in sight of the great settlement overlooking the Ford of
Trim. In passing, one may speculate on the size of the 'ship', so-called in the
account. If it was the one in which Patrick and all his company had sailed
up the coast, we can only conclude that the Irish kings kept the Boyne in
better condition than it is now.

It is difficult for us to visualise the site without the many monuments
that today, in ruins, make the approach to Trim so remarkably beautiful, 'a
combination of scenery,' says Wilde, 'and an architectural diorama such as we
have rarely witnessed'. The scenery was there, more unspoiled than today;
the architecture we know very little about, but the fortress of Feidlimid the
chief, standing high over the river with the houses of the lesser kinsmen and
retainers all round it, must have made an imposing picture, for Feidlimid

was no less a person than the son of Laoire, the High King himself, and his establishment must have been in accordance with his royal station.

Loman's ship arrived, 'at the door of the house of Feidlimid' near the Ford. Wilde has this to say about the exact location of the Ford:

> The ancient name of the place was Ath Truim, the Pass or Ford of the Elder Trees; and a ford, or shallow in the river, a short distance above the bridge, and within the extent of the old fortifications, was probably the site of this pass, for above, and particularly below it, the river is very deep.

The bridge referred to is, of course, the old bridge, for the new one was not built in Wilde's time.

The translation from the Book of Armagh continues:

> And when it was morning, Foirchern, son of Feidlimid, found him [Loman] reciting the Gospel; and admiring [or wondering at] the Gospel and his doctrine, immediately believed, and a well being opened in that place he was baptised by Loman, in Christ; and remained with him until his mother came to look for him; and she was made glad at his sight, because she was a British woman. But she likewise believed, and returned to her house and told her husband all that had happened to her and her son. And then Feidlimid was glad at the coming of the priest, for he had his mother from the Britons – namely Scotnoe, the daughter of the King of the Britons.

This clear and unadorned narrative is worth a little study. Laoire, High King of Ireland, was married to the daughter of the King of the Britons; his son was married to another British woman. But neither of them was a Christian, and the boy Foirchern, son and grandson of Britons, admired, or wondered at the Gospel of Loman. The explanation may be that the Irish and the Britons, kindred in race, had long been allies against the power of Rome in Britain, and that the Christian faith had only spread among those of the native people who had close contacts with the conquerors and accepted their way of life. It would be natural to expect fierce opposition to the 'Roman religion', such as was in later centuries shown by the Danes, yet there is no evidence of this.

Feidlimid saluted Loman in the British tongue and asked him about himself and his kindred and the faith he preached. Loman replied:

I am Loman, a Briton, a Christian, a disciple of Bishop Patrick, who is sent from the Lord to baptise the people of the Irish and to convert them to the faith of Christ; who sent me here according to the will of God.

Feidlimid, we are told, immediately believed, which would suggest that he knew something of Christianity already; otherwise we must regard the entire incident as miraculous. The whole household received baptism in 'the well that was opened at that place', and Feidlimid dedicated to Loman and Patrick his whole territory and possessions 'till the day of judgement'. It was no mere formal dedication, for he crossed the Boyne to Cluain Lagen and left his fortress at the Ford to Loman. The young Foirchern dedicated himself to the service of God and remained with Loman till Patrick came.

I do not know if anyone has positively identified the site of the *dún* of Feidlimid; if it were very near the Ford it would be on the slope of the present St Loman Street, but the site of St Mary's Abbey seems a more commanding position. When Patrick came, a church was built – the first great church in Ireland – with land and property for its support. This church may have been on or near the site of the present Protestant Cathedral of St Patrick, though some suggest that it was the original St Mary's Abbey, rebuilt in later centuries, with its lofty yellow steeple.

Loman had four brothers on the mission in Ireland; one, Manus, was later bishop of Forgney on the borders of Longford, and another, Broccan, gave his name to the foundation at Ardbraccan. The latter afterwards travelled into Connacht, where he died. It appears that Loman himself did not live for very many years as Bishop of Trim. When he was dying he wished Foirchern to 'accept the chieftainship of his church' and, to please him, Foirchern accepted; but three days after the death of his master he handed it over to one Cathlaid, a pilgrim, and lived his life out as a humble penitent. The story of Loman is told in stained glass in the new Catholic church of St Patrick, which crowns the height on the other side of the river.

As for Cluain Lagen, where Feidlimid took up his abode after he had surrendered his possessions in Trim to Loman, it is given in Hogan as Clonlyon in the parish of Kilmore, Barony of Upper Deece. That high country, within seven miles of Trim, seems a very likely site for a noble house, but I have not had an opportunity to locate Clonlyon or to find out if it contains a great rath or other remains.

We shall, in the course of our story, have occasion to visit Trim again. Its glory today is in what is left of its early Norman importance, its castle and town walls, its Cathedral and abbeys, noble in ruin but eloquent testimony to the great truth that nothing made by hands can last for ever. We must use our imagination if we wish to recapture the dawn of a June morning when the world was young, and a lime-white palace looked down on the white foam of elderflowers fringing the unchanging river.

TELTOWN, ORISTOWN AND DONAGHPATRICK
ST PATRICK'S INCURSION NORTHWARDS

Donaghpatrick, on a height overlooking the lovely valley of the Blackwater, takes its name from the great church, *Domhnach* in Irish, founded there by Patrick himself. He left Trim on Easter Monday, and travelled the road to *Táilte* (Teltown), where a brother of the Ard-Rí lived. It was one of the most important territories of ancient Meath and the scene of the great Aonach at Lughnasa (August) which harked back to the days of the *Túatha De Danann*, a thousand years before Patrick's time.

It is notable that old accounts make mention of a feast being held at *Táilte* when Patrick arrived, and as the time is given as Easter Monday or Tuesday it would seem that the festival on Tara was not just a local one, but that that week was the time of some seasonal festival celebrated all over the country. I have suggested the likelihood of a spring festival in honour of the triumph of the sun over the spirits of winter, but in the present state of our knowledge we can say little about the religion of the pagan Irish. I have heard that there exists an abundance of local tradition about the miracles worked by Patrick at Teltown, but I do not know if it has ever been recorded.

Miracles notwithstanding, the ruler of Teltown was not favourably disposed to Christian teaching, and the saint soon passed on to the next hill site, where Conall, another brother of the Ard-Rí, had his *dún*. This was Rath Airthir, now called in English Oristown. Conall received Patrick hospitably and he and his household not only accepted the faith but Conall donated a site near his own house for the erection of a church. Patrick marked it out, sixty feet long according to an early account, and left an altarstone to be used in it for the celebration of Mass. The *rath* was raised and the enclosing dyke dug and soon a great church crowned the height.

It may have been of wood, but if so it was soon replaced by a stone build-ing, for there are early references to it as a *daimliagh* or stone house. Most authorities say, however, that the first *daimliagh* was the one which has left its name to the present day at Duleek.

The remains of the rath at Donaghpatrick may still be traced in the graveyard beside the modern (Protestant) church, and on the left of the road as we approach is the great rath of Airthir where Conall's castle stood. It consists of a large central mound surrounded by four rings, and resembles the great rath at Tara.

Indeed its commanding position over the river makes it more impres-sive. The whole district of Donaghpatrick, Teltown, and Ardbraccan is well worth a visit. There is a gracious charm in that undulating country of woods and river meadows; the churches and houses seem to fit so well into their surroundings that one can almost imagine that they all belong to the golden age of early Christian Ireland.

Patrick did not delay long to enjoy his triumph at Rath Airthir. Leaving some of his priests behind him to look after the building of the church, he followed the road by the river up to the *Ford of the Two Forks*, near the present Ceanannus Mór. There was, near the river, another great house, the Head Fort of Meath founded several centuries before by King Fiacha. The site is in the grounds of the present demesne of Headfort. The word *annus* in the original name seems to have been replaced in later centuries by *lios*, a word of similar meaning, and whence came *Kenlis* in early English, and the contraction Kells.

Patrick founded a church here and left it in the charge of three brothers and a sister. Their names are given as Cathaceus, Cathurus, Catneus and Catnea. These are obviously Latin forms, and in early Christian times it was customary to keep all records in Latin, the universal language of the Church and of the schools. The four *Caths* may have been members of a native family who accepted the faith and gave the site for a church. We know very little about the exact location or the further history of this founda-tion, but a century later, King Diarmuid gave a grant of land in the vicinity to Columcille, and on it arose the great monastic buildings which will be described in a later chapter.

Again Patrick pressed on. He must have been a man of boundless energy, or his zeal for the work before him must have lent strength to his ageing body, for in a very short time he had gone on by Delvin through the present

Westmeath and probably as far as the great fort of Usnach. On the way or on the return journey, he founded so many churches that it would be impossible in this short survey to refer to all of them. There is one at Kilpatrick, near Delvin, which deserves mention, not only because it retains the saint's name but because of the interesting ruins that still stand on the site.

The Book of Armagh names eight churches founded by Patrick himself in East Meath (*Bregia*), the first being the Tullock already referred to. Fr Brady says that, while some of the others are difficult to identify, it is almost certain that among them were Kilcarne, Assey, Platten, Duleek, Derrypatrick and Ratoath. Derrypatrick is near to Clonlyon (*Cluain lagen*), the place to which Feidlimid of Trim retired when he gave his fort to Loman and Patrick.

Duleek was placed in the charge of Bishop Kienan (Cianan), who had been ordained by Patrick on the Hill of Slane on the first Easter eve, and who had carried the Pascal fire 'and the first waxen lights of Patrick'. This is the Kienan who built the first stone church or *daimliagh*, and while it is unlikely that any of the original building survives, the remains still standing are very ancient. Duleek continued to be an important bishopric for 700 years. Kells and Ratoath also retained their importance, but of some of the others we hear very little in the records.

A church was founded at Slane at an early period, though possibly not by Patrick himself. The tradition is that when King Laoire went from Tara to Slane to extinguish the fire of Patrick, there was among his retinue a young nobleman named Erc. He alone saluted Patrick, and in return for his courageous gesture the saint blessed him. He afterwards devoted his life to the service of God, and may have founded a church at Slane. In the grounds of the castle is a little cell known as St Erc's Hermitage, where he is said to have lived a life of solitude and prayer.

We know that there was an important monastery at Slane in the seventh century, for Archdall, quoting a history of France, says that in 653 the King of Austrasia was banished to Ireland at the age of seven years, and received into the monastery of Slane. He stayed there twenty years and received the education befitting his rank, after which he was recalled to his own country and kingship. Later a round tower was erected on the hilltop to guard the church and monastery against the Danes, but in the course of a raid in 918 the whole place was burned down with all the people in it and all its precious relics, including its bell, described as 'the best of bells'.

THE EPOCHAL ERA OF ST COLUMCILLE
THE BOOKS OF KELLS AND DURROW

O Cormac, beautiful is that church of thine!

With its books, with its learning,

A city devout with a hundred crosses

Without blemish, without transgression.

St Columcille, from his exile in Iona, addressed the abbot whom he had left in charge of his beloved monastery at Durrow. That lyrical note gives us the key in which we must set our descriptions in the Golden Age.

Columcille was a man from the North, a prince of the royal blood of the Uí Neill, in line for the High Kingship of Ireland. He chose instead the life of a tonsured monk, dedicated to prayer and penance. He studied at Finian's school at Clonard in Meath, and, as was the custom, spent periods at other schools as well. But as was, perhaps, not so much the custom, he also studied under one of the old poets, so that with his knowledge of the native Irish classics and of the Latin Roman classics, his great genius found a literary expression exceeding any in the world up to then. Many of his compositions have survived to clothe the lists of saints and their foundations with a living beauty.

His first foundation was at Derry, the 'oak wood', but no tree was cut to make room for this church or cell. When his fame spread, the Meath branch of his family asked him to found a settlement among them, and he chose an oak wood, Durrow. Leaving Cormac in charge, he went to the banks of the Blackwater to found the monastery at Kells, near the ancient Ceann Annus. No site in Meath retains so well the peaceful dignity of early Christian times. The great tower crowning the height, the stone house, the sculptured crosses, seem ageless in their soft grey colouring, with all the overtones of brown and green that changing light gives to stone. The town beneath shelters in their benediction. It is easy to imagine the monks coming and going there, or the young Ultan travelling from Ardbraccan to see the new foundation, or the Abbots of Donaghpatrick or Dulane with their companies coming to imbibe the inspiring words of this amazing young man while partaking of the refectory's humble hospitality.

It was in the year 550 that this foundation was made, though the actual buildings we see today are later. At the beginning it was possibly all of wood, well-planed planks for the church, wicker and plaster for the cells and a well-sheltered bright building for the scriptorium, for in every monastery and church from the very beginning writing was important. A copy of the Gospels would be left, perhaps on loan, to be copied for use. At first the scripts were simply and plainly done, but there was always the feeling that as it was God's book that was being written, it should be well done. Columcille was to add to his other activities that of perfection in writing, and it was from his immediate successors in Durrow, Derry, Iona, Kells and elsewhere, that the school of illuminators grew. The work of this school reached its peak in that greatest of all books, the Book of Kells.

But that was still in the future. The first book associated with the name of Columcille is the famous Cathach. The legend has it that this was the book that led to the saint's exile in Iona. About the end of the fourth century, St Jerome made a translation of the Gospels into Latin. It was adopted in Rome and gradually spread westwards. The first Irishman to secure a copy was Finian, the Abbot of Moville. It was a very precious book and, as far as we know, the owner refused to lend it to Columcille for copying. We can appreciate that Columcille, being the great student he was, knew all about the importance of the new translation, and felt a scholar's desire to possess it. He made a copy in secret and when the fact was discovered and the law compelled him to return the copy, he mustered his powerful family friends and gave battle. As a penance, he later submitted to a sentence of exile from his native land. The Cathach is our oldest surviving manuscript and scholars are agreed that it may quite well be in the actual handwriting of Columcille.

We in Meath cannot lay any particular claim to it, but we have some rights in the Book of Durrow which dates from the next century. It takes its name from a monastery in the Meath diocese, and we may assume it was written, or at least illuminated, there. The original is in the library of Trinity College. Meath County Library has a reproduction copy. Nothing I can say will bring home to the reader the amazing beauty of this book. The pages measure only 9.5 by 6.5 inches and it is only when a page is magnified that we can begin to appreciate the workmanship. This includes the design of lettering and ornament, the geometrical basis of tangential circles and spirals, the perfection of the interlacing and the artistry with which these minute details are combined to give an overall effect of strong, rich composition. There are only four colours, dark brown, brick red, green and a bright yellow, but they are used to give a delicate yet boldly striking effect.

If the Book of Durrow were the only manuscript left from early-Christian times, it would be the wonder of the world. As it is, it is overshadowed by the Book of Kells, in which the patterns are more lavish, the figure drawing more sophisticated, and the range of colours very much greater. In particular, the use of gold and purple gives the work more magnificence than the more austere colouring of the Book of Durrow.

The question that interests most people is the dating of these works. Experts tell us that neither of them could possibly have been written by Columcille himself and that the Book of Durrow was not written till after 660 and the Book of Kells at least a century later. This, they deduce partly from the comparison of the style with that of surviving metalwork of the period, with carvings on crosses and with known developments in styles elsewhere. I have always felt that this is a little disappointing, and that I would like to believe, as most people believed through the centuries, that the great Columcille himself wrote our two great books. That he and his contemporaries did produce many illuminated manuscripts is, of course, undoubted, and there must have been hundreds of them in our monasteries, at the time of the Viking invasions but these pagan raiders had no respect for the manuscripts as works of art. They removed the beautiful metal covers and took them home as spoil along with chalices, brooches and such valuables, and discarded the manuscripts as useless. There are, however, numbers of fine manuscripts on the continent, preserved from the Irish monasteries founded from the sixth century on.

We know that the Book of Durrow was kept in the monastery there down to the time of the dissolution of the monasteries at the Reformation (1540). It was afterwards kept as a precious relic by the MacGeoghegans, one of the great Irish ruling families, who retained at least some of their importance down to the time of Cromwell. One member of this family, writing in the early seventeenth century, mentions that the book was used to cure sick cattle, by pouring water over it! One of Cromwell's followers, Henry Jones, became Protestant Bishop of Meath, and somehow acquired possession of the precious relic and presented it to Trinity College, in whose library it is now kept.

The Book of Kells has an even stranger history. At the time of its composition, there was constant intercourse between Kells and Iona. It may be that part of the work was carried out in the Scottish monastery; some think the writing may have been done there and spaces left for the illumination to be filled in here. In any case, it is, of course, the work of Irish monks, and numbers must have worked on it, for no one man could have done it in three lifetimes.

When the Vikings began to raid the Scottish islands, all the treasures on Iona were brought for safekeeping to Kells. The monks themselves came in numbers, and Kells was rebuilt and extended to become the headquarters of all the Columban monasteries. This was the year 801 and it is probable that the crosses and Columcille's house date from that time, but the question is by no means settled. The Viking raids became as bad here as in Iona and the Kells Round Tower probably was built as a defence. The book was well guarded or hidden and kept safe till the year 1006, at which date this entry appears in the Annals:

> The great gospel of Colum Cille was stolen at night from the west sacristy of the great church of Ceanannus. This was the principal relic of the western world, on account of its singular cover; and it was found after twenty nights and two months, its gold having been stolen off it, and a sod over it.

Its later history is similar to that of the Book of Durrow and it is now in Trinity College. There is a fine replica in Meath County Library.

Volumes have been written about the art of early-Christian Ireland and it would be a pity to pass away from the study of this period without touching on some of the interesting questions that are discussed by many expert authors: How were the inks made? Did the scribes use magnifying glasses? How far was geometry known and taught in Irish schools?

Here is a translation of a poem by a scribe of the twelfth century, which helps us to see the writers as very human, though their work has been described as the work of angels:

> My hand is weary with writing;
> My sharp, great point is not thick;
> My slender-beaked pen juts forth
> A beetle-hued draft of bright blue ink.
>
> A steady stream of wisdom
> Springs from my well-coloured
> Neat fair hand; on the page it pours
> Its draught of ink of the green-skinned holly.

I send my little dipping pen
Unceasingly over an assemblage
Of books of great beauty, to enrich
The possessions of art
Whence my hand is weary with writing.

A PATRICIAN LEGEND RECALLED
THE STORIES OF WELLS AND CROSSES

A Teltown reader has sent me a legend of the well known as *Tobar Pádraig*, at Hermitage, Moynalty. He says it is a true story, handed down from one generation to another:

All the locality went out to see Patrick and his priests. After he had finished preaching, they all wanted to be baptised, only there was no water. Patrick made a hole which immediately filled with water, and he baptised them all. In the area there were three corpses and Patrick was asked to bury them. He told the crowd that where his oxen would rest for the night he would build a church, and they could bury them beside it. So they journeyed on 'til they came to a fort near Drumlane, and there they met another crowd. Again St Patrick started preaching and the oxen were let loose and soon lay down. When St Patrick was engaged preaching and baptising, the crowd were burying the corpses, and were finished before Patrick.

As soon as Patrick was finished the oxen got up and started to graze so he ordered them to be yoked again to travel on, only then to find out the mistake of the crowd, who wanted the church to be built there. Now St Patrick said where the oxen 'would rest for the night' he would build, and before he left he blessed the graves and ordered a cross to be erected over them. So he travelled on until he came to Moybologue and there he built a church.

Of the remains of this church, said to be his first, a portion was still standing when I saw it twenty years ago. The well at Hermitage I visited ten years ago on St Patrick's Day. There were three old women there saying the Rosary. I wonder was there anyone there this St Patrick's Day. Fifty years ago there were big crowds there. The graves at Drumlane are marked with a large stone on which a cross is clearly cut; it is just a scratching-stone for cattle.

I am grateful to the sender of this account, which has the true ring of ancient belief. It is suggested that St Patrick, in his journey across Ireland, went from hill to hill: Skryne, Tara, Teltown, Hermitage, and Moybologue. This would seem the natural route, as it is most likely that every hilltop was crowned with a great rath, enclosing the home of a chieftain and his retainers, the nearest thing to what we would call a town.

It is curious that while we have innumerable stories of Patrick, Brigid and Columcille handed down, like this one, through the oral tradition, there are comparatively few about the other saints who have left their names in Meath parishes. Three holy women, Scire, Liadhan and Cuach, have given us Kilskyre, Killyon and Kilcock. The last is not in the present county of Meath but near enough to be worth mentioning. I have read that there is a well there called *Tobar Mococha*. I wonder if any rounds or stations are still made there, or if any stories of this saint are still extant.

There are records of a St Lasara of Trim, a sister of St Forthcern. She visited St Finian at Clonard and after long wanderings returned in answer to the command of God to found a monastery in Trim. I do not think her name or fame have survived to our time. St Loman, though now better known through revival of devotion to him, has left little trace in our folklore.

St Ultan of Ardbraccan has fared better, so has Erc of Slane and Fechin of Fore. But how much do we know of the saints who gave their names to Dunshaughlin, Kilmoon, Killabban, Stackallen, Ardbraccan, Balrathboyne and dozens of other places? I have referred more than once to the monumental work of Dean Cogan in his three-volume *History of the Diocese of Meath, Ancient and Modern* (1870). Every reference to our saints which he could find in manuscripts and in oral traditions is noted in his pages. But no one person in a lifetime can go into every townland and talk to every old man and every old woman and gather every faint memory and shadow of a memory that remains. It is indeed a labour of love to write down every little detail about former pilgrimages, cures, patterns and so on, even though you may not always be able to link them with the name of a saint.

The idea of choosing the site for a church by the accident of an animal lying to rest is common in the lives of the saints. In Armagh, it was a deer and her fawn. Elsewhere we hear of birds and even bees being regarded as giving indications of the Divine Will. This is the first time I have heard this type of story in Meath and it illustrates what I am trying to impress on my readers; that the seemingly unimportant things we have heard from the old people are all little fragments of the fabric of our almost lost heritage. Gather the fragments, and someone will piece them together.

In discussing stations or penitential rounds, such as pilgrims to Lough Derg are familiar with, the following information may be interesting and may possibly link up with some living tradition. *Uladh* (pronounced ulla in English spelling) meant, in old Irish, 'a tomb'. Later, the word was applied to the tomb of a saint over which was a cairn or a stone altar, where pilgrims came to pray or perform penances.

According to P.W. Joyce's *Irish Names of Places* many places are named after such tombs such as *Killulla*, in Clare, meaning 'the church of the tomb'. Sometimes, if there was more than one grave or altar, the word was used in the plural and got translated into English as 'The Ullas'. But he gives the name of a place in Leitrim called in English 'Halls', and explains that in this case the plural Irish form *Na hUlladha* was partly adopted in the English translation.

There are at least three townlands in Meath which may have got their names in this way: Halltown Dunderry, Hallstown in the Barony of Ratoath, and Gathahall in the parish of Ballivor.

HOLY WELLS AND THEIR ORIGINS
THE KILLYON PATTERN

For some weeks now I have been dealing with various aspects of life in Ireland during early-Christian times, and my references to particular places were primarily intended as illustrative of these aspects. Inevitably, many sites were not mentioned at all, and in this instalment we may visit a few of them in the pleasant company of William Wilde, and, like him, present the scene 'from our summer recollections … when the birds carolled high above us, and the long calm twilight of midsummer, with all its poetic associations, induced us to linger amidst these scenes of beauty, fairy legend and historic interest'.

Beginning at the source of the Boyne, one of the first places to attract Wilde's attention was the Hill of Carrick, which appears to drive its name from a great block of rock called the Witch's Stone, standing on its northern brow just over the great limestone quarry. This boulder may have been deposited there by natural means during the Ice Age, but it may also have been transported there in prehistoric times for purposes of pagan worship.

The legend is that it was cast by a witch from the neighbouring hill of Croghan at some early saint. This legend attaches to almost every great stone in Ireland, and Wilde points out that it is equally prevalent over Scotland and Northern Europe. We remember in particular the Old Hag of Loughcrew casting the stones from her apron and the curious quatrain in Irish attributed to her, which was familiar to the people in John O'Donovan's time, and is still remembered in a rhymed translation:

> Many wonders have I seen;
> I've seen Carn Ban a lake,
> But now a valley green.

A hundred years ago there were some remains on the Hill of Carrick which Wilde believed to be the remains of a hermit's cell – such are found near many monastic settlements. In Fore, for instance (to quote Fr Coyle):

> … there is a modern building called the Anchorite's Cell, now the tomb of the Greville-Nugent family of Delvin. In this spot there was kept up a succession of hermits down to the seventeenth century, the last being Patrick Beglin, whose residence there is commemorated in a Latin inscription inside the oaken door of the Tomb, dated AD 1616.

But the hermits of Carrick Hill, and the religious house that once stood there, are nameless. The Witch's Stone was blasted by some local vandal many years ago. There remain two sets of holes on the hillside, called 'The Mule's Leap', associated, like the stone, with a legend of a nameless saint.

In this locality are the six holy wells which 'baptise the infant Boyne'. One of them was known in Wilde's time as *Tobar Aluinn*, the beautiful well, another, *Tobar na Cille*, the well of the church, and a third *Tobercro*, which Wilde says is *Tobar Croiche*, the well of the cross. These, like all the holy wells of Ireland, were once places of pilgrimage. Some had the cure of a particular disease: headaches, eye trouble and so on. In some there was a special form of visit, certain prayers and 'rounds' to be made. In most, there was a particular date, probably the feast day of the saint associated with the well, but only remembered as a 'Pattern' (Patron) Day. The date often survives as an annual fair day when its origin has been forgotten.

Most authorities believe that the holy wells were sacred wells in the beginning, at which pagan rites were celebrated and that, when Patrick came, he blessed them and Christianised their use as sources of water for baptism. The descriptions in early records suggest that baptism by immersion was common in the early Irish Church. There is an old belief that if a cure is effected or a prayer answered, the pilgrim will see a fish in the bottom of the well; in some places it is said to be a trout, but an eel is also mentioned. This sounds very like a pagan origin but some writers hold that the monks used to keep a fish-pond within the enclosure to maintain supplies for their meatless meals, and that simple people regarded the fish of the saints as sacred creatures.

Until very recent times, there was also the custom of leaving votive offerings at a holy well. Commonly, if a tree overhung the well – and almost always there was a sacred tree – the pilgrim hung a scrap of his clothing on it. The best known of these 'rag wells' was at Clonfad where the bush was a well-known landmark up to a few years ago. Now it has gone the way of many other relics of our native devotions.

Another holy well to which annual pilgrimages are still made is Lady Well in Killyon. Wilde does not mention it, but he has this to say:

> In the demesne of Killyon, on the northern bank of the river, about midway between Clonard and Trim, are the ruins of an old church and friary, originally founded by St Liadhan, the mother of St Ciaran of Saighir, who is still the patroness of the Parish. From some of the Inquisitions and from Burke's 'Hibernia Dominicana' we learn that the Dominican monks of Trim retired to the Friary of Donore, as it is sometimes called. The two walls, which now remain, are picturesquely situated on a sloping ground, surrounded by some patriarchal ash trees; and nearly opposite these, on the southern bank, at Lion's Den, in the townland of Castle Ricard, we find the crumbling walls of an old battlemented house. Two very perfect tumuli, one near the church of Castle Ricard, also occur in this locality.
>
> Below the friary, on the northern bank, the square border castle of Donore forms a conspicuous object, as the ruins are in better preservation than most of the other castles of the Pale.

This description shows us that Killyon is very typical of the Boyne Valley sites. First there are the tumuli, showing that the place was of importance in pagan times and had probably been an important chief's residence at the time of St Patrick. The site was donated to Liadhan, a young kinswoman of the chief; she founded a convent there, and a church was built. When the Normans came, they built a monastery of their own on the Celtic site. (It may have been derelict by then; if not they drove out the monks.) They had a succession of dwellings, castles, or other strong houses during the Middle Ages.

In Cromwellian times, the sway passed from the Ricards to new settlers who enclosed the demesne and built the manor house. A church of the new religion took the place of an ancient church beside the pagan tumulus, and the successors to the Norman monks crept back to a secluded spot where they hoped to escape the vigour of the Penal Laws. They ministered in secret till, in the late eighteenth century, the Catholic Church was able to reorganise its parishes. Then the Dominicans of Donore became the first pastors to officiate in the thatched chapels of Longwood, Killyon and Ballivor.

FOUR

ARTEFACTS AND ARCHITECTURE

HOW THE FARMERS WERE HOUSED

The name of the Royal Dublin Society is so closely connected in our minds to the great shows in Ballsbridge that we are apt to forget the other contributions it has made during the past couple of centuries to the improvement of economic and social conditions in Ireland. Not the least of these was the sponsoring, at the beginning of the last century, of descriptive surveys of the counties.

The Dublin Society, as it was then called (the Royal was added, I think, at the time of Queen Victoria's last visit), made out a list of subjects deserving of enquiry: soil, agriculture, pasture, farms, houses, and general conditions, including food, wages, villages, education, and historic remains. Gentlemen in each county were invited to undertake the surveys, and in Meath the choice was Robert Thompson of Oatland. His work was published in 1802, and copies of it are now comparatively scarce. There is, of course, a copy in the Local Studies collection at the headquarters of the Meath County Council Library Service, but I am fortunate in that a friend has given me one on long loan.

It is a beautifully produced book, with the leather binding showing no trace of wear after a century and a half; the frontispiece is an engraving of Bective Abbey, and there is a folding map of the county on which it is interesting to note that part of the parish of Longwood, now in Meath, was then in Kildare. There are also numerous drawings of the cattle and sheep then bred, and the latest improved ploughs and other implements then in use.

Mr Thompson did his work with scrupulous fairness and great attention to detail. Every chapter is a temptation to copious quotation. Here, for example, is the beginning of the section headed 'Farm Houses and Offices':

That description of men whom I shall here style the common farmers consists of those who occupy from twenty to one hundred acres, and in a few instances one hundred and fifty acres of ground, at the fair value between landlord and tenant; and this class is, I think, with respect to their circumstances, worse lodged than any part or the community. There is no point of rural economy to which the attention of the society might be more usefully directed than in endeavouring to promote the comforts and ameliorate the condition of that most useful body of men, with respect to their dwellings and offices. Their houses are for the most part extremely wretched, and in general this arises from too great a burden being thrown by the landlord upon the tenant. When a farmer, under the present system, enters upon a new farm he generally has a house and offices to build, perhaps the whole to fence, and this upon a lease of twenty-one or thirty-one years, a term now considered good. It is not to be expected that the tenant upon such a tenure will build with the most durable materials, or put himself to any extraordinary trouble or expense in procuring the most approved plan. He builds that same kind of low, mud-wall, dark, dirty and smokey tenement which, under the same circumstances, his father lived in before him, in which he was reared; to this house he adds a stable and cow-house of the same materials.

These farmhouses are generally formed from the earth or clay of the surface of the spot on which they are built, in order to save the expense of carrying it from any distance; hence the ground floor is commonly six or eight inches below the level of the surface outside the walls, and consequently subject to all the unwholesome effects arising from damp, to which the whole family are in a great degree subject from, their straw beds being, in most instances, placed upon the bare floor without even a mat or bedstead to protect them from its influence. This farm-house, and these offices, seldom last longer than the lease, frequently not so long, without propping and repairs, so that the farm-house tumbles when the lease expires nor is it the wish of the farmer that it should be otherwise, as in the re-letting of these grounds, which he has occupied, perhaps a stranger is preferred in consequence of his paying some trifle more than the old tenant.

Sir John Dillon has built at Lismullen a very good farmhouse, fit for the residence of a farmer, who holds one hundred acres of ground, which is slated and lofted, and from the disposition and number of the windows calculated to save the tax, at the same time admitting sufficient light. This house, he assures me, cost no more than twenty guineas but, as he procured the timber from his own demesne, a great saving accrued to him; however, from every calculation, I think such a house could be built for about forty pounds.

In the remainder of that section of Thompson's survey, mention is made of two other gentlemen who encouraged their farmer-tenants to improve their dwelling houses: Michael Tisdall of Charlesfort and Baron Hussey of Rathkenny. These seem to have been exceptions in an age when property in Ireland had its rights but not its duties.

I shall have occasion to quote Thompson again on a variety of subjects, but for this week I would ask readers to think about the age and history of the farmhouses in their neighbourhood. Remember that the miserable hovels described above were not the cabins of the labourers; they were occupied by families farming up to a hundred acres of Meath land in 1798. Now, apart from houses built or repaired with the aid of housing grants during the past thirty years, what is the history of the comfortable farm-houses that we associate with holdings of this size?

Some are slated and two storey, with kitchen and parlour below, and two or three bedrooms above. Others are long, one-storey, thatched houses, with the walls, whether of mud or stone, well white-washed, and with sufficient accommodation and furniture for decent living and frugal comfort. When, or by what slow degrees, did the change come about? In passing, we may question whether our modern architects have produced anything quite as comfortable and draught-proof as the traditional house.

A few weeks ago another of my friends in Brannockstown gave me an item which he had found in the thatch of an old house. He surmised that it was a tool for scutching flax, and when I brought it to the National Museum the expert told me that that is just what it was. He was most interested in it, as few have ever reached the museum, though, strangely enough, only a few days pre-viously, another had come in from Garadice, found in the same circumstances.

The item looks like half a blade of a scythe, with a handle inserted, but the whole thing is made of wood, and the splicing of the blade into the handle is very cleverly done. We discussed finds of flax in bogs, and it appears that experts have only heard of these, and have not had an opportunity to examine them, and relating them to depth and other conditions which would help to solve the mystery of their existence.

THE CROSSES AND OTHER WONDERS
KELLS HOLDS GREAT RELICS OF GLORIOUS PAST

The two great treasures of early Christian Ireland – the Book of Kells and the Tara Brooch – are associated with Meath but neither is housed in the county. We can hardly grudge them to our capital city where they can be seen by a wider public. But we have other treasures, no less beautiful and which cannot be taken from us, in Columcille's house and the sculpted crosses of Kells.

As one walks along the main street of the town, it comes as something of a shock to see, against a background of modern shops and in the midst of busy traffic, this grey sentinel of a thousand years, calm and beautiful, ageless and changeless, as the faith it symbolises. It is the Cross of Christ, carrying the story of the race of Adam and surrounded by the Ring of Eternity.

The cross is of sandstone, shaft and head carved from a single block, in perfect proportion of height and width, which gives a feeling of satisfaction to the least artistic observer. The various scenes depicted in the deeply cut carvings fit harmoniously into panels, with perfectly executed pattern designs introduced for decorative effect.

Centuries have weathered it and only a guide can easily identify the subjects of all the carvings. Many readers will have followed the details of this and of the other crosses at the churchyard under the guidance of Miss Helen M. Roe, who knows them so intimately and loves them so much. There is Adam and Eve being tempted by the serpent; there is Abraham offering his only son as a sacrifice, prefiguring the greater sacrifice of Jesus of Nazareth.

Daniel in the Lion's Den emphasises in another way the idea of the Redemption and prepares us for the scenes from the life of Our Lord, culminating in the Crucifixion. Moses receiving the Tablets of the Law; the Magi bringing gifts; the hermits in the desert fed by heavenly bread; the baptism of Our Lord – all the scenes are selected to give, in a striking visual manner, the whole Christian teaching on sin and redemption, man's duty to God and God's unfailing care for His children who trust in Him. We can imagine the preacher standing at the foot of that cross, now in the market place, with his congregation around him as he tells the story, pointing to scene after scene, pausing for moments of pious contemplation, followed by prayers of heartfelt thanksgiving.

Columcille's house is another of Meath's most precious monuments. It resembles the famous Kevin's Kitchen at Glendalough, in having two storeys, the vault helping to support the high-pitched roof. It is one of the few perfect stone churches or oratories surviving from early Christian times, and, like the crosses, it gives the impression of having stood there since the beginning of time, while of later churches, castles, and mansions hardly a vestige remains. This survival is all the more remarkable when we glance through the notices in the Annals:

807: The Church of St Columba at Kells was destroyed.

903: Kells forcibly entered by Maelsechnaill and many were killed about the oratory.

918: Kells plundered by the Danes and the Daimhliag (stone church) was demolished.

949: Godfrey, son of Sitric, with the Danes of Dublin, plundered Kells, Donaghpatrick, Ardbraccan, Dulane, Castlekieran, Kilskyre and other churches in like manner; but it was out of Kells they were all plundered. They carried upwards of three thousand persons with them into captivity, besides gold, silver, raiment and various wealth and goods of every description.

968: Kells was plundered by Aulive with the Danes and Leinstermen.

996: Kells and Clonard were plundered by the Danes of Dublin.

1015: Kells, Clonmacnoise and Clonfert were burned.

Further entries of the same kind go on and on even after the defeat of the Danes. Some of the burnings recorded may have been accidental, in those days of frail wood and wattle buildings, for example:

1144:   Kells was burned thrice this year, but there is no doubt about the
        significance of this entry.

1170:   Kells, Clonard, Teltown, Dowth, Dulane, Kilskyre and Castlekieran
        were plundered and burned by Dermod Mac Murchad, King of
        Leinster, and the English.

The Golden Age of Christian peace was long over by this time, and the
wonder is that any relic of it survived the centuries of turmoil which proceeded that last date, 1170. Another and worse invasion began then which
was to all but exterminate the entire Gaelic world.

But the stone house stands on the hill of Ceanannus beside the round
tower, and the cross casts its benediction on the town where children of
Gael, Dane, and Norman share the heritage of Columcille.

Before we embark on these dark pages of our history, there are some
other points of the pre-Danish period that deserve notice. These invaders
appeared on the coasts of Scotland before they touched Ireland, and so the
monks from Iona carried their precious treasures over to Kells for safety. It
appears, indeed, that many of the monks at Iona were slaughtered by the
Danes in 807 and that the Abbot, Cellach (himself, of course, an Irishman,
and, if his name gives a clue, perhaps a Meathman), fled with the survivors
to Kells. He rebuilt the monastery there which had been destroyed by fire
shortly before. It may be that it is to this rebuilding we owe the crosses.

When some of the first Danish invaders had settled down and adopted
Christianity, the influence of their own native styles of art was felt in Irish
metalwork, and there are three famous and beautiful objects connected
with Kells and dating from some time after the victory of Clontarf that
illustrate this. The first in point of time is the Crozier of Kells, which
bears an inscription identifying it with the church in Kells and dating it
to the middle of the eleventh century. It came into the hands of Cardinal
Wiseman in the middle of the last century and is now in the British
Museum.

The other two objects are book shrines, or cases made to hold valuable
manuscripts. One is the famous Cathach and the other the Misach, both
said to have been made in Kells in about the year 1070. The former bears
an inscription which, translated, begins, 'A prayer for Cathbharr O'Donnell
by whom this shrine was caused to be made.' Its history as the Cathach or

battle mascot of the O'Donnell family through many centuries, though not exactly Meath history, deserves to be told in full and I have no doubt Miss Roe will tell it in her forthcoming book.

THE ECCLESIASTICAL REMAINS AT SLANE
SOME NOT-SO-WELL-KNOWN FACTS

Listeners to a recent Thomas Davis lecture will remember reference being made to a young prince of Austrasia who was spirited away as a result of a conspiracy between a wicked bishop named Grimoald and the brother of St Gertrude. The plotters met in the abbey of which St Gertrude was the abbess, and the incident occurred about the time of the murder of the Irish saint Faelan.

I hasten to add that this murder was the work of bandits and that St Gertrude succeeded in finding and punishing them. How, from the record left by St Gertrude herself, archaeologists have, in the last few years, traced the exact road by which Faelan travelled and the exact spot to which he and his companions were lured by the robbers, is a piece of detective work stranger and more fascinating than any piece of modern fiction.

What links St Gertrude to the history of Meath is the plot to place a usurper on the throne of Austrasia. It was about the middle of the seventh century, some fifty years after the great mission of Columban in that part of the Frankish Empire. The prince was brought to Ireland, perhaps through the connivance of some Irish monk in one of the Columban foundations in the neighbourhood, and placed in the abbey of Slane. Sir William Wilde quotes Archdall, a former rector of Slane, as stating on the authority of Mezeray's *History of France* that Slane was:

> … for many years the residence of a royal prince; for we find that in the year 653, Dagobert, King of Austrasia, when at the age of only seven years, was taken by Grimoald, mayor of the palace, and by his direction he was shorn a monk, rendered unfit to hold the reins of government, and banished into Ireland. From oral information we learn that he was received into this abbey, where he received an education proper for the enjoyment of a throne; he continued here during the space of twenty years, when he was recalled into France, and replaced in his government.

While on the subject of Slane, Wilde describes a tomb which he believes to be of greater antiquity than any Christian tomb in Ireland, except one at Saul – Patrick's first church in County Down – and another at Donaghpatrick:

> … a fragment of which occupies a precisely similar position to the adjoin-
> ing church there. This tomb at Slane consists of two large gable-shaped flags,
> about three feet of which rise above the ground, and separated by an interval
> of about six feet. Each of these stones is grooved exactly like the gable of a
> house, the grooves appearing to be intended for the reception of the ends of
> horizontally inclined flags which formed the roof.

Wilde adds that at funerals it was the custom, when carrying the corpse round the graveyard, to lay it down for a short time at this spot. A similar custom prevailed in most of the old graveyards, but, as these are one by one giving way to new parochial cemeteries, the hallowed spots are liable to be forgotten. This is a pity, as the custom of stopping for the *De Profundis* at a particular spot gives a clue to the burial place of a revered person, and it has been, in many cases, the pointer to a long-concealed tombstone of great antiquity.

It is pleasant to be able to comment on the admirable way the ecclesiasti-cal remains at Slane are preserved. It is worth while visiting them, not only for their own importance but for the magnificent view from even ground level on this historic hilltop. Those young enough to climb the stair will be rewarded on a clear day with a beautiful vista extending to the mouth of the Boyne and the sea beyond.

Of the round tower of Slane, burned by the Danes in 948, no trace remains. Many other round towers probably existed at the river sites of Meath which met with a similar fate. In some cases the abbeys themselves do not seem to have survived the plundering, though some remained as parish churches. Kilskyre is an example of this.

Its foundress, St Scire, was a direct descendant of Fergus, brother of Niall of the Nine Hostages, and she herself is said to have been the friend and advisor of St Columcille, who would also be of the royal blood of Niall. It is even said that she attended the celebrated Convention of Drumcett where the future of the Bards was decided.

Reference has been made to the importance of the Bards in Celtic Ireland in both pagan and Christian times. They enjoyed very special privileges: lands were allotted in each *tuath* for their maintenance, and when they journeyed from one royal house to another they were entitled to bring a large company of student bards and to demand free entertainment, as well as valuable rewards for their poetic compositions. While their importance as chroniclers was very great and their scholastic attainments very high, it is easy to imagine that they gradually came to abuse their power. A chief bard (or his lady) might express a *mian* (desire) for the king's most precious jewel, and refusal might result in the composition of an *aoir* (satire) which would hold the unfortunate king and his family up to ridicule for generations.

So the kings, and possibly the churchmen, were driven to suppress the Bardic order altogether, but Columcille, returning blindfolded from his exile in Iona, pleaded for them, with, we hope, the backing of Scire, and a settlement was arrived at. The bards were to retain their ancient prestige but to curb their exorbitant demands.

We do not know as much as we would like to about the history of the Bardic order and Bardic schools in Meath. As elsewhere, of course, chiefs were the patrons of the bards down to the breaking up of the Gaelic order in the seventeenth century. Danes and Normans who settled in Ireland adopted the custom observed by the Irish chiefs of keeping poets and harpers.

It seems likely that after the Cromwellian settlement, many of the Meath families were forced back into the hill country to the North – from Kells to Kingscourt, Nobber, South Monaghan, South Armagh and North Louth. Along this whole line a tradition of Irish language poetry remained down to our own time. Manuscript works from this region are to be found scattered throughout library collections – some have been edited and published by such scholars as Fr L. Murray of Dundalk and Henry Morris of South Monaghan. In a volume published by the latter in 1916, he says that about nine years previously, a box of books and other items was purchased at an auction near Castleblayney. It contained eight large manuscript volumes written in Irish and comprising about 400 poems, some by the great Peadar Ó Doirnín. The purchaser had so little appreciation of their value that he gave the books to the children to play with, and that was the end of them.

Before saying a final goodbye to the monastic schools, we must not forget that Dagobert was not the only royal prince to come to Ireland for his education. Noblemen sent their sons here freely to what they believed rightly to be the fount of learning. One prince, Alfrid of Northumbria, has left a record of all the places in Ireland he visited, paying tribute to the welcome he found in both lay and monastic schools and in the palaces of chieftains. Mangan has made a fine translation of *Alfrid's Itinerary*, as he calls it, from which I quote the quatrain on Meath:

I found in Meath's fair principality,
Virtue, learning and hospitality,
Women of worth, both grave and gay men,
Learned clerics, heroic laymen.

BECTIVE OF TODAY AND YESTERDAY
EXAMPLE FOR ARCHITECTS AND ANTIQUARIANS

One of the most impressive Meath monuments is Bective Abbey, on the banks of the Boyne, midway between Trim and An Uaimh. It is a favourite resort for Sunday cycling parties, attracted no doubt by the lovely setting, as well as by the well-preserved turret stairs that lead out to a high platform commanding a magnificent view of the river and the richly coloured landscape beyond.

Before embarking on the history of this great Cistercian house, I cannot resist quoting Wilde's description of it, as it was a century ago. That great antiquarian had the eye of an artist and the lyrical pen of a nature-loving poet:

The tints which usually play upon the walls of Bective are of a richer and more varying hue than we have ever seen elsewhere. The square grey towers, gables and chimneys, rendered in some parts perfectly golden by the most brilliant orange and yellow lichens, and in parts festooned with the dark green drapery of the Irish ivy, rising out of the light feathery: tonnage of a plantation of young larch, and standing in the midst or a field of corn, which stretches between the ruins and the blue waters or the Boyne, form, upon a summers evening, one of the most lovely objects in nature.

Bective Abbey was founded in about the year 1148, 134 years after the battle of Clontarf. The history of those years is usually given in textbooks in a chapter entitled 'Kings With Opposition' and those who remember studying history in their school days have probably a confused memory of wars between O'Connors, O'Briens and MacLoughlins for the High-Kingship. They may even remember seeing it stated that these wars were proof that the Irish could never agree among themselves, and that the Norman conquest was not only a just punishment for their iniquities but a happy rescue from the chaos of tribal strife into the ordered government of the feudal system.

The facts are rather different. Throughout Europe in the Middle Ages, there were periodic wars of succession, struggles between rival claimants to the throne. The Wars of the Roses in England a couple of centuries later is only one example from Britain, while in much later times there were wars over the Spanish and Austrian successions.

In Ireland, the example of Brian Boru had shown that the old order was dying. It was a natural evolution that there should be a High King who would not only rank first in dignity but would form a strong central government, cutting out the powers of the lesser kings. The various struggles between ruling families were, therefore, an effort towards real unity, and when in 1166 Rory O'Connor was crowned at Dublin, the new order was well and truly established.

It is significant that the crowning was at Dublin. Tara was no longer even a symbol. Neither was Cashel or any other of the ancient royal seats. Ireland had but one king. During this century and a quarter, Meath had become dismembered, the descendants of the great Maelsechnaill were not seriously in the running for the High Kingship, but fought among themselves for the kingship of Meath, and gradually the outlying western parts of their territory were shorn from them by the rising O'Connors of Connacht.

By the time Rory was crowned, Meath had suffered many partitions, and in the new order there were various strong families in different parts of the ancient kingdom, all directly acknowledging Rory O'Connor as King of Ireland. Prominent among these families were the MacGeoghegans (their name survives in Castletown-Geoghegan), the O'Kearneys, also called Fox of Iebhtha, and the O'Farrells of Anghaile. A similar development occurred in every other part of Ireland, where such families as the O'Byrnes, MacCarthys, and O'Donnells rose to prominence. Near neighbours to us were the O'Reillys of Breffni and the O'Carrolls of Oriel (partly Louth).

But the intermittent wars that brought about these political changes did not by any means occupy the whole time and energy of the people. It is true that many of the smaller schools and churches destroyed by the Danes were never re-established, but the greater ones weathered the storm and the successive kings endowed them generously. Old buildings were replaced by larger stone ones, and the chieftains also built fine limestone buildings for themselves. It was an age of building on the continent, and Irish architects were quick to follow new ideas.

During the Danish period, the seas, patrolled by Viking ships, were not amenable to travel, but now princes and abbots frequently made pilgrimages to Rome and to the Irish monastic houses on the continent. Successive Popes sent legates to synods of the Irish bishops who were endeavouring to bring back order into the Church.

Kells was the meeting place of one of the most important of these synods. Its chief aim was to define the limits of the various Sees in the light of the many political changes. Thirty-eight dioceses were formed in four provinces, ruled by Archbishops (Armagh, Cashel, Tuam, and Dublin), with the Primacy still attached to Armagh. Except that some small dioceses have been amalgamated (such as Down and Connor) the arrangement made at the synod of Kells (1152) has lasted down to our own time.

The school of Armagh was recognised as the chief school of Ireland for a long time; it was rather a university than a school, and only those who graduated from it were entitled to the rank of professor in other schools. As early as the tenth century, it is recorded that only four men were entitled to this rank, three in Armagh itself and one in Slane. In the next century, Kells has one, and Monasterboice another, and after that they become more numerous, till, as we shall see, schools and professors were wiped out by the Norman invaders.

Reform was needed in the lives of the people as well as in the physical organisation of the Church. Wars are not conducive to spirituality, and even defenders of faith and morals have been known to be corrupted by the vices of those they fought against. But there were sufficient holy men in the Church to begin reform from within. The greatest of these was, of course, Maol Maodhog, Archbishop of Armagh. (His name is badly rendered in English as Malachy, and it is as St Malachy that he is familiar to most people today.) He visited the great monastery of Clairvaux where St Bernard had brought about a great reform by restoring the Rule to something of the strictness of the time of Columban. St Bernard has left on record that Malachy told him his people in Connor were:

Christians in name but pagans in reality, uncouth in their ceremonies and rebellious to discipline. They neither paid first fruits nor tithes, nor contracted marriage legitimately nor made their confessions.

We would not like to accuse either of the saints of pious exaggeration, but in the short period of eight years Bernard says that everything was changed for the better, 'Churches were built, and supplied with priests, confession was practised and marriage solemnised.' There is much more in the passage in praise of this quickly reclaimed people. It is worth adding that Bernard, the greatest man of his time, who was sought after by Popes and emperors, thanked God that it was given to him in his life to meet such a man as Malachy.

Houses of Bernard's new order (called Cistercian) were springing up rapidly on the continent, and in Dublin, St Mary's Abbey adopted their rule. Malachy secured from the king of the time a large tract of land near Drogheda, on the territory of O'Carroll. There, in 1142, the famous monastery of Mellifont was established. A few French monks came to direct building operations and teach the *Rule* to the Irish. The King of Meath was quick to invite the new order into his own territory – it was a small territory by now and he was only king by courtesy, but he was a Maelsechnaill still. Land was provided on the banks of the Boyne at Sean-Droicead, and the building was begun on the usual plan of Cistercian monasteries, where church, kitchen, dormitories, etc., were all under one roof. It was called the Abbey of Beatitudine and dedicated to the Blessed Virgin.

Its name has been shortened to Bective, and in later years some structural changes were made, which any visitor can easily notice. But substantially the impressive remains that stand today are the work of those Irish builders of 810 years ago. The very carving in the cloisters, owing to the hardness of the Ardbraccan stone, has withstood the ravages of time, and Bective stands as a textbook today for architect and antiquarian alike.

CRAFTS OF THE LAST CENTURY

Among the objects in the Meath Archaeological and Historical Society museum in Trim were many that show the skill of local craftsmen in the last century. There were sconces and noggins, scutching tools and grissets, all simple things familiar in the farmhouses of eighty years ago but objects of curiosity and admiration to the present generation.

Before the advent of paraffin oil and candles made from paraffin wax, the rush-light was the usual source of illumination in the houses of the poor. The rich had candles made from beeswax, and I often wonder what astronomical numbers of hives must have worked to supply the elaborate candelabra that hung in the halls of all the great houses.

The rushes for candle making were cut and brought home green. Women and children peeled them at night by the fireside, leaving one narrow sliver of skin on each, as otherwise the pith would break. They were then put to dry on the 'hurl' – a shelf-like platform by the sides of the large chimney brace. (One old man told me that in his young days he saw real 'hurls' of wickerwork stretching from wall to wall under the rafters. These were taken out in harvest time and mounted on big stones to scutch flax on.)

When the rushes were well dried out, sometime in the winter, they were dipped in tallow. This might be procured from a sheep killed in the farm-house for Christmas or it could be bought cheaply in the town on a fair day. The tallow was melted in a grisset, an oval-shaped shallow pot with three legs and a long handle. Its longest axis was hardly the length of the average rush, but by holding one end of the rush in each hand it could be drawn through the grease. The rushes were put back on the hurl to harden out and were then used as required. There was an iron holder with a nipper top which could be opened and closed to grip the rush–light firmly.

This was mounted on a wooden stand to have the light at a convenient height for a worker sitting on a stool. The frame was sometimes made by a carpenter, but the one I saw few days ago in a house where such things are treasured, that was simply a three-branched piece of an ash tree, the branches forming the legs of the stand.

Resin candles were also used, and the resin could also be bought on 'standings' at the fairs and markets. Old people who remembered them told me that they smoked a lot and so had to be fixed on a stand on or very near the hob so that the fumes would go up the chimney.

LINEN WEAVING

Women who worked outside in the daytime did their spinning, knitting, and sewing by such poor light at night. The farmers' wives who had servant girls could work by daylight. Home spinning was usual in every house a century ago and was not altogether dead until about the year 1900. But for most of that period, all handiwork was fighting a losing battle against the cheap, machine-produced products of the growing industries of England.

Still, a hundred years ago, most farmers grew a ridge of flax and put it through all the processes of 'drowning', 'scutching', and 'hackling' though the last of these was done by a 'specialist' in each parish. There are still hackles to be found. Then the fibre was spun into thread on the small linen-wheel, which was a work of art itself. The trade of wheelwright was a highly important one in those days. The weaving of the thread into linen was done by a weaver, and a hundred years ago there were many, but today I know of only one or two families who have preserved even a fragment of the old looms. The 'cup' was kept longer than any other part, as a drink from it was believed to be a cure for whooping cough.

The linen was used for sheets, shirts and what little table linen was required — a cloth to put on the table when the priest had breakfast after a 'Station' Mass, and the cloths required when a sick person was being anointed. I have a scrap of a linen sheet which came from a Big House, and is marked, in ink, with the owner's name and the date 1848. I was assured by the donor that it was woven in Killyon. It is fine and evenly done and the hand stitching on the hem is beautifully neat.

Some of the linen was dyed for bedspreads and for women's garments. Some of the dyes at least were home-made; a lady from Donaghmore has described how a yellow dye was made from the blossoms of the furze, and various lichens gave different shades of brown. But logwood, from far-off Honduras, could be bought in the shops to give a black dye.

The bedspreads were lined and sometimes padded with wool and then quilted. I have seen a quilting frame, two long wooden rails with cross pieces on which the material was stretched, while a woman, standing at the work, made parallel or zigzag lines of running stitch all over it. I was told that it would take a whole winter of spare time to make one of these quilts, and I have seen one which was then a hundred years old. So, even if the work was slow, the result was lasting.

STRAW AND WICKER

I don't know if the men practised as many of these fireside crafts as the women did. The labourers had very little time, for they worked from dawn until dark, and if the place of employment was far from home they were too tired after a hard day and a long walk to do anything but eat a scanty supper and go to bed. Farmers with a little more leisure may have produced articles of straw or wicker as occasion demanded, but there were professional basket-makers who kept sally gardens to supply the materials for potato baskets, turf baskets, calf baskets, cradles, etc.

Particular Irish names for some of these still survive: a *cliabh*, a *creel*, a *goban*, a *cish*, and a *bardog*. Bardogs were the baskets slung over the back of a horse or ass, and they are still to be seen in Connemara. It may be noted that the Irish word for a cradle is *cliabhán*, showing that it was a wicker article originally.

Basket-makers were not held in very high estimation among the community; neither were tailors, since their equipment was small and cheap, compared with that of the carpenter or blacksmith. I have heard an Irish expression in the south describing the tailor as the man of the scissors, measure and thimble, which shows that in all times and places there is contempt for the man of little or no property.

Sugán chairs must have been made in Meath, but I have never seen one. I have, however, often seen straw skips in which bees were kept before the introduction of the modern bar-frame hives. I have also seen an old man in this parish making straw doormats. A Kilkenny man, settled in this county, has a very nice armchair for a baby made entirely of straw ropes, but it came from his native county. No doubt many houses have articles of ancient home craft which I have never seen and I would be very grateful if they would tell me about them, or lend them for exhibition.

THE CRAFT OF THE SMITH

A few weeks ago I was one of a small party invited to show the sights of Meath to a group of foreign visitors. Naturally we took them to Ardmulchan, the loveliest place in the whole beautiful Valley of the Boyne. They were appreciative, as all discerning people are, of the wide, winding stretch of water far below the tower-crowned height on which we stood. It was still and peaceful in the evening light, reflecting green hills where one might think that never had any man walked but in quiet and meditation, if it were not for the huge fortress of the D'Arcys standing formidable and impregnable across the water. 'There's a picture', said one of our guests, 'that only the Old Masters could do justice to.'

But it is not of scenic beauty or even of historical associations I wish to write now. As we followed in the path from the road to the Height of

Maolchu, an Austrian gentleman in the party drew everyone's attention to the iron gate leading to the churchyard field. 'Look', he said, 'at that wonderful piece of iron-craft.' It was just a five-barred gate to me and I had never noticed before that the strengthening was done not by the modern diagonal bar but by two semicircles of iron, the larger reaching the fourth crossbar, and the second concentric with it, reaching to the third.

One of the Meath men present said he had often seen a blacksmith make such gates years ago, and he gave us a detailed account of how the bars were rounded on the anvil, the bolt holes made with a very simple hand drill, and the bolts fitted and hammered in. I am unable to describe the processes without the aid of diagrams, but when one's eyes are opened to the existence of this particular work there will be no difficulty in seeing specimens all over the county. We saw one within an hour at the entrance to Dunmoe Churchyard.

THE SOC-MAKER

A friend has given me this account of another vanished craft. In horse-drawn ploughs, the points wear out rapidly, and new ones can be bought in the shops. But up to sixty years ago these points were made locally – they were always known by the Irish name of *socs* and here is the description of the process as I got it:

When I was a boy there was a man in the village who made socs for ploughs. He could make mould-boards, too, but there wouldn't be so many of these wanted, so the soc-making was his principal trade. He lived in a little mud-wall house on the very edge of the street, and the forge was attached to the house, mudwall and thatch, too. I don't think it had a chimney, for I remember seeing smoke and steam coming out through the roof and the door.

He used to get fine sand for his moulds. It was a reddish sand found in the banks of the ditches, and was fairly sticky. He had two boxes for each mould – a good stout wooden one with a bottom, and another exactly the same size with no bottom, and not perhaps as deep. The boxes might be about a foot square and six or eight inches deep.

He packed the sand into the lower box and then put the model – a wooden soc – into the sand, and pressed it down and packed the sand well round it so that the box was quite full and perfectly level with half the soc sticking up.

Then he sprinkled something – ashes, I think – over the surface of the sand to prevent the sand in the second box from sticking to it. Then he very carefully put down the second box (the one with no bottom) and there were eyes and bolts so that the two were fitted together firmly and dead accurately.

Then he packed in sand round the model carefully until the top box was filled level. He used a bit of stick and a trowel to leave a funnel-shaped opening in the sand down to the wooden model; this was for pouring in the hot metal later.

Very carefully he lifted off the top box and put it aside. Then he took out the wooden model carefully, and if there was the slightest defect, if a grain of sand had slipped, he evened it with a little trowel. He then replaced the top box, bolted it down, and carried all into the forge and left it near the fire. He made four or five similar moulds, as one grisset-full of metal would do that many.

The metal was got from breaking down metal pots which the soc-maker collected around the country. He had a round, flat-bottomed grisset made of earthenware bound with steel bands, and having a long steel handle. It was more than a foot in diameter and about eight inches deep.

The fire was started with turf, but on top of that he put coke or collum, putting in the grisset (with the handle sticking out) and packing on more collum over grisset, metal and all, until the whole thing was round like a beehive. He plastered it all over with yellow clay mixed with fresh cow-dung, but left a hole in the middle of the top. Then he blew up the fire with a bellows, like a blacksmith's bellows, and soon you would see a blue flame coming out on top, like the flame from a blowlamp.

It was part of the trade to know just when the metal should be hot enough, for if it was not at the right heat the top would cool during the pouring. He broke up the fire over the grisset, raked off the scum and dirt with one quick push of a long tool, and then holding the handle poured just the right amount into each mould.

After some time he took the moulds outside the forge to finish cooling. I forget how long that took. Finally he took off the top box, loosened the sand from the soc, and if necessary filed away any little irregularity.

This man worked up to or perhaps a little after 1900. By that time the machine-made points were being sold in the shops. Besides selling directly to local farmers, he used to take an ass-load of socs to local fairs. I heard old people say that they remembered seeing the soc-maker taking his wares to the fairs in a sack on his back.

THE SLANE MAKER

The art of slane making lasted longer, and I think it would be possible to get a description from a man who actually made slanes himself. It may be necessary in these days of turf-cutting machinery to explain that a slane (Irish *sleán* or *sleamhan*) was the kind of winged spade used in the hand cutting of turf. It had to be the right weight and shape and be set in the dead right slant to cut and throw the sod without undue force and without allowing it to slip. It had to be very sharp, and so the temper had to be just right to take and keep an edge. This was achieved by hammering, and not every blacksmith knew just how to get this temper. Clients came miles to a good man, and his slanes were known and valued by expert bog men.

He was in the tradition of those ancient smiths who forged swords for kings and warriors of old, and who were treated with respect mingled with awe. They were said to be able to banish rats, and the water from the forge had curative properties. Indeed it is still believed to be capable of removing warts, and perhaps it is.

In the dark days of '98 the smiths of Ireland made the pikeheads and were themselves the first to use them in the hour of battle. There were many like the brave Paid O'Donohoe who forged steel for Ireland in his forge at Curraha.

OLD HOUSES

In pre-famine days, when population was growing rapidly and people were becoming poorer and poorer, there was naturally no great development in house building. Cabins of mud were thrown up and covered with branches overlaid with furze and thatched with straw or rushes, or even covered with sods. There was often neither chimney nor window, and the door opening was covered by a rough square of wicker or plaited straw.

But when times settled down again these hovels were for the most part empty and ruinous, and there are few now alive who remember the worst of them. The houses of the less poverty stricken were of the traditional type which has lasted up to the present time in most rural districts of Meath. Caoimhín O'Danachair, who has carried out so much study on various aspects of Irish traditional life, traces the development of house building through the centuries. From time immemorial the hearth has been the social centre of the home, and the big kitchen, with its open fire, is associated with a culture difficult to carry into the modern living room with its refined amenities.

In Meath, the fireplace was against the middle gable wall in the two-roomed houses, and the single bedroom was behind this gable wall. The door from the yard into the kitchen was close to the wall carrying the fireplace, and directly in front of it was a cross-wall some five feet long, of the same height as the side walls. This made a narrow hall, from one end of which a door opened into the bedroom. The other end led to the kitchen, but there was no door.

The top of the cross-wall carried a strong beam of undressed timber, the other end of which rested on the back wall of the house. This beam supported a large funnel-shaped canopy tapering to the point of the gable and forming with it the chimney opening. Under this shelter was the hearth, usually at floor level, and with a hob some six inches wide built behind it against the gable wall to a height of about three feet. Against the cross-wall was a seat, sometimes permanently fixed, and over it was a little glazed opening to let in light and enable the person in the chimney corner to turn and look out the open door at any unusual sound.

THE FIRESIDE

Only in quite recent times have we begun to realise that the people who planned and built the houses of long ago were extremely intelligent in using simple materials to produce dwellings exactly suited to the climate of the country and to the needs of their daily lives. Simple as the chimney looks, the good craftsman knew exactly the height and width of the brace which would have the desired effect.

At night, when the door was shut, the family and neighbours wanted to gather round the fire; there was space under the great canopy for half a dozen stools, while the man of the house could stretch on the fixed form with a bag of chaff between his back and the wall. There were even a few little holes or recesses near the hob where he could keep his pipe and tobacco, beside the grisset and the smoothing iron and all the other small household goods which would not be damaged by a little smoke or ashes.

In many houses there was a second room opening from the end of the kitchen farthest from the fire, and in this there was a table and a few chairs, so that tea could be served in it on special occasions. The bed in this room would have the best, perhaps the only, counterpane: quilted linen, patch-work, or knitted cotton. I have seen specimens of these preserved by guilds of countrywomen who appreciate the workmanship which was unfortu-nately despised a generation ago, so that in most houses they were thrown out and replaced by shoddy, factory-made articles.

HOUSES OF OTHER LANDS

In the Folk Museum at Arnhem in Holland, exact replicas of old houses from various parts of the country have been built. It comes as a surprise to the Irish visitor to find that in even large farmhouses the cattle were housed under the same roof as the people. We are accustomed to think of this arrangement as proof of the most degrading poverty. It appears to have been common here a couple of centuries ago. The part of the kitchen farthest from the hearth was at a lower level than the rest, and there the cow and calf were kept at night, with the liens roosting over them on the 'hurl'.

In spite of all the contemptuous references to the pig in the parlour, I think it was always usual to have a separate small pig-house, called in the last century the 'pig-craw' (Irish *cró*, a shed). One small confirmation of this comes from the old cure for the mumps. The sufferer was brought into the piggery and the disease wished on to the animals with the incantation, (*Leicne, leicne, chugat a' mucla*, Mumps, mumps, to you the pigs).

In Ireland there was a very special cause for houses remaining small and unpretentious. In the years following the Famine, landlords were more rapacious than ever in seeking rents, and any sign of prosperity might be an excuse for a rent increase. It was only after 1880, when at last, through the exertions of the Land League, the farmer was reasonably protected from both rack renting and eviction that farmhouses began to improve.

Possibly the first step was the erection of a cowshed, and the conversion of the lower half of the kitchen into a bedroom (the second or best room I have described). In some old farmhouses it is still evident that the wall separating this room from the kitchen was of later construction than the rest of the house. This is particularly true of townlands where there was a bad landlord; on the good estates the whole farmhouse and sheds may be of earlier construction.

LIFE IN THE FARMHOUSES

These little homesteads were on farms of three to ten or fifteen acres, and a hundred years ago these were numerically the largest group in the country. The few who had thirty to fifty acres were secure enough in their possessions, for they were the kind of tenants the landlords wanted. Unfortunately, many such farmers were already imitating the ways of 'gentlemen farmers'; they employed servant boys and servant girls at even worse wages than the big houses, and treated them with almost equal contempt.

I have seen a bell in the yard of a forty-acre farm to call the men to work, and an old woman told me that when, as a young married woman, she had worked there binding in the harvest she was cut a quarter-day as she had to feed her children in the morning and so could not make the seven o'clock bell. That memory would be of about the year 1880. The men slept in a loft over the cow stable, and their food was often potatoes three times a day. The farmers themselves would have bread, and there might be tea in the evening for the women of the house. Naturally not all farmers were like this.

In some houses there was one table for all; cabbage and bacon was beginning to supplement the potato diet, and wheaten as well as oaten bread was to be found on the breakfast table. In the nighttime, family and servants would gather round the hearth, where there would be good chat and story-telling, maybe music and dancing; the young people would play games with string and rushes, or ask riddles or say rhymes all in an age-old tradition, and all associated with the whole body of European culture, though naturally the people themselves did not realise that.

It is a pity that now, when scholars the world over are becoming more and more aware of the importance of rural cultures, we are destroying our links with the past as rapidly as our finances permit. We are not even trying to preserve a few of our old house types, as has been done in most countries of Europe. Some of us hoped that a full folk museum would be established here near the Hill of Tara, but there appears very little chance that it will ever be done now. A golden opportunity to keep even one period house, thatched and furnished in eighteenth-century style, is now open to us by the committee who have purchased Stella's cottage at Laracor. But not more than a dozen Meath people have shown sufficient interest to give even a five-shilling subscription.

THE GABLE

A footnote for those who like to notice the community of words rather than the community of material things: I have used the word 'gable' several times in this article. It means, of course, 'the pointed wall of a house'. The old Irish 'gabel', a fork, is still in use in gawlogue (*gabhalóg*), 'a forked stick'. Old French had *gable*; Anglo-Saxon *geafel*, and there are almost similar forms in languages as far apart as Icelandic and Greek. The *gaff* used in spearing fish is from the same root.

FIVE

NORMAN MEATH

HENRY'S BARONS FIND ACCOMMODATION

Less than five miles separate the Abbey of Bective from the Castle of Trim. In terms of time they are separated by little more than half a century. Yet, between monastery and fortress hangs the shadow of invasion – the clash of a conflict that has darkened the history of our country throughout the succeeding centuries.

In May 1169, a band of adventurers from the Welsh marshes crossed the narrow sea to land at Bannow in the extreme south of Wexford. There were 2,000 of them – mail-clad bowmen, born and bred to war and conquest – and before many days they had forced the Norse inhabitants of Wexford town into submission. They were few and to contemporary eyes must have appeared no more than a band of mercenaries drafted in to assist in a small civil conflict. But that small band was the advance guard of the Norman Conquest, and soon all Ireland was to feel the full force of it. Meath was to be the chief sufferer.

A century before the battle of Clontarf in 1014, the Danes had been conquering many countries of Europe. A body of them had settled on the banks of the Seine, and the King of France had to grant them permanent territory on his coast opposite England. There they settled, just as their kinsmen did in Dublin, Wexford, and other coastal towns. In time they became Christian and adopted the French language, laws, and customs. Their leaders intermarried with French nobility, and, as France, like other countries, consisted then of a number of small states, the settlement (known as Normandy) began the process of becoming part of the developing French nation.

England at the time of Clontarf was under Danish domination, but some years later the native Saxon kingdom was restored under the saintly Edward the Confessor. He had been reared in Normandy and was related to the reigning Duke William, known to history as the William the Conqueror. In 1066, William, with his well-armed soldiers, invaded England, conquered it without difficulty, and where there was resistance he used merciless violence so that the men, beasts, and crops were destroyed and whole tracts laid waste. In this conflict many Irishmen fought on the side of the native population against the invader.

Though the Norman soldiers were well disciplined, they were not in the least submissive to their king. Once the conquest was over, every baron was a law unto himself: he built his own castle and defended it against the king. An Anglo-Saxon chronicle of the time records:

> They filled the land full of castles. They greatly oppressed the wretched people by making them work at these castles, and when the castles were finished they filled them with devils and evil men. Then they took those whom they suspected to have any goods, by night and by day, seizing both men and women, and they put them in prison for their gold and silver and tortured them with pains unspeakable … They spared neither church nor churchyard, but they took all that was valuable therein, and then burned the church … Neither did they spare the lands of bishops, of abbots or of priests, but they robbed the monks and the clergy … The bishops and clergy were ever cursing them, but this to them was nothing, for they were all accurst and forsworn and reprobate … The land was all ruined by such deeds and it was said openly that Christ and His saints slept.

This chronicle referred to the years up to 1154, and it was just a year later that Henry, King of Norman England, announced his intention to invade Ireland. It is, therefore, worth quoting in view of the pious reasons advanced by these turbulent Norman barons when they wanted to justify their entry into Ireland. In the quotation there is one passage deliberately omitted. It is the detailed description of the actual methods of torture used by these Christian knights on the conquered people of England. It is so horrible that even the toughest of modern readers would find it hard to hear. It is well to be mindful of the method of conquest when we look at Trim Castle and we may reflect what blood, tears, torture, and slavery went into the building of its great towers, walls, and bastions.

The correspondence between St Bernard and St Malachy referred to in a previous article was well known to the pontiff of the time, Adrian IV, friend and fellow-countryman of Henry. On the strength of that correspondence, not-withstanding the significant Church reform that had taken place in the interim, Pope Adrian consented to a mission to Ireland, regarding as virtuous the strug-gle to win back this erring people to the ways of God. (William the Conqueror had made a similar entreaty to the Pope of his time before invading England, and the chronicle I have quoted shows just how he carried out his mission.)

Henry was more French than Norman by blood, and wholly French in language. He had great difficulty in controlling his barons in England, some of whom were now the third generation in that country, though still French speaking. As a means of pacifying them he planted the most violent of them on the lands bordering Wales, which was not yet conquered, and returned to his affairs in France. He kept the conquest of Ireland in mind as a future outlet for the energies of his uncontrollable barons.

It was at this stage that the King of Leinster, the infamous Diarmuid na nGall, cornered by the enemies his tyranny had made, fled to France and asked the aid of Henry the Norman. Henry was at war with his French barons and was only too glad to have the Welsh border rebels taken off his hands for the moment, especially as they were to engage on the new con-quest which he had long contemplated.

The first invaders were subjects of a French ruler, their leaders French-speaking Normans and half Welsh, and many of the rank-and-file were hired soldiers from Flanders. Their chief was de Clare (nicknamed Strongbow) and among the other leaders were the Geraldine group, closely related and bearing names like FitzGerald, FitzHenry and Fitz-Stephen, ('Fitz' means 'son' as in the modern French *fils*).

The details of the two years from 1169 to 1171 are too convoluted to go into here. The Irish had no standing armies; the Normans were professional soldiers. Soon, with strong reinforcements, they conquered Leinster and Meath, or at all events ravaged them from Dublin, Wexford and Waterford. So successful were the adventurers that Henry, fearing they would slip completely from his control, came over to protect the Irish from their aggression. He was welcomed by the Irish chiefs for that reason and also as a great king, and many of them accepted his invitation to a wicker pavilion which he erected outside the gates of Dublin, where they were entertained with great pomp and ceremony. The southern chiefs were all there; so alas was O'Melseachlain of Meath, and even the hardy old one-eyed warrior Tiarnan O'Rourke of Breffni. The O'Neills of Ulster, however, stayed away.

Henry convened a synod at Cashel in order to display his interest in reforming the Church, though no important decrees were issued, and neither Gilla Iosa, the Primate of Armagh, nor the other northern bishops attended. The main outcome of his visit was that many chiefs and clergy paid him homage, which they understood as courteous tribute to a great king who made himself their protector and the champion of law and morality.

This homage was to be interpreted very differently in the future by Henry and his successors. At the same time, unbeknownst to the Irish, Henry was parcelling out the whole country among his barons, and when he departed, each baron with his mercenaries set out to conquer the territory he had been granted, to hold as vassal to his liege. The wars of plunder in Meath began with Hugh de Lacy's arrival, just at the moment when Henry was making abject submission to the Pope for his share in the murder of Thomas à Becket, Archbishop of Canterbury. Such were the foundations on which Trim Castle was built.

THE NORMAN PLANTATION AND TRIM

The castle of Trim is popularly known as King John's Castle, though the building that stands today never sheltered that ill-fated monarch. Its construction is sometimes attributed to Hugh de Lacy, the first Norman Lord of Meath, but the castle he built was but a temporary structure, replaced after his death by the permanent stone fortress erected by one William Peppard.

This de Lacy, however, figures very largely in the history of Meath. He is reputed to have been a true Norman, unlike many of the other original invaders who were of mixed blood, and largely Welsh. When King Henry visited Ireland with the ostensible purpose of checking the excesses of his barons and proceeded to parcel up the whole country among them, he rewarded de Lacy with the whole territory of Meath, as it had been held by Murcha Ó Maelsechnaill – the Irish ruler of the ancient kingdom. It was a big endowment, comprising the present counties of Meath and Westmeath with parts of Offaly and Longford.

In return, de Lacy was to maintain and equip fifty knights for the King's service, for that was the usual method of land tenure under the feudal system; the King being, in theory, the owner of the whole country.

De Lacy had yet to conquer the province allotted to him, as the Burkes, Butlers, de Courcys and others had to do in other parts of the country. The method was to make a fast march into the undefended territory, where the mail-clad horsemen spread terror before them, burning and slaughtering, sparing neither young nor old, women nor children. Then, having reached a suitable place for an encampment, the party would settle there, forcing the common people to assist them in erecting their fortress. This consisted of no more than a high flat-topped mound, surrounded by a deep ditch, outside which was a larger, flat area, surrounded in turn by a bank and ditch. The technical name for the mound is 'motte' and the outer flat surface is called the 'bailey'. The ditch is called the 'fosse' and the bank is termed the 'vallum'.

Atop the bank and around the slopes of the motte were strong timber palisades. In the centre of the motte was a strong wooden house or tower for the commander and his soldiers. There might be another wooden house in the bailey for more troops who would be the first to face the attackers. This whole structure was called a castle, and such was the first castle of Trim erected by de Lacy in the year 1172, that is, immediately after he was granted the lands of Meath.

He had, of course, many kinsmen and fellow adventurers, each with his following of soldiers, and to each of these he made a sub-grant of part of his territory, and soon there were castles like that of Trim in each portion; all garrisoned for defence against the Irish, who, it will be remembered, had as yet no standing armies and were quite unaccustomed to this kind of warfare.

Chief among those barons who got the lands of the Irish families were Gilbert de L'Angle (afterwards called Nangle) and his son Joceline, who got the district around Navan and Ardbraccan, formerly held by the Coindealbhain (Kindelan) family; Gilbert de Nugent, who got the lands of the O'Finelans of Delvin, and Hugh Tyrrell who got Castleknock. There were many others such as the Petits, Tuites, and Husseys.

The land of each baron was called a barony and as, in general, each baron got the *tuatha* belonging to an Irish family, the present baronies (Lune, Delvin, Morgallion, etc.) are the oldest territorial divisions we have. Duleek seems to have been the second castle to be built, and soon after its erection de Lacy had to go to England to make his peace with the king, who accused him of aspiring to independent sovereignty in Meath, and threatened to replace him with a more loyal subject.

In his absence, the command at Trim and Duleek was given to Hugh Tyrrell, 'whom he loved so much' ('*k'il tant amat*' are the words in one old chronicle). By this time the Irish under Rory, the High King, had collected forces to resist the enemy, and advanced into Meath. Tyrrell torched his castles and fled to seek aid from Strongbow and the other Norman lords of Leinster. Rory had a blood victory and withdrew to Connacht where his troops dispersed, as was the custom. It appears that, as yet, the Irish did not realise the magnitude of the threat; they still relied on the promise the king had made the previous year to control the raiders and prevent further conquest. One account of this incident at Trim says, 'Earl Strongbow when he came there, found neither castle nor house to lodge in; wherefore he made no stay, but pursued the enemy, of which one hundred and fifty were slain.'

In any case, the conquest continued. The Irish chiefs still seem to have relied on law and justice rather than the sword, and there are references in chronicles, both English and Irish, to meetings between de Lacy and the King of Meath and between de Lacy and O'Ruairc of Breffni. The first is recorded as taking place at Tara, and the second at Tlachtgha (Hill of Ward), The incident of Griffith's dream is, I think connected with the Hill of Ward meeting, though it is given otherwise in some accounts. O'Ruairc was the close kinsman of the King of Meath, and it was his wife who had been, carried off by Diarmuid, the King of Leinster. He was a brave old man, and naturally felt a particular antipathy to the invaders. Still, he was willing to come to conference, and the meeting was arranged.

Each leader was to leave his bodyguard at the bottom of the hill and meet unarmed at the top, with only an interpreter. While the talk was in progress, de Lacy's soldiers were creeping uphill. Their commander, Griffith, stabbed O'Ruairc in the back just as he was mounting his horse after the interview. The justification for this act of treachery was that Griffith had had a dream the previous night in which he saw his beloved master, de Lacy, being murdered by the Irish, and, to forestall such an event, he got his blow in first. The explanation, naïve as it is, is given in all seriousness by Stanihurst, who, as the Abbé MacGeoghegan says in his history, 'was in heart as much an Englishman as if born in London'.

MacGeoghegan, who was chaplain to the Irish Brigade in France and wrote with all the evidence available to him there at the time (about 1748), is of opinion that it was the King at Meath and not O'Ruairc who was thus murdered. He adds, 'He was then beheaded, and his body interred with the feet upwards. His head was sent to Dublin and thence to England, as the head of a traitor and a rebel.'

De Lacy's own end was swift and violent. He continued his complicated schemes of conquest, intrigue and revolt for many years, and this description of him by his friend Gerald Barry (better known by the Latin name Geraldus Cambrensis: Gerald of Wales) is particularly enlightening:

> He was of a dark complexion, with black and deep-seated eyes, a flat nose, and his right cheek down to his chin badly scarred by an accidental burn, he had a short neck and a muscular and hairy chest. He was low and badly made. He character was firm and resolute and he was as sober as a Frenchman. He was always most attentive to his own business; and most watchful, not only over his own department but also over everything that was done in common. Although skilled in military affairs, his frequent losses in expeditions show that he was not lucky as a general. After his wife's death he indulged in battles of general profligacy. He was desirous of money, and avaricious and, beyond all model and moderation, ambitious of personal honour and distinction …

One of the things to be done in common was the erection of castles, and while superintending digging operations at Durrow he was attacked by a young member of the local noble family of the O'Cearnaigh, who cut off his head with one stroke of his axe. In the English account, 'he was treacherously murdered by a labouring man'.

The story of his burial and the controversy over his remains must wait until we refer to the relations between Norman invaders and the Irish Church. De Lacy's violent death occurred in 1186, some fifteen years after he had been granted the Palatinate of Meath, and it seems unlikely that it was mourned by his friends or regretted by his sovereign lord King Henry.

IRISH BISHOP 'ONLY A SAINT'
THE NORMANS AS 'STATESMEN'

Before the coming of the Normans, the Bishops of Meath resided at Clonard. It will be remembered that some years previously the boundaries of the Sees of Ireland had been fixed at various synods and, as the occupants died out, the smaller Sees were incorporated into the new order. In 1169 there was, however, still a Bishop of Kells.

The Normans appropriated the ecclesiastical and the temporal sovereignty of the parts of Ireland they succeeded in conquering, and so in the year 1191, on the death of Bishop Maolciaran of Clonard, Simon Rochfort, a Norman, was appointed. From that date to the Reformation, the Diocese of Meath was ruled by foreigners, some born in Ireland of Norman-Irish or (later) Anglo-Irish stock, many of them pure Englishmen who never set foot in Ireland before being appointed to the Bishopric.

The appointments were usually made on the advice or with the approval of the King of England, and often the bishop also held high office under the government. One historian boasts that whereas the Irish Bishop of Dublin Laurence O'Toole was only a saint, his English successors were statesmen. Rochfort, however, had the reputation of being, 'a most excellent prelate, of humble and meek behaviour'.

In 1191, the conquest of Meath was by no means finished, and Clonard was fairly exposed to attack from the O'Connors and other strong Irish chiefs to the south and west. In the year 1200, the town was attacked and burned, and two years later Rochfort transferred his place of residence to Trim. He founded a priory there for the Canons Regular of St Victor, and the church of this priory became the Cathedral church of Meath, dedicated to Ss Peter and Paul.

The site was called New Meath (now known as Newtown) and the ruins of this great church are among the most impressive in Meath. Near it, across the river, are the remains of the contemporary foundation dedicated to St John the Baptist. Some time later O'Dobhailen, Bishop of Kells, died, and his territory was incorporated into the Diocese of Meath.

The Norman barons and lesser landholders built churches for themselves, sometimes on the sites of existing churches where the native clergy were supplanted, and sometimes beside their own fortresses. The clergy serving these were Norman, and each was endowed with land and the right of tithes from the local landowners. These were parish churches and around them the dead were buried.

Fr Brady makes it clear that our old graveyards are indications of a former parish church rather than a monastery. Many of the present Protestant churches are on or near the sites of these first Norman churches, which were taken over from the Catholics at the Reformation. In turn, the Norman churches themselves stood on the sites of earlier Irish ones. Fr Brady gives as examples Dunshaughlin, Derrypatrick, Kilpatrick, Donaghpatrick, Kilskyre, and Kilmoon. He adds that Mullingar is an example of the kinds of places that had no previous ecclesiastical importance, and the only reason for their selection was that they were Norman strongholds, as indeed were all the places mentioned.

The Norman barons endowed many monasteries for the various religious orders recently founded among their French kinsmen. Besides the foundations at Newtown there were new monasteries endowed in Navan, Duleek, Clonard, Fore and elsewhere. St Mary's and St Thomas's in Dublin received grants of land in Meath. Bective and Mellifont, founded before the invasion but with French tradition, were also endowed and were destined to be Norman – not Irish – houses.

There was, all told, a great deal of property involved, and the control of it led to much litigation during the following centuries. Many parishes were controlled by the monasteries rather than by the Bishop and some of the controlling monasteries were outside the diocese. On the other hand, the convent of Lismullen, founded by a Norman lady, had, as part of its revenue, the Manor of Dunsink near Dublin, and there were many similar cases.

It would seem to be a characteristic of the Normans that they showed the greatest generosity in giving part of their plunder to the service of religion. For instance, in the year 1200, Walter de Lacy made a grant of land near Dunshaughlin to the Abbey of Thomas Court 'in pure and perpetual alms, for the good of his soul, and of Hugh, his father, and his mother, Rosa de Munemnene, who lies buried in the Church of St Thomas'. There are many records of such endowments, all for the spiritual welfare of the donors and their families.

It was in this peculiar atmosphere of violence and repentance that the controversy raged over the mortal remains of the first de Lacy, killed at Durrow in 1185. I give the record from a little book called *Some Notices of the Castle of Trim* compiled by Dean Butler and printed by H. Griffith, Trim, in 1840:

> Hugh de Lacy's body was long detained by the Irish, but was, at last, in the year 1195, recovered, and buried with great solemnity in the Abbey of Bective by Matthew O'Heney, Archbishop of Cashel, the Pope's legate, and John Cumin, Archbishop of Dublin; but his head was carried to Dublin and buried in the Abbey of St Thomas the Martyr, in the tomb of Rosa de Munemnene,

his first wife. A great controversy arose between the two abbeys respecting the rest of his body, which was at last decided in the year 1205, when it was adjudged to the abbey of St Thomas by Simon Rochfort, Bishop of Meath, the Archdeacon of Meath and the Prior of Duleek, who had been appointed judges in, the case by Pope Innocent III.

Bishop Rochfort himself is buried in his Cathedral church in Newtown; one of his successors rests in St Mary's Abbey, and another in Mullingar.

The native Irish were excluded from the Norman monasteries and from holding office as secular priests wherever Norman power extended. They were not allowed to travel abroad for study; in fact the law in England specifically forbade their entry into Oxford University. The equivalent Irish university in Armagh fell into decay during the wars of invasion. But a considerable portion of the diocese of Meath was still fairly well in the hands of the native Irish — all the fringe of hill and bog that encircles the plain of East Meath — and here the Church remained Irish. The English kings had no influence and the English bishops did not always make personal visitations.

THE OLD CASTLE OF TRIM
DESCRIPTION OF A MIGHTY RUIN

Our greatest authority on Irish castles is Mr Harold G. Leask, who held the position of Inspector of National Monuments in Éire. In one of his books he gives a list of the number of castles known to have existed in each county. Sixty-one castles in Meath are shown on the Ordnance Survey maps of over a century ago, but he adds that there were probably many more. In Westmeath the number is seventy-five and in Offaly seventy-eight.

Not all of these were erected by the first Norman invaders. Castles were useful for defence only up to the introduction of cannon, but residential castles were erected long afterwards, even into the seventeenth century. Those interested in dating a particular castle from its architectural features would do well to examine it with Mr Leask's book to hand. Within the limits of this short unillustrated article, it is enough to say that, in general, the oldest castles are the more massive and comfortless, while the latest ones are more like houses than castles, and their turrets and crenulations were designed for appearance rather than for defence.

Trim, of course, belonging to the early period, was completed by William Peppard in 1220, just fifty years after the Norman invasion. When King John visited the town some years before, he stayed at Porchey outside the town. This name has survived to the present time and seems to be derived from the Norman French word for a door or gate. Beside it is the Sheep Gate, the one entrance to the Norman town that still survives, but it is doubtful if the town walls were erected in King John's time, though there may have been some sort of defensive ring outside the limits of the temporary castle grounds.

Trim Castle is the largest Norman fortress in Ireland, having an area of over three acres inside its walls, which have a perimeter of 1,500 feet. The following is Mr Leask's description:

> In plan the keep is unique; it is square with a smaller square tower projecting from each of its sides. Each side measures 65 feet in length and over 76 feet in height ... The eastern tower served as a fore-building, and also housed the castle chapel on an upper floor. The walls of this and the other towers are relatively thin in comparison with those of the main building which are over 11 feet in thickness ... In the thicknesses are the passages and stairways from floor to floor.
>
> Externally the building is plain and unadorned in limestone roughly coursed, sparingly punctuated by the very narrow original loops or the ragged holes which mark where once there were windows ... Inside the building there were three lofty storeys ... The openings have bold mouldings in wrought sandstone ...
>
> One of the gate towers – the south or Dublin gate – which is probably a little later in date (than the rest of the castle) is remarkable, indeed unique in Ireland. It consists of a main tower, nearly round in plan, placed astride the curtain wall and pierced by the entrance passage way. This was contained outwards between two crenulated walls to a barbican on the outer edge of the moat or fosse. There was a counter-balance drawbridge which, when raised, cut off the inner gate from the entrance in the barbican, which was commanded by the defenders from above. This gate-tower was the residence for a time of the boy, Price Hal, later Kind Henry V, left there by Richard II in 1399, on his hasty return to England, which was to end in defeat and death.

The history of Trim for the next three or four centuries is a catalogue of violent deeds, burnings, executions, and reprisals, often between the Normans themselves, sometimes against the Irish 'enemy'. There were parliaments held in Trim, and the king's viceroys often abode in it; moneys were minted there, conspiracies planned, and ransoms arranged. Through the pages of the Annals we have whole litanies of Norman names: FitzAdam, Genevill, Butler, Verdon, Kempe, Wogan, Wellesley, Birmingham, Hussey, Cusack and so on. Here is a typical entry:

> 1368 – Thomas Burley, Prior of Kilmainham, and the King's Chancellor: John FitzReicher, Sheriff of Meath and Sir Robert Tyrell, Baron of Castleknock, were taken prisoner at Carbury by the Birminghams. James Birmingham, who was then kept in irons as a traitor in the Castle of Trim, was set at liberty, in exchange for the Chancellor; the rest were forced to ransom themselves.

In 1393, the Earl of March was allowed to collect tolls on goods coming in to Trim, Athboy, Skryne, and Navan, 'to be expended in surrounding the town of Trim – which is the general place of assembly of all the liege subjects of Meath – with a stone wall, in paving it anew, in improving the town, and in repressing the adjacent enemies and rebels.' Among the tolls is listed a penny a head on every hawk or falcon.

Trim suffered greatly during the Cromwellian wars. Some years later (1666) there is a record of a sale by Adam Loftus of Rathfarnham to Sir James Shaen, of the castle and manor of Trim and the lordship of Moyare for the sum of £7,200. The description says that the caste is 'environed by a wall now ruinous' and the following list of fields included with the manor is given: Rathfield, Maudlin's Field, Much Marishocke, Little Marishocke, Sherryfield, Derysland, Stonefield, Muchfield, Phelimynsland, Paurkfield, Horsecrosse, all together containing 320 acres.

There is a long list of townland names in the locality which space does not permit me to give. It may be that local people would be interested in tracing some of the fields and townlands under their present-day names; if so I shall be happy to let them have the source of my information. Where, for instance, is, 'a meadow called Broadmede, in the fields of Trim containing 24 acres' or 'Leytown alias Ballynaferagh, 30 acres'? Another place has the strangely spelled name of Vinerintida. Roristown was still Ballyrory, and Dalystown was Gallestown.

During the Williamite Wars a hasty effort was made to repair the town walls, the bridge and the drawbridge gate of the castle, an order being given on

21 January 1689 for the work, 'to be begun on Wednesday next, the 23rd day, and done with all expedition'. But after the defeat of King James at the Boyne, the need for walls and battlements passed, and there is no further record of the military occupation of the castle. During the three centuries since then it has gradually become the noble ruin we see today, standing, as Dean Butler says, in the midst of a peaceful country where the inhabitants 'trust their lives and properties to the gentle influence of united interests and mutual benevolence, rather than to the rude defence of walls and castles'.

THE ANCIENT CASTLES OF THE COUNTY
TRACING THE NORMAN BLOOD

When Tennyson wrote in the last century, 'Kind hearts are more than coronets, and simple faith more than Norman blood', he was implying that Norman blood was usually recognised as proof of nobility. That legend was well perpetuated here in Ireland among the great Anglo-Irish families, and persists even down to our own, more democratic age.

The families founded by de Lacy and his robber barons form a substantial part of the history of Ireland, and especially of Meath. Some of their descendants were patriotic from an Irish perspective; some remain, after more than eight centuries, no more than colonists with a strange loyalty to the land of their origin. The majority have a very mixed history of generosity and rapacity, self-sacrifice and self-seeking, the courage that produced martyrs and the easy faith that kept great possessions.

From the first conquest after 1170, there are three significant dates to remember in the history of Cruises, Nugents, Plunketts, Barnwalls and the rest: The Reformation, about 1540; the Cromwellian wars (1642-1652) and the Williamite or Jacobite wars of 1689-1691. Some of the Norman families changed their religion with Henry VIII; the majority did not.

In Cromwellian times many fought as loyal subjects of Charles I of England and were wholly or partially dispossessed, while others managed to remain on the strong side. The majority took the side of the Catholic King James II and some shared in his exile, but many took the easier way and retained their estates during the subsequent Penal Laws. Today, great families still live in their great houses on the sites of the first 'motte and bailey' fortresses of de Lacy's time. Others have come down in the world, in the material sense, and are so long intermarried amongst us that only their surnames give a clue to their origin.

As we travel around Meath, we forget for the moment the blood and murder, and feel only fascination at the sight of those ruined, roadside castles or those massive, opulent hulks visible through richly wooded demesnes.

There is Clongill out behind Wilkinstown, so big and so alone with not a tree or a bush to suggest life around it. There is Dunmoe, down on the river bank, just glimpsed from the main road to Slane, but well worth the steep descent to see it on the rock amid the graces of its long-forgotten owners. There are the Tyrrell ruins on the height across the river. There are small, frowning square towers like Donore and Frayne with dark histories of war and secret meetings. There is Moymet, once proudly held by the powerful Dillons, and there is Delvin of the Nugents.

Though the castles of Slane and Killeen and Dunsany are gracious, and the castle of the Prestons was a place of learning, all of them have their dark histories.

Here are a few notes on Meath castles which were founded in the time of de Lacy himself, according to a compilation entitled *The Beauties of Ireland* by J.N. Brewer, published in London in 1826. Not all of the places mentioned have remains of the original castles.

Dowth or Douth, is on the River Boyne, two and a half miles from Slane. Sir Formal de Netterville entered Ireland with Henry II. His son Richard married Catherine, daughter of Hugh de Lacy, Lord of Meath and settled on the estate of Dowth, which has remained a seat of the elder branch of this family ever since. Nicholas Netterville was created Viscount Netterville of Dowth by King James I in 1622.

Killeen Castle, the noble mansion of the Earl of Fingall, is situated near the small town of Dunshaughlin. This castle was originally built by de Lacy about the year 1180 and was for many ages the seat of the Cusack family. From them it passed to that of Plunkett, by the marriage of Joan, daughter and sole heir of Sir Lucas Cusack, Knight, Lord of Killeen, Dunsany and Gerrardstown, to Sir Christopher Plunkett who, in 1432, was Deputy to Sir Thomas Stanley, Lord Lieutenant of Ireland. In this family the estate has since remained. Lucas, the tenth lord baron of Killeen, termed Lucas More (the great) was created Earl of Fingall by King James I in 1628. The castle of

Killeen, in its existing state, has few visible traces of high antiquity, but the ancient or gothic style of architectural arrangement has cultivated in the extensive alterations made under the direction of the present earl. Large and tasteful additions, comprising several fine apartments, have been recently carried out based on designs of the architect Mr Francis Johnston. His Lordship has also improved the demesne by plantations to a great extent, which are in a thriving condition.

Dunsany Castle was originally erected in the twelfth century, probably by Adam de Feipo. It has been re-edified in a style allusive to the Gothic but adapted to modern taste and habits. The estate was long vested in the Cusack family but has passed with Killeen to the Plunketts.

Skryne is now a place of little importance but was formerly the chief seat of the de Feipo family. Adam de Feipo, on whom Hugh de Lacy bestowed large possessions in this part of Meath, built a castle here, of which the ruins still remain. The de Feipo family passed out of history early, and after several changes the estates at Skryne came by marriage to the Nugents in the time of Queen Elizabeth I.

Slane: The manor and its dependencies were long possessed by the family of Fleming, whose ancestor entered Ireland with de Lacy, and who took from this place the title of Lord of Slane, fixing his residence at a castle in the vicinity of the town. These proprietors forfeited the estate in the unhappy year of 1641 and it was soon after acquired by its present possessors, the family of Conyngham, later ennobled by the title of Marquis Conyngham.

Moyrath castle (parish of Kildalkey) was originally built, according to the *Annals of Innisfallen*, in the year 1219, by Viceroy Lord Geoffrey Morres, Baron de Montemarisco. The manor and castle of Moyrath were purchased by William Oge Nugent, second son of William, first Baron of Delvin, and from that time became the seat of a branch of the Nugent family, denominated after this place. William Oge was knighted and married before 1382 to Joan, daughter of Sir Thomas de Tuite of the Sonnagh in Westmeath, by whom he had, among other issue, Thomas Nugent, progenitor of the baronet family of Nugent of Moyrath.

Delvin castle was erected in 1181 by Sir Hugh de Lacy, Lord of Meath. Here is Clonyn, the fine seat of the Marquis of Westmeath, chief of the noble family of Nugent, descended from Gilbert de Nugent who came over to Ireland in the train of de Lacy in 1172.

This list by no means exhausts the register of barons endowed so handsomely by de Lacy in the course of his conquests.

THE NORMANS' SELFISH OPERATIONS
AN ADMISSION BY GERALDUS

When de Lacy granted Delvin to his brother-in-law Gilbert de Nugent, the church there was granted to the abbey recently founded at Colp near Drogheda. This abbey, in turn, was a dependency of the priory of Llanthony in Monmouthshire. That was the typical Norman method of reforming and reorganising the Church. A little later, according to Archdall (quoted by Dean Cogan):

> Sir Gilbert gave the church of Darrideneth, with two carrucates of land next adjoining, to the monastery of St Thomas (Dublin); as he did to the monastery of the Virgin Mary the church of Dissertale otherwise Ballicur, and four carrucates of land, with the island in which stood the little grove for the health of his own soul and the souls of his brother Richard, his Lord Hugh de Lacie and others.

This is also typically Norman. They took property by force of arms and then gave part of it to the Church for the health of their own souls; it is not recorded that they prayed for their enemies.

The name of Nugent appears frequently as rector of various churches and abbeys in the neighbourhood, though in the reign of Henry IV, there was a John Mortagh Vicar of Delvin, whose name is obviously Irish. The Nugents kept to the ancient faith at the time of the Reformation, but managed to hold their property right through Cromwellian and Williamite times during the Penal Laws.

I do not know if Darrideneth and Dissertale survive as place names and, if they do, in what form. Only local people can supply such information, as there are few students with sufficient leisure to investigate on the spot. Dissert or Dysart is a common place name all over Ireland, and signifies a lonely place or a place of retreat from the world during early Christian times. The Dysart which is now a parish some miles from Mullingar was formerly called *Disert-Maoltuile*, from, presumably, the first holy man who made it his retreat, and his name is still preserved in a holy well there (*Maoltuile* is often anglicised as Flood). In Norman times, we find John de Fresingfeld presented to the parish of Dysart and a later rector was named Moynagh.

The Norman Husseys got possession of the territory of Galtrim, which was then a very important place, and had an ancient church dedicated to the Blessed Virgin. Some rectors mentioned during the next few centuries are Thomas de Meelton, John Swayne, and John Randolf – none of them bearing Irish names. Dean Cogan remarks, however, that the Husseys of later centuries, 'were a fine old Catholic family, and gave many excellent priests to the Church'.

Among other Meath places where Norman churches were established in the time of de Lacy are Ratoath and Dunshaughlin, and the tithes of these were granted to the Abbey of St Thomas in Dublin. This great abbey is again referred to in the following record:

In 1200, Walter de Lacy (son of Hugh) confirmed the grant of the churches of Donaghmore and Trevet and the lands of Donamore, near Grenoke. The same Walter granted the church of Dunshaughlin with the grange as his father had granted it. He also granted the churches of Ratoath, Donamore Grenock, Killeglan and the church of the town of Magliswine (Ballymaglasson) and Knockmack, with all their appurtenances, etc., and the church of Scurlogstown and Laracor. He confirmed to the abbey the following churches, the grants of different persons *viz*. Sydden by Hay Teeling; Dovanashine (Kilshine) by Robert de Mandeville; and Trevet by Walter de Esotock; and a lease forever of the lands of Donamore, near Grenock, and a piece of land near Dunshaughlin. In 1205, Reginald de Turbeville made a grant of all the tithes of the five carrucates of land in Delvin, which Gilbert de Nugent gave him on his marriage. In 1205, Theobald Walter granted the church of Ardmulchan, with the chapels and other ecclesiastical benefits thereunto belonging. In 1207, Eumanic de Feipo granted the Church of SS Peter and Paul, 'with all the tithes of his land adjoining Loughseudy'.

A 'carrucate' is the amount of land which one team of horses or oxen could plough in a season. It is often called simply a 'plough-land'. One might imagine from such lists of endowments that the first Normans, however savage in warfare, did, in fact, a great service to religion in Ireland. But, as MacNeill says, 'there was much building and much writing of official documents, but no progress in learning or the arts, not one school of note, in an age when universities were springing up all over Christendom'.

The Irish were excluded from preferment in the new churches, and therefore the religious progress of the previous half century was checked completely. This is not alone the opinion expressed by Irish annalists. The Norman cleric Geraldus Cambrensis had every reason to exaggerate any faults there were in the Irish Church, and to give every credit possible to his own kinsmen. He had toured many parts of the country as tutor to Prince John (the John who visited Trim) a very few years after the coming of the first conquistadors. He found every fault he could with everything Irish, but had to admit the exemplary purity of the clergy, which was in great contrast to the very unpriestly ways of many of his own brethren.

Some years later, when John was king, Geraldus addressed an appeal to him to remember the pledges his father had given to the Pope, but which had remained unfulfilled. He implored him for the good of his own soul to do something to avert the ruin into which the conquest had plunged the Irish Church; this petition, of course, went unheeded.

It may be remarked that the building of castles and churches and the general assumption of sovereign power occurred within the first fifty years after the first Norman landing in 1169. It was a war of one generation. Geraldus, describing it, calls his chronicle *Hibernia Expugnata*, 'Ireland fought to a finish'. If he had lived a little longer he would have had to change this title. In a short time the conquest was all but undone; in a couple of centuries the English authority was recognised only in a few walled towns and in the district immediately surrounding Dublin.

It is, therefore, one of the puzzles of history that the Normans, who in 1066 conquered all England in one battle, and who seemed to overrun Ireland with equal ease, failed so completely to hold their conquest here. Their first success was due to physical superiority, their subsequent failure to inferiority. The physical superiority came from the fact that they had a standing army, trained in the arts of war. They were paid soldiers recruited on the continent and among the already conquered peoples of England and

Wales. Their lives were of no account to their leaders when advantage was to be gained from their sacrifice. In this they were modern indeed. The Irish at that time, like other free and peace-loving peoples, had no standing army. If there was a small account to settle by force of arms, a chieftain might gather his men for war, but not at a time when crops were to be sown or harvests reaped.

The Normans used heavy armour and long bows. They built castles from which they could not be dislodged with any implements of war then known. All this was sudden, and the Irish were totally unprepared for it, though we may wonder why, with the example of England and Wales before their eyes, they did not realise that some day invasion must come. However, they didn't, and though they fought every inch of the way, it was not until after fifty or more years that the tide began to turn. They learned the new methods of war and began to employ professional soldiers from the Norse Kingdom of Argyle and the Hebrides. These were called Gall-oglaigh (foreign soldiers), the name usually anglicised as 'gallowglasses'.

The moral superiority of the Irish may be estimated by comparing the position of the Normans in Ireland after one generation with their position in England after a century. In the latter country they were still French-speaking; in Ireland they rapidly adopted the Irish language – the son of the first Nugent was called William Oge – and they were eager to seek marriage alliances with the sons and daughters of Irish chiefs.

The idea of nationality grew and hardened in the face of conquest. A free country is unselfconscious in this respect but the trial of war develops national sentiment. Soon the chiefs of north and south were uniting against the common enemy, and the success of the Irish forces, backed by this national sentiment, could be summed up by the admission of a Norman lord, 'Better a castle of bones than a castle of stones.'

THE URBAN AND RURAL STRUGGLE
HOW THE 'MERE IRISH' FARED

The changing status of towns is a feature of early Norman times in Ireland. Clonard, Kells, Trim, Duleek, Dunshaughlin and other places were monastic centres and a large population grew up around them (with 3,000 students in Clonard, for example). There must have been considerable buying and selling of the necessary food and clothing for them. In Danish times these towns declined with the scattering of the great schools, but the seaports grew in importance as the outlet for foreign trade. This was largely due to the skill and experience of the conquered Danes in all matters pertaining to the sea.

In Norman times, the conquistadors settled where they could on older settlements like Trim and Kells, and these towns became fortified strongholds. But in war or peace people have to eat and drink and be clothed, so naturally there were markets in the towns or merchants from them went into the country to buy produce from the hostile Irish. So a new class of people enters the picture; the traders and the makers or manufacturers who converted the raw material from the country to the finished product – millers, weavers, spinners, tailors, bakers, carpenters, masons, leatherworkers, smiths, and other craftsmen.

The successive kings of England were very favourably disposed towards the growing towns for they were an easy source of revenue for them. It was easy enough to collect levies from them on markets and on exported goods in comparison to the difficulty of collecting anything from the powerful barons who had conquered a considerable portion of the country and held it for their sole benefit. Each lord was, to all intents and purposes, an independent king, and they fought one another to increase their possessions just as much as they fought the Irish chiefs.

When John came to Ireland as king (he had already been here as prince) his chief business was to subdue the de Lacy brothers. To that end he brought with him a fleet of 700 ships. The Irish princes made common cause with the king and pursued the de Lacy forces from Trim through Louth and northward to Carrickfergus. From there the brothers fled to France, disguised themselves as workmen and found employment in the Abbey of St Taurin Evreux. The abbot discovered their identity and through his influence John forgave them and restored their estates to them. Walter paid a fine of 2,500 marks for his lordship of Meath and Hugh 4,000 for his Ulster possessions.

Because such occurrences were frequent, the kings found it wise to strengthen the towns and keep them on their side. Charters were granted to many large towns, on payment of a large sum of money to the king. This empowered them to elect their own officials and magistrates, convene their own law courts and pass laws to regulate their own trade. Each business or craft had its own guild which regulated standards, terms of apprenticeship and such matters. To these old charters our modern towns owe their right to have a mayor and corporation, though the maces and town flags of today are but interesting survivals. Dublin received a charter on the first visit of Henry II in 1172. In a list a century later, the important cities are given in this order: Dublin, Waterford, Cork, Ross, Drogheda, Trim and Kilkenny.

In Ireland, the native Irish were excluded from the towns, not only from being members of corporate bodies, or 'freemen', but from taking part in any trade or from being apprentices or even servants in the towns. The idea was that the towns should be English strongholds of middlemen, wealthy traders and loyal subjects of the king, with almost complete freedom from the power of the great landed nobles.

It did not, of course, work out quite this way in practice. English and Anglo-Norman nobles were intermarrying with Irish nobility and lesser Normans were being absorbed through trade and intermarriage. So by degrees, Irishmen found their way into the trade guilds of the towns and their names began to appear on the rolls of freemen.

While the process of assimilation was going on, increased national consciousness of the Irish chiefs was also developing. Native princes began to keep standing armies of their own and, with these forces, availed of every opportunity to rid themselves of English rule. A close alliance existed between the Irish chiefs and the Bruces of Scotland, whose struggle against English rule was not dissimilar. After Robert Bruce, with the aid of Irish allies, won the decisive battle of Bannockburn (1314), his brother Edward was invited to bring over an army and assist with Irish liberation.

He was offered the crown of Ireland, which was not strange since the Bruces were closely allied by blood and marriage to many Irish families. They were related through marriage to the de Lacy family of Meath who took the Irish-Scotch side against the Anglo-Irish and English forces. Prominent Meath families on the latter side were the Mapes (Maperath) and the Birminghams of Carbury.

In the three-year campaign the Scottish forces destroyed crops as they went along and it was famine rather than arms that later led to their defeat. They plundered all before them and left a rather unhappy memory of what had been such a promising expedition. The first winter was spent at Loughsweedy in Westmeath where Bruce and O'Neill of Ulster entertained for Christmas, 'the most considerable chiefs of Ulster, Meath, and Connacht'.

The following year, King Robert arrived from Scotland and with an army of 36,000 men marched down through Meath, crossing the Boyne at Slane and taking Castleknock on the way to besiege Dublin. When this force had later been reduced by famine, it was a Birmingham who followed the depleted forces across the Boyne to the final defeat at Faughart near Dundalk. The towns of Kells and Granard were among those burned by Bruce during the campaign. At another stage it is recorded that the O'Connors Faile (Offaly) were massacred at Ballyboggan, 'by the English of Leinster and Meath'.

During the campaign, the English prince Mortimer came to Trim to chastise the de Lacys of Rathwire for siding with Bruce and he confiscated their lands. But it appears that later they made peace and were forgiven for their defection, except for one of them, John, who was smothered at Trim by order of Mortimer.

Meath must have been completely devastated during these three years and there must have been terrible suffering through famine and disease. No memory of those days now survives in legend or tradition. Perhaps the later horrors of Cromwellian times eclipsed them in popular memory.

FACTIONISM AMONGST THE INVADERS
'MERE IRISH' NOT THE ONLY SINNERS

The expression 'more Irish than the Irish themselves' has been used so often in regard to the invaders of Ireland that many of us may have the impression that the whole colony covered its connection with England and became an integral part of the Irish nation. This is an over simplification, and, as far as Meath is concerned, the saying hardly amounts to a half-truth.

It is true that, as the Irish reasserted themselves, the settlers, being the weaker element, became absorbed. This happened on the borders of Meath where the O'Connors on the south, the O'Farrells, the O'Reillys, Farrellys and others on the west, freed their territories completely. In the year 1432, when an O'Neill of Tyrone was inaugurated king, he received the allegiance, not only of these Irish rulers but also of the foreigners of Westmeath: Nugent, Baron of Delvin, Plunkett, and Herbert.

The corridor from Trim to Athlone was closed, to the great detriment of English influence in Connacht. In East Meath, however, from Trim to the sea, or roughly in the circle bounded by the Boyne, the Anglo-Norman lords were now English in outlook, and little is heard about whatever of Irish blood and tradition survived there.

Most of the chronicles are from English sources and are, in the main, records of civil war between the English settlers themselves and of complicated relations with the various factions in the frequent civil wars in England. This is worth emphasising if only to counteract the often-repeated statement that the Irish, alone of all the peoples of the world, could never agree among themselves.

One English king, Edward II, was, with the connivance of his wife and son, deposed in 1317, just after the Bruce victory in Scotland and during the Bruce campaign in Ireland. He was put to death by the running of red-hot irons through his body. Less than a hundred years later, Richard II was deposed and died in prison, some say of starvation, which was a usual method of killing among the English of the period. Forty years after this, the long and bloody wars for the succession, known in history as the Wars of the Roses, began again.

Some quotations from accounts of events connected with Meath may help to give the reader an idea of the state of this part of Ireland during the two centuries following the death of Bruce in 1318. In 1329, Lord Butler, who was allied in marriage with the English royal family, led a powerful army into Westmeath, with the intention of subduing that county. He was met by MacGeoghegan near Mullingar and was defeated and lost his life in a bloody encounter.

Among those of his officers slain were three Ledwidges, two Petits, two Nangles, two Whites, and a William Freyne. At almost the same time, Bermingham, earl of Louth, was massacred with 160 of his followers (all described as 'English') by their own countrymen, the Gernons and Savages. This Bermingham had previously been Lord Justice of Ireland, and Sir John Darcy was his deputy. But later we hear that the Berminghams defeated the English of Meath at Carbury.

Often, during the period, an English royal prince was Lord Justice or Lord Lieutenant of Ireland, but had a deputy from the colony such as a Darcy, Butler, or Fitzgerald. Sometimes the deputy was English, the prior of Kilmainham, or even the Bishop of Meath. In 1331, there were two Barnewalls and a Tyrrell among those killed in an encounter with the O'Tooles near Dublin, but:

... these disturbances were partly quelled by William Bermingham at the head of a large body of forces. The same year a Hugh de Lacy was in the army of the lord Justice which defeated the Irish at Finea but that was their only victory; the Irish were victorious in Leinster and many English were arrested on suspicion of being in league with them. Among those were Fitzgerald and Burke, as also William Bermingham, who was condemned and executed notwithstanding the services he had rendered to his king and country.

About this time, the Lord of Trim was Roger Mortimer, through whom, by marriage, the de Lacy heritage passed to the Crown of England. This is said to be the reason for the fact that East Meath continued to be an English province, part of what was later to be called the Pale. Prince Lionel of England, a kinsman of this Mortimer, brought over huge forces to subdue Ireland. This was one of many such expeditions, none of which met with any notable success.

Lionel tried to substitute Englishmen fresh from England for 'Englishmen born in Ireland' but after many defeats he had to abandon this policy and invite the 'old English' to his standard by conferring titles on Preston, Cusack and others. At this time an old Meath name, O'Kelly, appears. Ralph O'Kelly, born in Drogheda, became Archbishop of Cashel.

In 1367, Lionel convened a parliament at Kilkenny at which was enacted the famous statute forbidding the 'English by descent' having any contact with the ancient Irish, intermarrying with them, speaking their language, adopting their names, or admitting them to their religious houses. Even some of the old English of Meath were guilty of these 'crimes', for one family of the Berminghams called themselves Mac Fheoris (now MacGorish); the d'Exeters were Mac Jordan (Sheridan) and a branch of the Nangles had become the MacCostellos. There was no Irish Bishop of Meath, though an O'Kelly reigned at Cashel, but Irishmen were being admitted to the local foundations from time to time. The statute was not, of course, always enforceable but the idea which prompted it always existed in English policy, and new English were often put in the chief offices of state over the heads of the old English. One such lieutenant promised 'to protect and govern' the colony for £11,213 per annum, but he was forced to admit his failure to either protect or govern, and gave up the undertaking within two years.

The pressure on the English was such that many went to live in England, and a law had to be passed by which such absentees would have their lands confiscated unless they left deputies to defend their castles, for the law said, 'the loss of Ireland would be of vital importance to the king and crown of England'. One to suffer under this law was a William Carew of Ballymaclo in Meath, but he was afterwards pardoned and restored.

King Richard II (who was afterwards deposed) brought no fewer than 34,000 regular troops to help the colony and extend its boundaries. But, as every casual reader of history knows, the genius of MacMurrough Cavanagh was too much for this unfortunate monarch, in spite of his great army, and he added neither one pound of revenue nor one acre of land to the English province. He bestowed some titles on his supporters, Christopher Preston and William Nugent among them.

It was during Richard's sojourn in Ireland that he heard of the seizure of his throne by Henry, Duke of Lancaster, and because a son of this Henry was in Richard's train, he imprisoned him with the son of the Duke of Gloucester in the castle of Trim. On his deposition shortly afterwards, the two princes were released. The first named of them was the later Henry V of England, the subject of the Shakespearean play.

There was soon trouble for England in both Wales and Scotland and the merchants of Drogheda availed of the opportunity to do a bit of piracy and raiding across the water. They brought home some plunder, we are told, but, at the same time, the Irish had many successes against the English of Meath. One curious incident of the time is 'The War of the Caimín'. Mac Firbisigh records it thus:

> An abuse was given to the son of the Chief of the Berminghams, in the great count in the town of Ath Truim by the Treasurer Meath, that is Barnewall's son, so that he did beat a caimín (that is a stroke of his finger) upon the nose of Mac Fheorais, or Bermingham's son, which deed he was not worthy of, and he entering on the Earl of Ormond's safeguard so that he stole afterwards out of the town, and went towards O'Connor Faly and joined together, and it is hard to know that ever was such abuse better revenged than the said caimín; and thence came the notable word Cogadh an Caimín.

During this war, the Berminghams and O'Connors 'preyed and burnt' a great part of Meath. By the year 1120 the colony was bounded by a circle through Dunlavin, Trim, Collon, and Dundalk and such was the pressure of the 'Irish enemy' on its frontiers that a dyke was built some years later as a defence. The dyke was surmounted by a paling from which the colony came to be called 'The Pale'. A century later, a report says that the area within the Pale, where English language and dress were used, was only twenty miles long. It comprised much of East Meath, but even there, another report says, the greater part of the population was native Irish.

TRIM DESTROYED
VICTIM OF LIGHTNING STRIKE

A parliament in the Middle Ages was very different from an assembly bearing the same name in modern times. It was not elective or in any other way representative. The king (or, in Ireland, his lieutenant) summoned his noblemen and higher clergy to a meeting which they were not always willing to attend. Absence, which implied that they did not favour the measures to be enacted, was often punished by 'royal displeasure' which could be quite unpleasant.

The Acts passed, however, are an indication of the conditions of the times. One lord lieutenant held a parliament in Trim on the Friday after Epiphany in 1447, in which it was enacted that the men should shave the upper lip, under pain of being considered among the Irish enemy. An Irish homicide or robber, though naturalised, might be looked upon as an enemy and consequently be put to death. The sons of labourers should be forced to follow the professions of their fathers.

A law was also passed against false coin, including against 'the coin of the O'Reilly', which shows that at least one Irish chief was powerful enough to mint money on the very border of the English province.

The use of the word 'naturalised' indicates that some legal process was necessary to make an Irishman a 'native' of his own country, but evidently no process could give him the full benefits of citizenship.

In spite of such laws, which we find repeated in almost every parliament, the Irish were not yet conquered. Two years after the enactment just quoted, no less a personage than the Duke of York, heir apparent to the throne of England, crossed the Irish Sea. He had a commission to remain ten years in the country, and keep for the use of his army all the revenues thereof without rendering any account of them, so that his great military talents might be effective in completing the conquest. He also got £2,000 per year from the English treasury, and already owned great castles in Ireland, including Trim and much of Meath.

After some time, he penned a letter, still extant, asking for more money, so that, as he says, 'it shall never be chronicled by the grace of God that Ireland was lost by my negligence'. He details that:

> the Irish enemy, MacGeoghegan, with three or four Irish captains, associate with a great fellowship of English rebels, and with great malice and against all truth have maligned against their allegiance and vengeably have burnt a great town of my inheritance, in Meath, called Ramore, and other villages thereabouts, and murdered and burnt both men, women and children without mercy, the which enemy be yet assembled in woods and forts waiting to do the hurt and grievance to the king's subjects, which they can think or imagine.

Still this Richard of York seems to have done something for the English lords of Ireland, for when the civil war broke out in England a few years later, we find them on the Yorkist side. It was under a Yorkist king that Robert Barnwall was created first lord-baron of Trimblestown in County Meath. His castle is now an imposing ruin a few miles from Trim. Many other frontier castles were built at this period to keep out the Irish enemy, but at the same time the king's subjects had to pay an annual tribute to O'Connor for permission to live in peace, £60 from Meath and £20 from Kildare.

In 1467, Edward Plunket was charged with treason, for forming alliances with 'the hostile Irish' and providing them with arms and horses. A few years later, when a military society was established in Ireland for the defence of the English provinces, one of its thirteen members was Edward Plunket Seneschal. Others were Preston, Lords of Gormanston, Alexander Plunket and Barnaby Barnwall. Some time later an O'Connor was granted forty pence for every plough land in Meath, evidently for assisting the Earl of Kildare against the Irish. It is between the lines of such contradictory records that we must try to read the history of Meath.

Two local places appear in the history of this time – Castlerichard (Castlerickard) granted to Butler, Lord of Dunboyne, and Portlester, as titular estate of one of the great Eustace family of Kildare.

When, in 1485, after the Wars of the Roses, Henry Tudor was crowned King of England, the Anglo-Irish lords were still partial to the House of York. So when Lambert Simnel was proposed by an English faction as the rightful heir to the throne, it was to Ireland he came first to get recognition. He was crowned in Christ's Church after a sermon preached by the

Bishop of Meath and when he went back to England it was with a strong expedition raised here. In the subsequent defeat of this army, Plunket, son of the Baron of Killeen, was among the slain. Then the king sent over his representative to receive the submission of his Irish subjects, first in Dublin and then in Trim.

Oaths of submission were sworn in Trim by Nicholas Herbert, prior of St Peter's of Newtown, Richard Nangle, Abbot of Navan, and James, Abbot of Castlemartin 'of the order of Bective'. The king was not fully satisfied, so he sent for certain nobles to be reprimanded personally. Among these were the barons of Delvin, Killeen, Dunsany, and Trimblestown. They were pardoned and entertained to a banquet at Greenwich, the young pretender whom they had crowned being called in to serve as a waiter at the table.

Further parliaments and expeditions followed, and a new conquest was deemed necessary. The English colony was smaller than ever and the majority of the original Norman stock were absorbed. Only the great lords and the 'new English' officials were left and the whole process had to begin all over again.

Two events, however, occurred at this time, which were to have an impact on world history. The first is noted thus in our records, 'Six muskets were sent from Germany to the Earl of Kildare, and were made use of by his guard while they stood sentinel in his apartments.' The following year Christopher Columbus made his voyage across the Atlantic and neither Ireland, nor Thule, was henceforth the extreme region of the earth.

Happily unconscious of the new era that was dawning, the Burkes and O'Connors, O'Neills and Butlers, O'Donnells and Berminghams, Irish, Anglo-Irish, and English fought their wars with the old weapons in the old way.

The Annals record plagues and storms with monotonous regularity, and in 1506 a disastrous fire, caused by lightning, consumed the town of Trim, 'the most considerable in Meath'.

SIX

CROMWELL

CROMWELLIAN ATROCITIES IN THE COUNTY
HARROWING CONTEMPORARY DETAILS

Some weeks ago I had a most interesting letter from Mr James F. O'Malley, of An Uaimh, on the subject of the Cromwellian atrocities in Meath. He says he was lucky enough to come across an ancient pamphlet (undated), entitled *A collection of Some of the Massacres and Murders Committed on the Irish in Ireland since the 23rd October, 1641.*

This pamphlet was originally published in London in 1662, which is within twenty years of the events recorded. Ten years later, Dr Lynch, in his *History of the Irish Bishops*, describes this pamphlet as an accurate and truthful narrative. The horrors described have never been denied, and such scrupulous writers as Curry and Cogan are completely assured of their authenticity.

Sir Charles Coote had his headquarters in Trim, and from there his soldiers sallied forth, wreaking vengeance on man, woman, and child; sparing neither the aged nor the infirm; butchering alike the loyal gentry of the Pale, and the poorest day-labourers. Here is one quotation:

Mr Thomas Talbot, of Crawly's Town, about eighty years old, being protected, and known servitor to the crown, was killed at his own door by some of Captain Morroe's troop. The soldiers under Grenville's command killed in and about Navan eighty men, women and children, who lived under protection.

The list goes on: 200 at Dunamore, Ardmulchan, Kingstown and Harristown; 40 reaping the harvest at Bonestown, Dunshaughlin; 70 tenants of Mr Francis McEvoy at Rathcore; 100 at Mulhussey; 42 men, women and children and 18 infants at Doramstown. There is a whole page like this, but with horrible details of the torture of the old, the blind, and the bed-ridden which I will not quote. Man's inhumanity to man is something that ordinary sinners like myself find it difficult to understand.

To give the rest of the account would not be fair to our young readers and is rather outside the scope of this series, for my aim is to help to keep alive the living traditions of the parishes. All this happened 300 years ago, and seems to have left no details in the memory of the people; only the idea of terror associated with the Curse of Cromwell. It would be most interesting to find if there is a concrete tradition which survives, and for that reason I add a list of names of murdered persons: Mrs Ellinor Taaffe of Tullaghanogue; Walter Dulin; Walter Evers (near Trim); Mrs Alison Read, Dunshaughlin; Conor Breslin, Mulhussey; Eleanor Cusack, Clonmoghon; James Dowlan, Donagh Comyn, Darby Denis, and Roger Bolan, slaughtered by the garrison of Trim (no addresses given); Patrick White, Clongill.

The Anglo-Irish of the Pale were very reluctant to join forces with the native Irish chiefs, and this persecution in Meath was intended to drive them into rebellion as the prelude to confiscation of their great estates. So the Lords of the Pale agreed to meet the Irish chiefs at the Hill of Crofty, near Duleek. Thence came Rory O'More, Philip O'Reilly, Fox, Byrne and MacMahon, with their troops of cavalry, in full armour. Lord Gormanston came forward to meet them with the challenge, 'Why come ye armed into the Pale?' That was the preliminary to the parley. What a subject for a painting, though no artist in Ireland has thought it worth portraying.

The alliance was not a success. The Anglo-Norman Lords wanted to dig with the two feet, and they were prepared to let Eoghan Rua down at any moment in order to save their prestige and their property. The final result may be read in that most illuminating book, *The Cromwellian Settlement of Ireland* by John Prendergast, Dublin, 1865. This book is out of print, but may be consulted at the county library headquarters by serious students.

You will read of the land-hunger of the English, greater than that of all other peoples. To satisfy it, the Irish were cleared to Connacht, to the slave-ships, or to famine graves. The Lady Dunsany was dragged out of her castle like any common Irishwoman; John Lutteral was transplanted from property worth £2,500 a year, and the council, as a concession, gave compensation of £10 each to his four sisters. Barnewalls, Cusacks, and many others with Norman names are recorded as making special appeals to be allowed to remain, even on fragments of their former huge estates; in most cases they were refused. Hanging was the penalty for refusal to transplant, and there is one story from North Dublin typical of many. The Hores were ordered to transplant from Kilsallaghan Castle, but the lady head of the family hanged herself rather than face the road to Connacht.

Prendergast, visiting the place in 1852, found that the story was still well-known in the district, and a crossroads nearby was still called *Molly Hore's Cross*, for of course the poor suicide was, by Crowner's Quest Law, buried in disgrace at the crossroads. No wonder that many of the old Irish preferred to go to the armies of Europe as swordsmen. Many an old name died out of Meath in those years. Some families held on in poverty, and their descendants are still with us.

A typical example is the great O'Coindealbhain family, which survives in the many Conlans and Connellans in the Diocese, and, in a different spelling, in the Kindelans of Spain, honoured last year in Meath in the person of General Alfredo Kindelan. That many of the Anglo-Normans eventually proved their innocence and were reinstated will be apparent to anyone who can look through the Rate Books of Meath County Council and who has a little knowledge of family names.

I would ask parish historians to dig up any information they can about the pre-Cromwellian owners of local property. I know, in my own parish, families who have very definite traditions of the lands they owned before the confiscations.

THE MECHANICS OF THE PLANTATION
A FEW EXAMPLES QUOTED

During the Cromwellian wars in Ireland, the English parliament had an ingenious method of raising money to finance the army. Rich people in England were asked to 'adventure' money, for which, when Ireland was subdued, they would get portions of land to be taken from the natives. There were many willing to gamble on the chance of a very big return, but even so, wars are expensive things and money was still lacking; so the army in

Ireland, both officers and soldiers, were promised that they would be paid in land when the war was over.

This may have helped to keep up their morale – they would possibly have preferred ready money for immediate spending, but they had no choice. When the massacres of Drogheda and Wexford were over, and the last spark of resistance quenched, preparations were made to honour, if that word may be used, the pledges to adventurers and soldiers.

The Cromwellian government ordered a preliminary survey of all the lands of Leinster, Munster, and Ulster, except for a few places of which there were already recent records. It was a civil survey; that is, it was not a mapping out by sappers, but rather an inventory taken by commissioners, who had instructions to visit every barony, swear in juries, take evidence from existing landowners of the extent and quality of their possessions, and, if necessary, walk the lands to verify boundaries or other matters in dispute. All this was done in less than two years, and on the result was based the actual surveying by Petty for the apportioning of estates to the Cromwellian planters.

The complete records were deposited in Dublin, but half a century later, most of them were believed to have been lost in a fire. A duplicate set of books also existed, but these too were lost. Then in the year 1817, eighty-four of the originals were discovered in the library of Viscount Headfort at Kells. It was a wonderful find and the books eventually went to the Public Records Office, with copies made and deposited in the Quit Rent Office. The originals were lost in the fire of 1922, but fortunately the copies are safe.

In 1940, the Irish Manuscripts Commission published the whole material in a number of volumes so that the public might have a chance of consulting them. Volume V deals with County Meath, and there is a copy of it in the Meath County Council Library Headquarters. The simplest way to show how interesting the book is, is to give an extract, keeping the original spelling. Here is the parish of Emlough:

> The said parish bound on the east with the Red Moore on the west with ye lands of Norbintowne and Carlanstown on the north with the parish Kilbeg on the south with Grange of Rossmyn. And it contains these towns: Emlough, Cravelstowne, Reiske, and Balreiske. Proprietors in 1640, and their qualifications: Gerrald Fleming of Cubrah, Irish Papist; the Lord of Hoth, Protestant; William Betah of Donowre, Irish Papist (for the two last).

The acreages are given for each townland as follows: Emlough: 18 arable, 20 meadow, 100 bog and moore; Cravelstowne: 240 arable, 10 meadow, 40 pasture and 60 bog; Reiske: 36 arable, 20 pasture; Balreiske: 80 arable, 30 meadow, 80 pasture, 100 bog. Observations: 'Emlough: there being on the premises a vast chappell and weare [weir]'. Cravelstowne: 'a vast castle'. I omit the detailed boundaries of each townland, which are also given.

Those who know these townlands will be able to say if these acreages are correct, but I think they will find them on the small side, for here are the figures given in Griffith's Valuation of 1854, which is still regarded as accurate: Emlough: 493; Cravelstowne: 1,007; Reiske: 91; Balreiske: 525. Allowance must, of course, be made for the fact that the Civil Survey is in 'Plantation' measure and Griffith's in English statute measure.

Still, it would appear that the Lord of Howth underestimated the extent of his possessions. The jurors who investigated were local, and though their names for this county are not preserved, it would be inevitable that they should be the local landholders, and each landholder would give evidence of his own holding before the jurors, so in the absence of a very large number of commissioners it would be easy to have collusion.

The landholders must have known that they were to be dispossessed and that the bigger their estate, the less was the chance of holding on to them. While the survey was being made in 1654, there were commissioners sitting in Athlone, trying the cases of any landholder who wished to prove that he was innocent of any part in the rebellion, for to quote the Carte papers, 'as the whole nation was declared guilty of rebellion it lay on each claimant to prove the extent and nature of his estate'. This explanation of the discrepancy in areas is my own, and it may be quite wrong. If so I hope some learned reader will correct me.

One striking thing in the Civil Survey is that there were so few Protestant landholders in 1640, a full hundred years after the Reformation. For instance, in the Barony of Navan there are sixty Catholics and only ten Protestants. It is to be understood that there is no reference at all to the tenants, cottiers, servants, tradesmen, etc., but only to what we might describe as landlords. But these Catholics are almost all of Norman stock: Cusacks, Dillons, Darcys, Husseys, Nangles, Lutterals, many with titles like Lord Fingall and Sir Richard Blake.

The few Irish names include a Reyley, a Moore, and a Dowde. It is worth noting that in the landowners of Emlagh, noted in Griffith's Valuation, there is no Fleming or Betagh, but the Earl of Howth still owns Gravelstown. There are twenty houses given and the surnames of the occupiers are: Gaffney Smith, Reilly, Murtagh, Shaffrey, Crowly, Tiernan, Connor, Bennett, Macken, Kernan, Connor, Pollard, Brady, Jones, Kernan, Lynch, Rogers, Kernan, and Walsh. Some of these had big farms, others had not even gardens.

It is interesting to go through these lists for townlands with which one is familiar. Those who are middleaged will remember some of the 1854 occupiers and will have heard of others. The grandsons of some are still there; other names have disappeared completely. Such records as I have quoted give an added interest to the study of local history, and it is for that reason that I thought it useful to let readers know of just two of the many sources which are available to students in the Local Studies section of the Meath County Council Library.

WARS OF THE ELIZABETHAN PERIOD
THE GREAT VICTORY AT TYRRELLSPASS

The English regard the Elizabethan Age as the most glorious in their history. During the forty-five years that this extraordinary woman occupied the throne, England became a great power in western Europe. She defeated the hitherto invincible Spaniards on the sea and laid the foundations of her empire in the new western hemisphere. At home, the increase of wealth and the exaltation of victory created the atmosphere for the literary renaissance that produced Spenser and Shakespeare.

It was a period of bitter and bloody religious persecution, because absolute monarchy – which we might nowadays call hereditary dictatorship – could be put into effect only if all acknowledged the sovereign as head of the Church.

These forty-five years saw almost continuous war in Ireland, The Conquest, said to have been completed almost 400 years previously, had to be undertaken all over again. This time it appeared to be wholly successful, for the death of Elizabeth in 1603 coincided with the final defeat of the Great O'Neill, the test of the Gaelic princes of the North.

The story of the Elizabethan wars in Ireland belongs in part to the general history of Europe, and the most remarkable part of it is that Ireland alone 'resisted English expansion, wore out Elizabeth, broke generals like Essex

and Brugh.' I would recommend all interested in Irish history to study the
period for the part Meath played in the struggle. The Abbé Mageoghegan
quotes from an early *Catholic History of Ireland* the names of 'the principal
Irish who abetted or opposed the war.'

First is a list of the modern Irish princes who supported the interests of
the queen and the list is subdivided under the headings Munster, Leinster,
and Meath. We may presume that there were no 'loyal' Anglo-Irish in Ulster
or Connacht. The Meath names are: Preston, Viscount Gormanstown;
Nugent, baron of Delvin; Fleming, baron of Slane; Barnewal, Baron of
Trimblestown; Plunket, baron of Louth; Plunket, baron of Dunsany; Plunket,
baron of Killeen.

Next is a list of 'the ancient Irish princes who supported the cause of the
queen'. There are five from Munster, one from Connacht (the O'Connor
Don) and 'in Meath, O' Melachlin, a prince' This example of Irish defection is, however, counterbalanced by the Meath names in lists of those who
fought on the Irish side, 'In Meath – Mageoghegan, a prince' and among
those nobles, 'both equal in birth and virtue to those already named, though
not chiefs of tribes'.

The bravery of Richard Tyrrell and Richard Mageoghegan deserves to
be remembered with pride in the annals of Meath. Here is how the Abbé
Mageoghegan of the princely family of Westmeath describes Tyrrell's most
famous exploit, 'Some step was necessary to be taken to restore the English
power in Ireland.'

The queen appointed a new deputy, Lord Burrough in May 1597, and
invested him with supreme authority in both civil and military affairs.
Burrough (or Brough) was haughty and determined; he commanded for
a long time in Holland, against Philip II (of Spain), whereby he became
expert in the art of war. The Anglo-Irish of Meath (named above) were
eager to side with the cause of Elizabeth. They assembled at Mullingar to
the number of 1,000 men under the command of Barnewall, and marched
after the deputy who was on his way to Ulster at the head of a powerful
army, reinforced by fresh troops from England:

> In their route, however, they met with a signal defeat. Richard Tirrell [or
> Tyrrell] who was of English descent and lord of Fertullagh in West Meath,
> served at that time in the army of O'Neill and had already become formida-
> ble to the English.

O'Neill was fully aware of what was happening, and he dispatched Captain Tyrrell, 'at the head of 400 infantry, with orders to act in either Meath or Leinster, according to emergencies':

Tirrell marched through the whole of Meath without meeting an enemy, and having reached Fertullagh he encamped, in order to give his army some repose. The troops assembled at Mullingar being apprized of Tirrell's march, determined to take him by surprise. The baron Trimbelstown, who commanded them, looked upon this expedition as unworthy of himself, on account of the small number of the enemy he had to fight, and, therefore, commissioned his son to undertake it thinking it a good opportunity for him to signalise himself and so make his court to the Deputy.

At the dawn of day, Tirrell received information, through his spies, that the enemy were in full march to surprise him ... He made a feint of flying before them as they approached, by which movement he gained a defile, covered with trees, which has been since called Tirrell's Pass. He then detached half of his little army and posted them in a hollow adjoining the road, giving the command to his lieutenant O'Connor (of Offaly), a brave and intrepid man like himself. He then, in order to influence his enemy to pursue him, marched on with his division. While the English were passing the place where O'Connor lay in ambuscade, this officer sallied forth with his troops, and caused the drums and fifes to play Captain Tirrell's march. This was the signal agreed upon for an attack; the English army, having got between two fires, were cut to pieces; and so general was the slaughter that one soldier only escaped through a neighbouring bog, to carry the news to Mullingar, from whence the army had set out three days before. Tirrell had sufficient generosity to spare the life of the young nobleman who commanded his enemy, but brought him as a prisoner to O'Neill.

During the engagement, O'Connor's hand became so swollen that it became necessary to cut off the handle of his sword with a file before it could be disengaged.

The generosity of Tyrrell will only be appreciated if we remember that in these wars the massacre of surrendered garrisons was the order of the day. Ormond, for example, had hostages hanged; the surrendered Spaniards in the Desmond wars were butchered, even though the terms of surrender had been sworn to by the deputy; hundreds of instances could be quoted on the English side, and as might be expected there were sometimes reprisals on the Irish side, though very, very few cases of cruelty or torture. O'Neill never allowed wanton bloodshed, nor slew a man except in battle.

Those who know the scene of the engagement at Tyrrellspass will appreciate the tactics from a military point of view, and I am sure the brave captain is still remembered in song and story by the firesides of Fertullagh. The heroism of Mageoghegan must wait till next week. One remark of the historian of his family is worth quoting. It is in reference to the gentlemen who took the side of the queen:

> It is strange that all the ancient and modern Irish who abetted cause of heresy were Catholics, with the exception of three or four who had embraced the reformed religion. The latter were guided by their principles, the former by a blind respect for the shadow of legal authority.

The last phrase is a masterpiece of Christian charity. A more worldly writer might call it very open-eyed respect for their own property. And all of us might well ponder the very strange anomalies of so-called religious wars.

MEMORY OF THE LAST CONQUEST
THE MAGEOGHEGAN AT KINSALE

A little over twenty years ago, Very Revd Paul Walsh delivered a lecture at Castletown-Geoghegan on the genealogy of the family which gave its name to that village and parish. I am not sure if the text of the lecture has been included in the works of Fr Paul as published after his death, but through the kindness of *The Westmeath Examiner* some copies were bound at the time and are in the keeping of the Meath Archaeological and Historical Society.

I have looked up this work to find out what is known of the ancestry of Richard Mageoghegan, the hero of Dunboy, who is referred to in general histories as being, 'of the princely family of Moycashel'.

The modern barony of Moycashel largely represents the ancient Cline Fhiacha, anglicised in the Middle Ages as 'Kinaleagh' and often referred to as Mageoghegan's Country. The family first associated with it was the O'Molloy whose descendants are still numerous in the district, and the first mention of a Mageoghegan in the Annals is in the thirteenth century. They were tough men it seems, for an English source says that, 'no English or peaceful man could live among them'.

In the centuries that followed they gave priests and bishops to the Church, and brave soldiers to the country's service, as well as annalists to record its history. Some were caught up in the intrigues of Elizabeth's reign and accepted the queen's titles. The head of the family at that time was Conley Mageoghegan and he refused all inducements to surrender his title, or what was called by the English his 'captaincy'. 'His son Ross was more amenable, and so to him, by the force of English law, was given, over his father's head so to speak, all the rights, 'lately appertaining to the captaincy', which meant over thirty-four townlands, with extensive powers of administration. The parchment recording this begins, 'The Queen desiring to change the name of captain to seneschal, a degree or name more usual in places of civil governance.'

Ross was not, of course, accepted by the rest of the family, and they would be less than human if they did not grudge him his vast possessions which were supplemented by the confiscated property of the monastery of St Beecan (Kilbeggan). In 1580, he was murdered with, the English said, the consent of his father. The complicated struggles for possession which followed his death make sorry reading and are typical of the success of the policy of 'divide and rule'.

Yet it was a son of this Ross who was the hero of Dunboy. In 1599, he declared for O'Neill and soon all the Mageoghegan kindred were out on the patriotic side, except two uncles who were the English protégés in the family quarrels. Richard was in possession of the monastery lands of Durrow at the time but in a letter (quoted by Fr Paul Walsh) he wrote, 'O' Neill, to whom I am and will be obedient, hath chiefly entered into action for matters of religion and this house, being a religious house, must be restored to the Church.'

Richard seems to have served from this juncture under Captain Tyrrell, the victor of Tyrrellspass, who had followed up that adventure with distinguished service in the armies of O'Neill, both in Ulster and in the famous march to Kinsale. It will be remembered that when the Spanish force, which was to aid the Irish, landed at Kinsale, O'Sullivan Beare and other chiefs gave up their fortresses to them as a token of their sincerity, and as landing bases for the larger contingents that were to follow.

When the Irish army was defeated on the land side of Kinsale, it was hoped that the Spanish garrisons would hold out until these reinforcements arrived and until the Irish could remuster. The English were so reduced by battle and disease that they dreaded this possibility and so offered very favourable terms of surrender to the Spanish commander, which he accepted, handing over not only Kinsale itself but all the other strongholds on the coast. For this he was imprisoned on his return to Spain by order of the king because his action was judged plain treachery and came at the moment when the king had the new fleet ready and had sworn to support Catholic Ireland 'at the risk even of his crown'.

O'Sullivan Beare, in order that at least one point of entry should be kept open, got some troops into his castle of Dunboy by night and took possession of it from the Spaniards, 'without any hostility to them'. One of the officers was Captain Tyrrell. The place was put ready for defence and Richard Mageoghegan was placed in charge, while Tyrrell took command of light forces for observation in the surrounding countryside.

The English attacked by land and sea and from the numerous islands in the bay, and where they took an outpost all were put to the sword and the inhabitants of the district – men, women and children – slaughtered. They had 5,000 men and powerful artillery; in Dunboy there were 140 men. But Tyrrell's flying column was everywhere, and had there been a few more like him Dunboy might have been saved from its tragic fate. It would need the imagination of a novelist to recount the events of these brave days, and what a film they would make.

After three separate attacks had failed, the English president, Carew of unholy memory, ordered a fourth, and here is an account of the end – inevitable but heroic:

> The English artillery continued to play upon the castle from five in the morning until nine, when a turret of the castle was seen to fall. However, the firing was kept up still against one of the fronts of the castle till one in the afternoon when, the breach being affected and the plan of assault fixed upon, the detachment which was to begin the attack advanced. The Catholics disputed the entrance by the breach for a long time but were at length forced to yield to the overwhelming numbers of the English, who planted their standards on one of the turrets.
>
> Roused by despair, the besieged renewed the battle and fought with desperation until night, sometimes in the vaults of the castle, sometimes in the great hall, the cellars and on the stairs, so that blood flowed in every quarter; several of the besieged fell during the attack, among whom was Mageoghegan, their commander, whose valour equalled the greatness of his mind and high birth.

The castle was not yet taken, however, and the following day the English offered terms of surrender which the exhausted remnant of the garrison accepted. Mageoghegan, the commander, although mortally wounded, would not listen to any terms and, seeing the English enter in crowds and, struggling already with death, rose up, snatched a lighted match, and made an effort to fire a barrel of powder which was placed near him, his intention being to blow up both himself and the enemy rather than surrender. He was prevented, however, by a Captain Power in whose arms he was basely and inhumanly stabbed by the English.

Of the few left alive at this stage, not one was allowed to escape. The siege had lasted fifteen days and had cost the English over 600 men. No wonder that in their fury they left not a vestige of the castle. When the news reached Spain, 14,000 men were ready to embark at Coruña. The sailing order was countermanded because all hopes of a successful invasion were lost with the loss of Dunboy.

The defenders, one writer says, 'were worthy to have been citizens of ancient Sparta, from the mode in which they sacrificed themselves for the good of their country'. They are worthy to be remembered forever in Ireland, and no place more than in Meath, the home of the gallant Mageoghegan.

PURITAN ERA OF SAVAGE SLAUGHTER
THE LOCAL CROMWELLIAN MASSACRES

On a day in December of the year 1641, the people of Meath, gathered at the crossroads and on the hilltops, witnessed a strange and impressive spectacle. From early morning, troops of horsemen were passing. At the head of each was a nobleman in the colourful dress of the time, sword in belt and gun in holster, and with him his kinsmen and retainers, all armed and mounted for a great hosting. There was the Earl of Fingall from Killeen and his cousin of Dunsany; from the Trim direction came the Lord of Trimblestown, and from Kilbrew came his kinsman Patrick Barnewall and Segrave of Kileglan. They were all heading for Duleek.

To meet them came the gentlemen from across the Boyne – the Lord of Louth chief among them. Lords Gormanston and Cusack came westwards to the meeting place. Sir Christopher Bellew was there, Darcy of Platten,

Fleming Lord of Slane, Aylmer, Bath, Malone, and from the near neighbourhood Lord Netterville of Dowth. There were many more. The Hill of
Crofty was thronged with the Palesmen, the Catholic Anglo-Irish lords, till
now the proud masters of the land and contemptuous of the native chieftains from the bogs of Laois or the hills of Cavan.

On this day, however, they were uneasy. The events of the past year had
shaken their complacency. Over in England, the king was at war with his subjects. The Puritanical Parliamentary Party was in rebellion against him, and it
was men of this party who were in control of the government of Ireland. One
of them, Parsons by name, had boasted publicly that within a twelve-month
period, there would not be a Catholic left in Ireland. It was intended to root
out the 'old English' families as well as the natives, and for this purpose every
method was being used to drive the Palesmen into rebellion, for, said the
Lords Justices, 'the more in rebellion the more lands should be forfeited to us'.

The native Irish in the north had already risen. The Palesmen had protested their abhorrence of that action. But Puritan soldiers from Dublin
had nevertheless ravaged Santry and Swords, and when the Anglo-Irish
Catholics sent a written protest to Dublin, the bearer was seized and put on
the rack. He was Sir John Reid of Dunshaughlin. Another of their number,
here at the meeting on Crofty Hill, bore the marks of similar treatment
a few months previously. He was Patrick Barnewall of Kilbrew, a man of
sixty-five years of age. All through the Pale, innocent people, poor and rich,
were being tortured and murdered. There seemed no alternative but to take
up arms in defence of their very existence. They were reluctant to adopt a
course so opposed to their traditional attitude, and what made the decision
harder was the bitter necessity of joining forces with the native Irish rebels.

Their fathers had helped in the defeat of the great O'Neill; some of the
elder among them had been young soldiers of the Queen themselves. Now,
from out France and Spain, from Naples, Florence, and Lorraine, the kin of
the exiled Irish chiefs were returning to be avenged.

On Crofty Hill the Palesmen waited for the formal meeting with their
old enemies. They waited, and presently a troop of horsemen was seen
approaching. Armed men like themselves, the leaders of the Irish insurgents
were escorted by a troop of cavalry and a guard of musketeers, captains of
their people bearing the proud names of O'Reilly, Fox, Byrne, MacMahon,
and led by the bravest of them all, Rory O'More. Lord Gormanston rode
forward and put the formal question, 'Why come ye armed into the Pale?'

O'More gave the formal reply that the grounds of their coming and taking up arms was for 'the freedom and liberty of their consciences, the maintenance of His Majesty's prerogative', in which they understood, 'he was abridged, and the making of the subjects of this kingdom as free as those of England'. Lord Gormanston answered, 'Seeing these be your true ends, we will likewise join with you therein.'

What a great scene it was. The dramatist great enough to make it live again would have to show us the mental reservations in the minds of the chiefs who thus expressed their concern for 'His Majesty's prerogative', and the very complex emotions in the hearts of all. To the optimistic it may have seemed the beginning of a real union, the final absorption of the colonists into the body of the Irish nation. Some must have known from the beginning that the welding would break under the first strain.

For the moment all was well. Further conferences at Tara, Kells and Kilkenny, brought the approval of the Catholic Bishops and the establishment of a Provisional Government whose watch word was 'Loyalty to the King', and whose only demand was that Catholics should have liberty of conscience and security in their possessions. The aged Bishop of Meath, Dr Dease, was against the war, and it is said that his influence prevented his kinsmen of Westmeath from joining the confederate forces in their first operation, an unsuccessful siege of Drogheda.

Meanwhile the reign of terror continued. Sir Charles Coote had his headquarters at Trim, and a pamphlet published some twenty years later describes the most horrible atrocities committed by his soldiers. In many instances it is stated that the murdered persons were 'known servitors of the Crown', or were 'in protection'. This did not save them, as the whole idea was to foment rebellion and so leave the way clear for confiscation.

I do not propose to harrow the minds of my readers with the horrible description of tortures given in the pamphlet, but the names of some of the victims may be of interest.

Mr Barnenwall of Tobertinan and Mr John Hussey were hanged at Trim. General Lynch of Donower, aged 80, was killed by troopers, as was another aged gentleman, Thomas Talbot of Crawly's Town (a place I cannot identify). Eighty men, women and children were killed in Navan, and 200 in the district Donamore, Slane, Ardmulchan, Kingstown and Harristown. Mrs Eleanor Taaffe and some other women of Tullaghanoge were murdered by soldiers from Trim, as were some old beggars at Kilbride. Walter Evers, a justice of the peace, old and bedridden, was brought on a cart to Trim to be hanged. Mrs Alison Read, of noble family, at Dunshaughlin was killed, though she was an aged woman, and forty reapers at Bonestown in the neighbourhood were slaughtered at their work. Seventy tenants of Mr Francis M'Evoy, men, women, and children, were killed and 160 more at Rathcore. At Doramstown (Ardbraccan) the dead included eighteen infants. The son and heir of the Whites of Clongill was murdered, and outrages are recorded at Stedalte, Downastone, Duleek and other places.

Coote himself, the author of so much of the evil, met with a violent death before the war was very long in progress: This is how his friend Borlase, one of the Lords Justices, describes it:

> In April 1642 pursuing the rebels at Trim, he was unfortunately shot in the body, as it was thought by one of his own troopers, whether by design or accident was never known. And this end had this gallant gentleman, who began to lie so terrible to the enemy, as his very name was formidable to them.

So much for point of view. Fanaticism is a fearful thing, and the memory of those times should teach its own lesson. Yet, so far from hardening Catholic Ireland in defence of religion, the five or six years that followed showed the breaking up of the elements in the confederacy – on one side, the old Irish with the support of the Papal Nuncio, and on the other the Palesmen, who hated Owen Roe O'Neill and the Nuncio even more than they hated the Puritan government.

It ended in defeat. By 1649, Owen was dead, and Cromwell was loose on the land. In the interval, however, there was his Meath campaign which is even still remembered vaguely at the firesides.

CATHOLIC PALESMEN BETRAY OWEN RUA
TREACHERY LEAVES IRELAND DESOLATE

By the year 1647, the Royalist forces were nearing defeat in England and the city of Dublin was in the hands of the Parliamentary forces under Colonel Jones. Owen Roe O'Neill had been called down from the north, where his brilliant victory at Benburb had practically put an end to the Parliamentary opposition. He swept down into Leinster and soon had control of the hinterland of the capital. His main bases were Athlone, Portlaoise, and Trim, with all the castles and fortresses in between.

The Council at Kilkenny, jealous of his victories, ordered him first to Connacht and afterwards north again, hampering him further by want of money and food for his men. But in his absence, Colonel Jones sallied out from Dublin and got as far as Summerhill before he was faced by the Confederate army under the command of Preston. He won an overwhelming victory which the English Parliament considered so important that they voted to the victor a settlement of land to the value of £500.

The exact place of battle is given in most books as 'Dungan's Hill', and one account has Dungan's Hill near Lynch's Knock. I am sure there is a tradition in the district of the exact scene of the slaughter, for slaughter it was. The Revd Denis Murphy SJ, in his book *Cromwell in Ireland*, quotes from *The Exact Relation of the great victory obtained against the rebels at Dungan's Hill*. On 8 August 1647 he writes, '[Preston's] 3,000 foot [soldiers], being deserted by their own cavalry, retreated to a bog and threw down their arms. They were surrounded and cruelly put to death to a man.'

Preston is said to have been unlucky all during the war. He had been a soldier in the Netherlands, like Owen Roe himself, and is said to have been a good soldier there. He was an uncle to the Lord Gormanston of the time, and as such belonged to a class that hated Owen Roe and all he stood for, even more than he hated what should have been the common enemy. His want of co-operation may have been the cause of his ill-luck.

The whole story of the wars is a sorry history of intrigue on all sides; O'Neill stood for the complete restoration of the Catholic Church, and in this the clerical element of the Supreme Council at Kilkenny was with him, but the lay lords of the Pale were not, because much of the wealth of these Catholic lords had come from confiscated Church property. O'Neill also stood for the freedom of Ireland, and no element in the Supreme Council wanted that. He was, however, the greatest soldier in Europe and the most loyal, and when they could not do without him they had to recall him to their aid.

After Dungan's Hill he was ordered back from the north to defend the Pale. He had 3,000 men, and on his way he was joined by the O'Farrells and the O'Reillys. General O'Farrell was one of O'Neill's best officers, and

Myles O'Reilly is known in song and story as the hero of Finea. I do not know exactly the route the armies marched, but Brian O'Higgins describes a conference of officers at Kilbeggan about this time in *The 1951 Wolfe Tone Annual*.

He says that O'Neill's generals advised him not to risk any more lives, 'in defence of a parcel of trimmers and intriguers who should be left to their fate'. But O'Neill was too loyal to act thus, and his friend Bishop Heber MacMahon of Clogher persuaded the others to imitate the example of their leader. Then, 'Owen addressed them in grave and dignified words, reminding them that they and he were the sworn soldiers of Ireland, and that all Irishmen were entitled to protection against the common enemy.' Forthwith the army set out on its march. When they reached the awful field of Dungan's Hill, O'Neill, in a solemn charge, bade his men remember that, 'every whitening corpse which lay there silently called upon them to avenge the disaster of that unfortunate field'.

'Hold fast together', he said, 'and we shall overcome Jones as we overcame Monroe.'

If O'Neill actually brought his men to Summerhill, he must have withdrawn them again to a strategic position on the other side of the Boyne, some six or eight miles back. There, near where the Stoneyford River joins the Boyne, was the Fitzgerald Castle of Portlester, and this he made his headquarters. As the enemy arrived he withdrew still further, so that they crossed the Boyne without hindrance and followed the smaller river towards Earl's Mill. There O'Neill was waiting to surprise them, in the most advantageous position he could have chosen. It is difficult to describe a battleground without the aid of a map, but the actual deployment of the troops is well known locally and, like all O'Neill's field work, is a lesson to military men of our own day.

The result was a magnificent victory. The Parliamentary General Moore was killed at a spot still called Moore's Bush. His colleague the distinguished General Monk fled with the remnants of his army, and so the enemy was again bottled up in Dublin and the Pale was in Irish hands.

It would be pleasing to record that this victory was followed up with enthusiasm by the Confederates in general. Unfortunately, in a very short time, the General Assembly, at the instigation of the Trimblestowns, Dillons, Prestons and others, was declaring that, 'Owen Mac Art O'Neill is a traitor and a rebel, and all who adhere to him are put out of our protection.'

With O'Neill at Portlester was an officer named Fennell from the Ormond country. He had a strong force of horses at his command but allowed O'Neill's Ulster men to be cut down without interfering. It was he who afterwards bargained with Cromwell to open the gates of Clonmel, but in spite of this act, which he pleaded in his defence, he was afterwards hanged by the Cromwellians.

A canonball found at the scene of the battle of Portlester still survives, and in the woods around are the remains of the trenches cut by O'Neill's men. Similar military works may be seen on the Hill of Ward whence the Irish army is said to have entered the town of Athboy by Bunboggan Lane. Perhaps a specialist in military history could reconstruct the campaign for us, as has been done at the scene of the Battle of the Boyne. Meantime, it is to be hoped that the older people are keeping alive and passing on the traditions of these wars, in Summerhill and Athboy and Ballivor; in every parish from the Monaghan border, round by Moynalty and on to Finea where Myles the Slasher kept the bridge as bravely as the ancient Roman – one man against an army:

> Then flashed his weapon around him;
> It pierced through the breasts of the foe,
> It rang on their bucklers and helmets;
> It shattered their mail at a blow.
>
> He fought till the red lines before him heaped,
> High as the battlements, lay;
> He fell – but the foot of a foeman pressed
> Not on the bridge of Finea.

I hope the whole rousing ballad is still recited through Meath and Breffni. It is to be found in many collections and is given in full in the number of the *Wolfe Tone Annual* I have already referred to. The Palesmen served their country badly; they let down Owen Roe, the bravest and most chivalrous soldier that Ireland ever produced. His death, following this betrayal, just when Cromwell had landed with his Ironsides, left the country a helpless victim to hatred and fanaticism, and well the real native Irish knew it. Many are the laments for the lost leader from the Gaelic bards of the time. English-speaking readers will be familiar with the rendering of Thomas Davis which catches the despair of 1649:

We thought you would not die,
We were sure you would not go,
And leave us in our inmost need,
To Cromwell's cruel blow.

Sheep without a shepherd,
When the snow shuts out the sky,
Oh! why did you leave us, Owen?
Why did you die?

THE AFTERMATH OF THE SLAUGHTER
THE FATE OF THE SURVIVORS

After the Cromwellians had taken all the towns that resisted them, the remnants of the Irish armies remained for some time in the bogs and mountains
and other remote places. There were Cromwellian garrisons in almost every
town – 350 of them in all Ireland – and they had instructions to starve out
the enemy by destruction of crops.

This policy, in a country already ravaged by ten years of terrible warfare, aggravated the horrors of starvation and plague to such a degree that
the country was reduced to a howling wilderness. Children were eaten
by wolves even here in the east of the country, and there are eyewitness
accounts of unfortunate people eating carrion and even corpses.

But the garrisons themselves began to feel the pinch of hunger too, and
the English of Dublin were starving. Some cattle were imported there from
Wales but none of these reached the country towns. The officers, therefore, encouraged the soldiers to till the land around their posts, and all the
Irish not in arms were invited to come back near the garrisons and raise
crops. They were promised the benefit of their labour until such time as the
Parliament of England should decide their fate.

After a while (May 1652) terms were made at Kilkenny with the Leinster
armies – the Meath lords chief among them – by which those 'not guilty of
first blood' were to be allowed to return to their homes under protection
and to maintain themselves until the final settlement should be made. Those
not satisfied to remain at home under the Cromwellians might fight in
foreign armies. ('First blood' seems to have meant having been in rebellion

before the war became a king versus parliament struggle.)

It seems that many availed themselves of the terms, but the garrisons exacted so much every week from each family that they were almost worse off than in the bogs. Some of the gentry, for instance, came back and lived in the stables attached to their former homes which were now occupied by small garrisons. Every Saturday they had to contribute towards the soldiers' pay, and, when any hidden money they had was exhausted, they had to give their very clothes for sale in the marketplaces of the towns. On the other hand, some of the English officers naturally became friendly with their former enemies and even married their daughters, in spite of severe laws against fraternising.

Within a week or two of the Kilkenny Treaty, Sir Walter Dungan and others 'got liberty to beat their drums' in the different garrisons to rally their men for service with the King of Spain. They marched, with their pipers playing, to various ports and before the month was out, 7,000 had embarked. Within the next three years, 34,000 soldiers were transported to foreign parts; Spain, France, and Poland chiefly.

I have no lists of the Meath men among these exiles. Many readers will remember two lectures on Meath men in Spain delivered by Professor MacBride a few years ago – one in Trim and one in An Uaimh. The professor has spent years making researches into the history of the Irish in Spain and, no doubt, the full results will be published later.

For the moment I can depend only on my memory of this lecture. It seems that owing to the traditional belief that the ancient Irish came from Spain, the exiles were received as children returning to their motherland. They were given all the advantages of citizenship from the moment they arrived. The army was glad to have such famous and noble soldiers. Their children had every chance of education befitting their rank, and thousands of them rose to eminence in every profession and walk of life.

At a later period, the Spanish army was controlled by a preponderance of Irish officers. In the military archives and in the records of the universities and ecclesiastical colleges there are complete records of families from the year 1652 down to our own times. From Meath the professor had found the names of O'Reilly, Sheridan, Allen, Lynch, Conway and many others that I cannot now remember. In each case there is an exact record of the date of birth of the officer and the townland he came from. The most famous on the list was one Ultan Kindelan, whose baptismal certificate showed that he was born at Ballinakill and baptised at the then still Catholic church of Castlerickard by the Bishop of Meath. His direct descendant Lieutenant-General Kindelan became one of the greatest statesmen in Spain. He visited Ireland a few years ago to receive an honorary degree at the National University as a tribute not only to his own personal worth, but to the memory of the 30,000 Irish exiles of the Cromwellian settlement.

The Urban District Council of An Uaimh gave him a civic welcome to what had been the province of the Kindelan family in pre-Norman times, and in Ardbraccan he was presented with a stone engraved '*Tobar Ultain*', for, after a lapse of more than a 1,000 years, the family have not forgotten that it was on their land that the Saint of Ardbraccan raised his first little church.

So the exodus began. In the troubled years that followed, young nephews and cousins of the first exiles went to the armies of Spain and France and other continental countries. There was an Irish Brigade in France up to the year 1791. At home the misery continued. The English government conceived a plan for disposing of the destitute thousands.

At the time there was a shortage of labour in the West Indian Islands and Africans were being seized and shipped there. Why not Irish also? The idea naturally found favour with the isolated army of occupation in the colonies, as well as with the owners of plantations. So young girls and boys who had no means of support were seized and sold into slavery, numbering not less than 3,000 and some estimates double that. I am reluctant to go into details of this fearful traffic, but those who wish may read a little book called *Whence the Black Irish of Jamaica?* by Revd Joseph J. Williams, SJ published in America in 1932.

Some surnames from this book point to possible Meath origins such as Regan, Halpin, Moore, Cane, Darcy, Kelly, and Tirrel. We know that the survivors at Drogheda – said to have numbered only thirty – were transported to the Barbadoes, and that the same sentence was passed on any priests who were not executed. But the final settlement was yet to come. The soldiers were gone, so were the young widows and orphans. There remained the landowners who were past military age, and their former tenants and servants. These, as has been said, had returned to their homes where they occupied whatever space was left them by the Cromwellian soldiers, and had begun to till and rear a few calves, pigs, and poultry, while waiting for conditions to settle.

They may not have known that their doom had long been sealed. At the very beginning of the wars, Englishmen had been encouraged to adventure their money for the support of the army, and had got in return share certificates entitling them to land in Ireland. The officer and soldiers in the garrisons had been getting similar certificates in lieu of pay. Now the investors were getting impatient, so with all speed the order was given that every man, woman, and child in Ulster, Leinster, and Minister was to transport to Connacht by 1 May 1654.

At the same time a survey of the whole three provinces was undertaken, parish by parish, and arrangements were made for the allottment of the confiscated land, with part in each barony to go to the English investors and part to the soldiers. The division was made by drawing lots. A value was placed on the lands according to their reputed fertility.

In Meath 1,000 Irish acres were valued at from £600 (in parts of Westmeath) to £1,000 in the Barony of Moyfenrath (the Trim, Clonard, Enfield area). So the best land in Meath was given outright as freehold at from 12s to £1 per Irish acre to the Cromwellian soldiers and their English backers.

THE RESTORATION OF THE STUARTS
THE PLANTERS CONFIRMED IN POSSESSION

'The dismallest failure in English history' is Sir William Butler's description of the English experiment in government without a king, which lasted eleven years and ended with the recall from exile and coronation of Charles II in 1660.

Cromwell's one tangible achievement of establishing possession by English Protestant colonists of the three richest provinces of Ireland had long been the object of English politicians. No English ruler, king or protector, Catholic or Protestant, would wish to undo such a desirable and long-desired achievement.

The transplanted gentry could not be expected to appreciate this as clearly as we can now. Claims for restoration of estates poured in from Connacht, and the Catholic clergy even harboured hopes of getting back some of their confiscated property. The argument was that those who had fought and lost all in defence of the English Royal House would now be rewarded, and that the Cromwellian soldiers and adventurers would be punished for rebelling against their lawful sovereign.

One of the first acts of the new King, however, was a declaration confirming both the army and the adventurers in the land they had got in lieu of their money – excepting only a few named persons who had actively conspired to bring about the late king's death. At the same time, the declaration proposed restoring their lands to any Protestant gentry who had fought on the king's side. When this should be accomplished, any Catholics who could prove their 'innocence' were to be restored too, and compensation paid to the new owners.

The conditions required to prove 'innocence' were such that it seemed unlikely there could be half a dozen Catholics able to fulfil them. Even then, the 'innocent' were not to be allowed back to any property within the precincts of any corporate town. Unjust as this proposed arrangement was, it caused such an outcry from the Protestant planters that an Act of Explanation was passed, making the chance of restoration still more slender for the Irish Catholics. The preamble to this Act is worth quoting:

> That Almighty God has given his Majesty, by and through his English Protestant subjects, absolute victory and conquest over the Irish Popish rebels and enemies … that compelled by necessity during his Majesty's absence beyond the sea, certain of his subjects had undertaken the government, and deprived the said rebels and enemies of their estates.

And these same loyal subjects had now invited his Majesty to come home and had restored Ireland to his authority.

That quotation illustrates perfectly the spirit in which the Irish claims were to be met. A Court of Claims was set up, and of the 6,000 Irish claiming 'innocence', 600 were heard during the first five months. There was much hard swearing on both sides, but to the credit of the judges, about 500 of the 600 were adjudged 'innocent'. This caused such a storm of protest that the Court was dissolved, and the remaining 5,000 were completely excluded from any chance or hope of restoration. Exception was made for about twenty persons of outstanding position and influence, the kind of people who, in all ages, whatever king may reign, will come out on the winning side.

On the restoration of King Charles, his father's old deputy, Ormond, was restored to power. He had, it will be remembered, served his master well during the Cromwellian wars, sacrificing his Irish 'allies', betraying their trust, lying to them, and pretending friendship when it suited him. He had shared the new king's exile and now was sent by him to govern Ireland again in his name. Though one of the Butler family, unlike his kinsmen he was Protestant, having been reared as a ward of court.

It was to him now that the Irish Catholic bishops had to appeal for justice for their Church. He asked them to draw up a 'Remonstrance' – a kind of declaration of loyalty to the new king – and for that purpose, connived to bring about the return of many exiled bishops. They were all willing enough to declare their loyalty, but certain clauses in the declaration were objectionable to them as being insulting to the Vatican, and others contained a humble admission of their guilt in the late rebellion.

Bitter controversy raged for three years, and though the whole thing fizzled out eventually, it achieved Ormond's object of maintaining prejudice against the Irish Catholics. Years afterwards, he wrote that his aim in permitting that meeting was to work a division among the Roman clergy.

The details of this Remonstrance and the part played by individual clergy are of great interest and are dealt with very fully in Volume II of Dean Cogan's *History of the Diocese of Meath*. In the midst of the controversy, Dr Mageoghegan, Bishop of Meath, died and was succeeded by Dr Patrick Plunkett, son of Christopher, Lord Killeen, and his wife, Jeuct, daughter of Sir James Dillon, created Earl of Roscommon. Dr Plunkett had been appointed Bishop of Ardagh during the height of the Cromwellian wars, and was vehemently opposed to Owen Roe and the Nuncio.

He approved of the peace with Ormond but, after the Cromwellian massacres, did all that a good priest could to comfort his afflicted people, until he was forced to fly to the continent. He returned with the others to the meeting of Bishops to discuss the Remonstrance and seems at first to have been in favour of signing, but afterwards resisted Ormond with such vigour that he was arrested in 1669. He was allowed to live in Ireland after his release, and was appointed Bishop of Meath in succession to Dr Mageoghegan, in which position he worked tirelessly for the reorganisation of the diocese, till his death in 1679.

Although Catholics were treated unjustly in the matter of property during the reign of Charles II, there was no persecution of the Church as there had been in Cromwell's time. The laws were still on the statute books but were not enforced. Among other proofs of this is a letter written by Dr Plunkett to a friend in Rome:

The Viceroy of this Kingdom [it was no longer Ormond] shows himself favourable to the Catholics, not only in consequence of his natural mildness of disposition, but still more on account of his being acquainted with the benign intentions of his Majesty.

Masses were celebrated publicly and records survive of ordinations by Dr Plunkett in various parts of the diocese – Navan, Multifarnam, Balnagreny, Clonin (near Delvin) and Bealis, which is given as near Navan, though I do not know where it is.

Another letter, written by Dr Plunkett in 1668, throws some light on the kind of people who succeeded in getting back their estates. It is written to his relative Dr Oliver Plunkett, then in Rome, who was later to come to Ireland as Primate and meet a martyr's death at Tyburn:

As regards your relatives, the Earls of Fingall and Roscommon have re-acquired their lands and property, which were in the hands of Cromwell's officers, and to the great delight of all friends the Castle of Killiney has been restored to Lord Fingall. The Baron of Dunsany, not having recovered any of his estates, is reduced to great poverty; but the Baron of Louth has obtained a partial restitution of what he lost. Mr Nicholas Plunkett of Dunsaile has got back all his former possessions. The other Plunketts of Tutrath, Balrath and Preston have not as yet got back all their castles, which are still in the hands of the Cromwellians and Londoners.

SEVEN

O'HIGGINS

THE STORY OF AMBROSE O'HIGGINS

If Captain Drake had been invited to visit Longford Castle, as he visited so many other Meath mansions, it is quite likely that among the many servants he would have seen an elderly man by the name of Higgins. Drake, of course, would not have noticed him or found out his name. He would not have heard that Higgins's son was abroad in Spain seeking learning and hoping maybe one day to come home an ordained priest to minister secretly in his native diocese. In his own parish of Summerhill, his namesake, Revd Thomas Higgins, may have also looked forward to the return of the poor scholar whom he had helped on his way.

THE GOVERNOR OF PERU

It did not happen that way. Young Ambrose Higgins never came back. He never became a priest. But in distant lands he achieved fame that Drake could not have imagined in the most fantastic of his daydreams. He became Don Ambrosio O'Higgins, Marquis of Osorno and Baron of Ballenar, Viceroy, Governor and Captain-General of Peru and Chile, and Superintendent-General of the Royal Treasury in the richest province of the great Spanish Empire. He left a son who led the peoples of South America to final freedom, as Ambrose had delivered them from the worst evils of colonial oppression.

Today the name of O'Higgins is as familiar in names of towns, streets and institutions on the far side of the Andes as that of Washington is in the United States of America. But at home in Meath, probably not one in a hundred have ever even heard the names of either Don Ambrosio or Don Bernardo. A few old people can still point out the remains of the Higgins homestead, and there is one single book about them published in Ireland; it is from the pen of Mr Thomas Coffey, B.A., a Meathman well known to readers of *The Meath Chronicle*, and the title is *In South American Waters*.

MERCHANT ADVENTURER

In South America, there are innumerable books and essays dealing with the Higginses and their time, but as most of them are in Spanish I have had to be content with the only one in English I could find, *O'Higgins and Don Bernardo* by Edna Deu Pree Nelson, published in New York in 1954. The author has, naturally, little to say about O'Higgins's boyhood, and Summerhill is not even mentioned. It recounts that in Spain, the boy, through hard work, managed to keep himself and go to school. He studied Spanish, Greek, geography, and mathematics, and after some time got a job in a bank in Cadiz. While there, he had an opportunity to see at first hand the extent of Spain's colonial trade. There were merchants who held monopolies on shipping silks, wines, and dozens of other wares to South America. No country was allowed to trade directly with Spain's colonies, any more than the Irish of the same period were allowed to trade with any country except through English ports. The merchants of Cadiz were, like their counterparts in English ports, enormously wealthy, and Ambrose Higgins thought he would try his hand at the game too. He got in touch with a merchant who agreed to enter into a kind of partial partnership with him. Higgins was to travel with a cargo of goods to Chile and sell it directly there. It took three months to make the voyage to Buenos Aires, and from there it was more than 1,000 miles through the Pampas to the foothills of the Andes.

PEDDLER AND ENGINEER

It was winter. Wise men told the young stranger that he would never get across the 20,000 feet high range of mountains between Mendoza and his goal Santiago. He and his mules and his merchandise would be swept over the narrow passes into the yawning void. But Higgins made it. After a nightmare journey, he looked down on the smiling city with its magnificent cathedral and handsome palaces. He was later to see the miserable streets in which the native peoples were crowded in squalor and misery, worse than he had ever seen in his native land. So many were already battening on the poor of the city that Higgins decided to go out into the villages, walking with a single packmule, to peddle his wares.

He made enough profit to go back to Cadiz and buy another consignment. He was well enough known and trusted in Cadiz to be able to get some credit and start independently this time. But before returning to Chile, Higgins travelled to Madrid to apply for a government position. He had noticed during his time in Santiago that all the wealthy Spaniards there were government officials. Some were on enormous salaries, some were not, but all had prestige and used it to advantage in running lucrative businesses on the side.

Higgins, approaching middle age and determined to settle in South America, was naturally anxious to secure a steady income. After much waiting he was appointed assistant to an engineer who was being sent out to Chile to repair the forts which were designed to protect the long coast against smugglers. The engineer was an army captain named Juan Garland, an Irishman. To citizens of Spain it may seem strange that foreigners like Garland and Higgins should get Government appointments under the Spanish Crown.

The fact is that all through the Middle Ages, an Irishman reaching the shores of Spain became automatically a Spanish citizen. Professor McBride of U.C.D., who has done much research on the Irish in Spain, says that the reason for this extraordinary privilege was the belief that the Irish people were of Spanish origin:

> They came from a land beyond the sea,
> And now o'er the western main,
> Set sail in their good ships gallantly
> From the sunny land of Spain.

This account of the coming of the Milesians may be legendary, but the legend was deeply rooted in both countries. There was also the long-standing enmity between Catholic Spain and Protestant England to ensure a welcome for Irishmen fleeing religious persecution. Officers virtually controlled the Spanish army for centuries, and to this day Irish blood is the boast of the elite among the Spanish nobility. Readers will remember the visit a few years ago of the Duke of Tetuan, descendant of the O'Donnells, and Lieutenant General Kindelan whose ancestors had gone out from Meath more than a century before Higgins.

A MORE DISTRESSFUL COUNTRY

The engineer and his assistant reached Chile and started work on the forts. But the business Higgins had hoped to do failed because the agent he was compelled to employ proved corrupt. From then on we hear no more of peddling. Higgins was a capable engineer and in the course of his work he proved himself a born leader. The endemic rottenness of the administration was apparent to him, and he saw how it could be reformed to the benefit of Spain itself, as well as of the colony. There was, for instance, the position of the native Indians who were subject to the Government. Their employers bore no responsibility for their lives, and when one died there were plenty more to take his place. What Negro slaves there were in Chile were cared for as one would care for working animals, but the natives had no commercial value.

In outlying parts of the country there were the wild Indians, against whom there was intermittent warfare. We can't blame them for holding out as well as they could against the rule of the white man, and when they attacked it was with understandable ferocity. It was the masterly handling of this difficult situation which first brought Higgins to prominence.

THE RISE OF AMBROSE HIGGINS

There was plenty of engineering work to be done in Chile. With its long coast it offered a veritable open invitation to smugglers from England, Portugal and other sea faring countries. The forts constructed for defence ages before were in poor repair. Then there were the wild Indians on the southern frontier, often in open warfare with the Spanish colony. To the east, the passes across the Andes were so badly maintained that the poor *peons* (labourers0 who conducted mule-caravans across from Buenos Aires were in constant danger of their lives. Higgins had learned this for himself on his first journey to Chile with his peddler's pack. Now, as assistant to Garland, he did his best, and when Garland died on his way back to report progress in Madrid, Higgins carried on alone.

He was hampered by want of money, for the Spanish officials and wealthy settlers were far too short-sighted to raise funds for anything but their own luxurious living. He had as yet no authority to force them. But fortune played into his hands.

As army engineer-officer, Higgins confronted the outbreak of an Indian uprising promptly and effectively. He organised a militia of local peasantry, trained them into a lighting force, and restored order without any great loss of men or money to the Spanish Government. Furthermore, when he met the Indians he spoke fairly to them, made a peace treaty, and kept it. This was something to which they were not accustomed.

Soon his name was honoured among them, and he was invited to their own conferences, which was something no Spanish officer had ever before been allowed to do. The Spanish Crown rewarded him with a captain's commission, and thereafter he climbed, slowly but surely, the ladder of success.

GOVERNOR OF CHILE

The story of the years that followed is one of achievement in the face of constant opposition from vested interests. Everything the grandees could do to thwart the upstart Irishman, they did with the energy of hatred. But Higgins was a man of courage and determination. He repaired the mountain road from Buenos Aires to enable a regular mail service to Santiago. Along the route, stone houses were constructed and stocked with dried beef, sugar, tobacco and *mate* (the common drink of the country), to which mail couriers had access.

Because the work was carried out honestly it cost only a fraction of what the Spanish Government had anticipated, and the 180-mile road vastly improved Chile's year-round communications. Higgins gained further promotion as the years passed. When the Governor of Chile died, intrigue at the Spanish Court gave Higgins reason to fear that his aristocratic enemies would secure the appointment of someone who would lessen his power.

One day a courier arrived from Buenos Aires over the mountain road and he handed Higgins the leather mail pouch. In it was a letter bearing the Royal Seal of the Spanish Court, and opening it he read:

> Don Carlos by the Grace of God, King of Castile, of Aragon, etc. Due to the death of Don' Benavides, the office of Governor and Captain-General of the Kingdom of Chile and President of my Royal Audiencia, has become vacant, and giving attention to the merits of the Brigadier of my Royal Forces, Don Ambrosio Higgins Vallenar, commandant of the Frontier, has been appointed to succeed him…

VICEROY OF PERU

For the next part of the story I quote from Mr Thomas Coffey's essay:

> Assuming the reins of government Higgins at once made a town of the entire north of Chile, shedding the light of a kindly countenance on the poorest and most abandoned of his subjects without distinction. Having himself drank deeply of the bitter cup of affliction in his early youth, his great heart went out to those in sorrow, as only an Irish heart can.

Higgins emancipated the Indian *peons* who up to then had been forced to work without pay and in a state of semi-starvation on the great estates. He devised the *inquilino* system under which each labourer was given a piece of land free of rent and seed to sow it each year. In return he worked when required on the estate for a small wage which, with the fruits of family labour on his own land, put him beyond the reach of hunger and enabled him to keep his family in reasonable comfort and security.

Under Higgins's regime, progress was felt in every field of activity, which in turn enriched the Spanish court. The slums of the old cities were cleaned, new towns sprang up, smuggling was greatly diminished, there was peace with the Indians, fisheries were developed, and the natural resources of the country began to be used for the benefit of all classes. In old age, reward came in the form of the greatest gift in the King's power to bestow. Higgins was appointed Viceroy of the rich province of Peru.

SPANISH NOBLEMAN

Even in the modern democracies there are those who dearly love a lord, and in countries that are still ruled by crowned heads it is said that men will pay dearly in money and service for the privilege of prefixing 'Sir'.

In the Spain of Higgins's time such titles were even more coveted because, in theory at least, they could not be bought. One must be able to prove that he already belonged to a noble family – that his ancestors had been gentlemen, in the technical sense of the word, for several generations. Rather a difficulty for the former errand boy from Summerhill, but it was overcome and the King of Spain was able with a clear conscience to make his Governor of Chile the Baron of Ballenary.

I give the account from the Deu Pree Nelson biography without comment as to its veracity:

> The King, having reviewed the facts presented in the Governor's application … found that Higgins was a legitimate descendant in direct line of Juan Duff O'Higgins, Baron of Ballenary of the County of Sligo, Ireland, of the old and illustrious house of O'Neill.
>
> What more could His Majesty ask than all the important witnesses to the facts: Chichester Fortescue, a geneologist, Lord Lieutenant-General, Governor and Viceroy of Ireland; the Catholic Archbishop of Dublin and the Spanish Ambassador to the Court of London? If the parish records were missing, as the application plainly stated, was it not because the Protestant government had not allowed records to be kept at the time Higgins was born?

With the new title of Baron of Ballenary, Higgins had the right to use the 'O' prefix of Irish nobility, and has therefore come down to us in history as Don Ambrosio O'Higgins. He showed his gratitude by making a large contribution to the expenses of the Spanish war against France. It was the period of the rise of Napoleon, and in the struggle that followed, another boy from Summerhill was to win his spurs on the battlefields of Spain. Ambrose O'Higgins died in 1801 at the age of eighty. It is likely that he had heard in his letters from home that young Arthur Wesley had got a commission in the British army. But no one then dreamed that in a few years Arthur, Duke of Wellington, would have trod 'upon an Empire's dust' on the field of Waterloo. It was perhaps as well Ambrose did not see what the years were to bring to the courtly Spain he had loved and served so well.

ANOTHER O'HIGGINS

If Ambrose O'Higgins left Chile a happy Spanish colony, those who succeeded him were not able to maintain it in that condition. It is only one man in a million who can resist the temptation to selfishness and tyranny inherent in all colonialism. Before many years, there was discontent in all the South American colonies, and patriot leaders were flying from the whole continent to form secret revolutionary groups in London, Paris and Washington.

THE WIND OF CHANGE

What it is now fashionable to call 'the wind of change' was blowing over the Spanish Empire. Nationalism as we know it was a growing force among the young thinkers: the masses of the people had been sufficiently raised above slavery under O'Higgins's regime to be ready for the new doctrine. The struggle was long and bloody, and in it Chile took the lead.

It was ironic that the last dispatch the aged Ambrose read in the Viceregal Palace at Lima contained the astounding news that his son Bernardo was one of the conspirators plotting to overthrow the regime he himself had built up during a lifetime. Deu Pree Nelson suggests that, though it was a hard blow, the old man understood. At least in his last will, made a few days later, he left his estate to the boy he had never before acknowledged.

DON BERNARDO

It is a fantastic story. I give it as it is told in the Deu Pree Nelson biography, and I have no means of verifying it, for Mr Coffey does not mention it at all. According to Spanish law, no official serving in the American colonies might marry a native-born woman without a special license from the Crown, even if she was of pure Spanish blood. Many Spaniards from the very beginning of the conquest had, of course, married native Indians, and the big majority of Chileans were of mixed race. There does not seem to have been any racial prejudice against Indian blood. The reason for the marriage law was that it was believed that an official having a Chilean wife would be more interested in the welfare of Chile than in ruling it for the profit of Spain. So while a licence might be granted readily enough to a junior official, it meant the end of his chances of promotion.

When Ambrose O'Higgins gained the rank of Lieutenant-Colonel he made the acquaintance of a very lovely young lady, daughter of a Spanish nobleman settled in Chile. They became engaged and O'Higgins went to the Governor's house to ask the Governor to help him in obtaining an immediate licence. But before he had time to mention his business, the Governor told him that letters had just arrived from Spain commending his services, and advancing him to the rank of colonel.

'Spain has been slow to recognise your ability,' said the Governor, 'but now you have been noticed by the Crown, work as tirelessly for Spain in the future as in the past, and you will have any position you choose.'

O'Higgins was so dazzled that he did not even remember the licence until he was out of the Governor's presence. Then he realised that he must choose between a legal marriage and a career which would help him to do all the good he had been dreaming of for the Chilean people. He chose his career.

The biographer does not say if a secret church marriage took place. If it did it remained secret, and it appears that only two or three confidential friends ever learned of the relations between the rising statesman and Dona Isabel Riquelme. When a son was born to them, the father had the certificate of his birth signed by the priest declaring that this was his son, Bernardo, but omitting the name of the mother. This document he kept secret all his life. The mother reared the child for some years, but, possibly for fear of discovery, the father ceased to visit her altogether. As she was not married according to Spanish law she later married again, and the father had Bernardo removed to the home of a trusted friend many miles away.

He saw him once only during his years in this house, and then only in company with a whole party of children. He never saw him again, for spies were everywhere and one indiscretion would be the end of his career. A rumour that something was suspected made him send the child to Spain to be educated, and later, to be more secure, he had him removed to London. The boy bore his mother's maiden name, but from an early age he knew the truth from a conversation he overheard. It says much for his character that he kept the secret even from the exiled Chilean patriots who became his friends in London.

When he returned to South America, just after his father's death, he found his mother a widow with one daughter. The winds of change had blown so far that he was not afraid to reveal the whole truth. For the rest of his life he was honoured as the patriot son of a patriot father and his mother and stepsister lived with him and shared privations and glory alike. That is the story told in the book *O'Higgins and Don Bernardo*.

A SOLDIER WITHOUT AMBITION

The young O'Higgins was an idealist without personal ambition or a great opinion of his own ability. He was ready to die for his country if only he could serve her in the humblest capacity. But in one of the early battles against the Royalist troops, when Carrera, the leader of the revolutionaries, proved incompetent, O'Higgins cried out, 'Live with honour or die with glory', and rushing forward to the head of the troops, turned defeat into victory.

He did not take any credit for this action, the first of many in which, though Carrera was commander, O'Higgins was the hero. If he had had full command, victory might have come in these first days of revolution. As it was, Bernardo could do no more than save the patriot troops by a brilliant retreat across the Andes. In Buenos Aires they were joined by revolutionary leaders from the other South American states, for the winds of change were, by now, blowing over the whole continent.

Plans were made for the most daring feat ever recorded in military history: the crossing of the Andes with a whole army. They chose a pass more than 13,000 feet higher than the Great St Bernard over which Hannibal had led the men of Carthage against Rome.

DON BERNARDO O'HIGGINS

It was midsummer in the southern Andes – the month of January, 1817. But on the heights the cold was intense; biting winds swept through the narrow pass; now and then avalanches of boulders came with terrifying, thunderous roar from the heights above and blocked the pathway. Up and up the almost perpendicular slope crept the long column of men, 5,000 of them, in single file. There were almost as many mules, bearing arms and munitions, provisions for fifteen days' march, a cable bridge and grapples for crossing ravines, artillery pieces and the narrow gun carriages for mounting them.

THE PASSAGE OF THE ANDES

As the altitude increased, the men could barely crawl forwards, gasping for breath as blood spurted from their ears and nostrils. Now and then a man, overcome by dizziness, stumbled over the edge of the path and his dying scream echoed and re-echoed from the depths of the canyon below. But always when Don Bernardo passed a cheering word back along the line there was a '*Viva la Patria!*' from every parched throat. Where O'Higgins led every man followed with confidence. On the fifteenth day a valley appeared beneath them: it was Chile. The miracle had happened: an army had crossed the Andes.

THE LIBERATION OF CHILE

The patriot troops, with the element of surprise on their side, won a decisive victory. Very soon Chile was independent, and much against his will, O'Higgins was named dictator of the new Republic. However, it was not as easy as this brief account may suggest. In Peru the Spanish forces were still powerful and they had ample means to transport unlimited troop numbers by sea to any of the ports on Chile's long coastline.

The new government was unopposed and though energetic and enthusiastic, lacked warships. The ladies of Santiago sold their jewels to make up the price of their first ship, a battered British vessel. Another was added and Captain O'Brien (an Irishman obviously) took charge of the 'fleet'. They put to sea and captured one Spanish vessel, then another and another, until there were eleven. Meanwhile, the economy of the country was being developed; schools were established, land divided, and a fine standing army trained to take part later in the liberation of Peru. At the end of five years, the country was over its initial difficulties and well on the road to a peaceful and prosperous future.

THE BRAVEST DEED OF ALL

However, as so often happens, men who had done little in times of danger jumped on the bandwagon, and sought prominence and power in the new regime.

At the delicate stage when intrigue threatened to lead to civil war, O'Higgins entered the Government House where the opposition party was meeting secretly. Removing his badge of office from his tunic he said:

> There will be no talk of bloodshed over me. You do not terrorise me by talk of sedition, by threats or secret meetings. I despise death today as I have scorned it on the battlefield. But if it has not been given me to consolidate the new institutions of the Republic, at least I have the satisfaction of leaving it free and independent, respected abroad and glorious in victory. I thank God for the favour He has given to my government. I pray that He may protect those who succeed me.

He turned and walked from the room and from public life. Twenty years later he died in Lima. There, as well as in Chile, his name is remembered. Mr Coffey says he had the privilege of inspecting the *O'Higgins*, the flagship of the Chilean Navy. At Valparaiso and in Peru monuments to both Ambrose and Bernardo abound.

THE HIGGINS FAMILY

What claim had Ambrose O'Higgins to be a descendant in direct line of Juan Duff O'Higgins, Baron of Ballenary in the County of Sligo of the old and illustrious house of O'Neill? And what claim has Meath to be the birthplace of this great soldier and statesman?

MacLysaght, in his work *Irish Families*, states that the name 'Higgins' has been said to be of Norse origin, and akin to the word 'Viking'. But he says – and his authority in the field is acknowledged – 'Higgins' or 'Higgin' is an anglicised form of a genuine old Irish name, *Uige*, of which the genitive form might be *O hUigean*.

The Higgins were a sept of the O'Neills of the Midlands whose descendants spread as far west as Sligo. For centuries, the name of O'Higgins keeps turning up again and again, borne by poets and men of learning. There was Tadhg Mór O'Higgin in the fourteenth century, Tadhg Óg in the fifteenth, and no fewer than five others in the sixteenth — all great poets. One was also Archbishop of Tuam. In more recent times there were churchmen, physicians and chemists of the name, and in our own day there are still O'Higginses distinguished in many walks of life.

THE ANNALS OF THE POOR

When it comes to tracing the direct ancestors of any particular Irishman, we are up against very great difficulties. In Gaelic times there were very exact records, but it was the policy of the English to destroy anything that might keep pride of race alive, so throughout the Middle Ages there was deliberate destruction of documents and stern suppression of bards who kept genealogies alive in the oral tradition. Families were so often dispossessed and forced from their native districts that they lost that connection of place and family so important to genealogy.

In the case of the Higgins family, all we know for certain is that the parents of Ambrose lived in the Ballina district before coming to Summerhill in County Meath. It is not quite certain whether the move was made before or after the birth of Ambrose. The late Pádraig O'Higgins, who came to Meath from the west many years ago and settled in Summerhill, has made a study of the origins of his famous namesake. He is of the opinion that Ambrose was born in Summerhill, in the house now in ruins that is well remembered as the Higgins's homestead. Most of what follows is taken from Pádraig's notes as published in *Ríocht na Midhe* in 1956.

TRANSPLANTED

The castle of Dangan, still known as Lynch's Castle, fell into Cromwellian hands and was for some time the residence of Bishop Jones. He sold it to a County Down planter named Rowley who married the heiress of the neighbouring Langford property in 1683. It may be one of the family of this Rowley who brought the Higgins family up from Ballina.

One of the Rowley ladies married into the family of the Earl of Bective, and tradition has it that the young Ambrose was attendant or page boy to her and that she helped him on his way to Spain. But the question of why the Higgins family came up to Summerhill at all persists. Had the Rowleys or the Langfords estates in the west on which they were employed? Or could it be that the Higginses were originally Meath people who had been dispossessed and gone to Connacht a generation earlier?

This seems likely, when we consider that a Revd Thomas Higgins was parish priest of Summerhill from 1722 to 1762. It may be only coincidence, but Pádraig O'Higgins states in his note that the priest and Ambrose were of the same family. There are other recorded instances of families returning and being welcomed by the new owners, particularly if they were tradesmen, because the planters were in desperate need of skilled craftsmen.

LOCAL TRADITION

Whatever the explanation, we know that in the same year, 1722, Squire Rowley called in Cassall, the famous German architect, to design a new mansion for him on the Langford property. Ambrose was then a baby of a year old, and as the new castle took ten years to complete, he may perhaps have already begun work in the old castle of the Lynches as a child helper around the kitchen.

Local tradition is extremely vague about the circumstances in which the boy left home, but it is remembered that he walked to Dublin and from there worked his way to Cadiz. The reason may be that O'Higgins did not really achieve fame until he was over sixty years of age, and by that time many who remembered him would have already been dead. We know that some of his brothers were married and that at least two of Ambrose's nephews served in the Spanish army.

Nephews are also mentioned as having joined him in South America, and there is a tradition that he helped his people at home when he became wealthy. But the last years of O'Higgins's life were the dark years of 1798 and the Union and people were in no circumstances to think of or rejoice in the greatness of an Irishman at the other side of the world. The connection with Spain was practically severed by this time, and consequently few Irishmen went to the South American colonies.

EIGHT

FAMINE

THE GREAT STARVATION

The potato blight appeared for the first time in Ireland in the autumn of 1845. During the next five years a quarter of the population would perish from starvation and the diseases that follow starvation. That is the bald outline of the story. But the how and why of the famine need a great deal of explanation.

We are familiar with accounts of famine in places ravaged by war or visited by some natural catastrophe, but, to the credit of the global community, every effort is made to assist such stricken areas. People give generously of their food, clothing, and money; volunteers bring medical aid to the sick and look after the homeless.

The Irish Famine is different because there was no war, no earthquake, and no general shortage of food. The potato crop failed but the corn harvest was abundant and the cattle export trade as big as ever. Yet nearly two million people died.

POPULATION AND POVERTY

Landlords were anxious to increase their tenant numbers when Catholics were enfranchised in 1793. Forty shillings worth of valuation gave the right to vote, and the more voters a man had at his command the greater his influence. Tenants were compelled to vote as directed, and the landlord could sell the votes to the highest bidder. Therefore, sons of tenants could be granted leave to live on a bit of unprofitable land.

They could build a cabin on it, marry and rear a family, supporting them by the labour required to drain and dig and plant on bog and mountain, with the constant risk of bad seasons and semi-starvation. As they reclaimed they had rents imposed upon the land they made. But there was no alternative, for there were no industries to absorb the natural increase of population.

The increased demand for food created by the Napoleonic Wars gave rise to increased employment on larger farms for the poor. The post-war economic slump – at its worst in 1823 – forced many to cross to England and Scotland to work in the harvest and return with the £3 or £4 they earned for the rent of the cabin and potato plot.

Steamships were just coming into use at this period, and there was such competition for passengers that the steerage rate was as low as five pence a head. Sometimes as many as 1,500 people were crowded on board small steamers of 200 tons, and accidents were frequent. In the census of 1841 it was estimated that 57,651 labourers sailed to Britain that year, and of these nearly 14,000 embarked at the port of Drogheda.

No doubt many of these latter came from Connacht, but there is a tradition of Meath men going too. This – let it be noted – was before the famine. Farmers were little better off than labourers. Half of the holdings were less than five acres. Another third were between five and fifteen acres. Only 7 per cent of farms were over thirty acres, and if we remember that these include the huge estates of the gentry it becomes evident that a middle class hardly existed in pre-famine Ireland.

EVE OF FAMINE POPULATION

According to the census of 1831, the population of Meath was 176,826, and while the method of enumeration was not as careful as that in present use, we can accept the figures as a fair enough estimate.

If the head of each family had a vote we would expect to find 20,000 or 30,000 names on the register; in fact, the total number of registered electors in 1836 was only 1,868. Of these, only 581 had property valued at £50 and over; 308 were in the group £20 to £50, and the remaining 979 had between £10 and £20 valuation. That means that at least 90 per cent of the people lived on holdings of less than £10 annual value, and had no share at all in the political or civic life of the country.

Up to 1832, a valuation of £2 per annum carried the right to vote, which prompted landlords, in their quest for greater power and influence, to encourage tenants to subdivide their farms among their sons.

It was standard practice for a parliamentary candidate to pay a substantial sum for a landlord's support. This scandalous state of affairs had been worse before the Act of Union (1801) when there were no fewer than fourteen MPs for Meath, two for the county and two each for the boroughs of Athboy, Duleek, Kells, Navan, Ratoath and Trim. Athboy was the sole possession of Lord Darnley, and none of the other towns had more than two or three landlords.

After the Act of Union, however, there were only two members for the whole county, and the elections, by open ballot, were held at Trim. The advantage to Catholics of being allowed to enter parliament for the first time in 1829 was offset by a bill which disfranchised the Forty Shilling Freeholders, the vast majority of the farmers of Ireland, leaving only the tiny electorate outlined above.

THE GRAZIERS

Neither O'Connell nor anybody else seems to have made any protest against the fate of the Forty Shilling Freeholders. They had no longer any *raison d'être* from the political point of view; they were becoming, every year, less and less necessary as a labour force, for changing economic climates were making it more profitable for the large landowners to raise cattle than to grow wheat for the English market.

The advent of the steamship made the export of live cattle to England feasible. Gentlemen looked with contempt on tillage and only reluctantly ploughed what was necessary for their own use and for winter fodder for livestock. Many did not even do this much; they fed the cattle on a wide range and did no stable feeding.

As the strong farmers prospered, they imitated gentlemen, for being graziers put them in a higher social grade than that of the tillage farmer. So, by the time of the first appearance of the potato blight, we may take it that the 581 freeholders of £50 and over were in the cattle trade.

A gentleman named Garnett was among those who gave evidence at the Devon Commission which investigated the state of Ireland shortly before the famine. He occupied 1,300 statute acres in Meath, and only tilled what he required for his own use. Mr R.W. Reynell of Killynan had 3,000 acres in Meath and Westmeath, of which only 150 acres were in tillage.

The Meath graziers bought their cattle in October at Ballinasloe fair, one of the world's largest, and sold them in the Dublin market in June. A second consignment bought in May was sold in December, a practice which has continued down to our own time. The larger farms also kept sheep. Few graziers made any attempt at drainage or improvements because 300 acres could bring £1,500 a year without effort.

THE LABOURERS

At the other end of the scale were the labourers in and around the towns, some of whom had no patch of ground for growing potatoes. There was little employment for them on the farms, and tariffs had already killed other industries.

Here is an extract from the report of a commission of enquiry into the state of the poor shortly before the famine. The place described is Kells:

Cabins of single rooms are there frequently occupied by a large family, with sometimes a widow or an old man lodging with them, or occupied altogether by several widows, or by one or more, and one or two old men, and all (pigs included) sleeping in different corners of the room. The families are those of labourers, who generally get but very little employment; and the old men and widows subsist chiefly by begging, except those who are wholly or in part supported by their children who give them all they can spare of the wages they earn at service ... A number of these cabins are situated in little courts at the back of the main row of cabins which form the front of the street or road. These courts are seldom more than six or seven feet wide, and that space which forms the only passage or entrance to the cabins is usually blocked up with the heaps of manure made by the pigs, and with the rubbish and filth thrown out of the houses at the very doors.

BOG HOLDINGS

It was not only in towns that large numbers of the poor lived in extreme poverty. The evicted and the unemployed took refuge in unreclaimed bog where they would build a hut of sods and lay out a small plot of potato ground around it. By using ashes and any other manure available, the plot was made more fertile, and a new bit was taken in the next year, and in a few years there was a tiny holding, enclosed by a hedge and producing a little oats for the rent which the landlord clapped on as soon as the squatter had brought his little bit of wilderness into cultivation.

The report quoted above states that in the bog near Kilcock there was, 'an immense population, and nothing can equal the wretchedness of the poor'. Lewis reports in 1836 that there were in Meath 561,527 statute acres of cultivated land, and 5,600 acres of unimproved mountain and bog. It was on the fringes of this waste that a big proportion of the population existed.

FAMINE

In the late autumn of 1845, a letter signed by Very Revd Dr McEvoy, P.P., Kells, and dated 24 October, appeared in the Dublin newspapers:

> On my most minute personal inspection of the state of the potato crop in this most fertile potato-growing locale is founded my inexpressibly painful conviction that one family in twenty of the people will not have a single potato left on Christmas Day next ...
>
> With starvation at our doors, grimly staring at us, vessels laden with our whole hopes of existence, our provisions are hourly wafted from our every port. From one milling establishment I have last night seen no less than fifty dray-loads of meal moving on to Drogheda, thence to go to feed the foreigner, leaving starvation and death the soon and certain fate of the toil and sweat that raised this food.

Dr McEvoy's description of Kells might reasonably be applied to every district in Meath. His prophecy of starvation and death was to be fulfilled in greater measure than even he could have foreseen. For 1845 was only the first of the Black Years.

COMING OF THE BLIGHT

The potato blight had appeared in Germany some three or four years previously, and had spread westwards through Belgium and thence to Britain. It also visited Canada, and is said to have long been known in Western America. The European countries, then and later, guarded against starvation by buying up supplies of cheap food as a substitute for the potato.

Ireland was the only country where a majority of the population depended on one crop. The young had no hope of employment; some emigrated permanently or seasonally; those who could not go reclaimed a bit of mountain or bog and grew potatoes on it. Rack-rented farmers set plots and cabins at rack-rents to poor families, thus ensuring cheap labour in the busy seasons. The poorest begged, and the 'charity' was potatoes. The new workhouses were a last resort.

Evictions became more numerous every year and big farms became bigger as grazing gradually became more profitable than tillage. This state of affairs was naturally well known to the British Government and its representatives in Dublin. There had been so many Commissions on the State of Ireland that someone said if Blue Books could be eaten there would have been no famine. But no precautions were taken to avoid catastrophe.

RELIEF AND RED TAPE

The blight appeared first on the Wexford coast in the middle of September 1845, and within a month the papers were full of letters from every county in Ireland. Once the disease appeared, a whole crop might be rotten in twenty-four hours, though in places it was a little less severe, and perhaps a fifth of the crop might remain edible at least for a time. Fr O'Rourke quotes one misfortunate woman from County Meath in his history of the famine as saying, 'Awful is our story; I do be striving to blindfold them in the boiling. I trust in God's mercy no harm will come from them.'

That brave, anonymous woman, trying to put her troubled thought into an unfamiliar language – what was her fate? Awful was their story in 1845, and more awful was it to be in 1846 and 1847.

Dublin Corporation met and sent a deputation to the Lord Lieutenant. O'Connell's party met and made recommendations. They asked for no charity, but only that own money be applied to providing work for the people, and food be retained in the country which they could buy with their wages:

> The proceeds of the woods and forests in this country are £74,000 a year, money which instead of being applied to Irish purposes has gone to improve Windsor and Trafalgar Square – two millions of Irish money having been already expended in this manner ... Let a loan of a million and a half be raised on this £74,000 a year, which at 4 per cent, would leave a portion of it for a sinking fund ... Let the absentee landlords be taxed 50 per cent and the resident ones 10 per cent.

Among the suggested works was the construction of the railways, long projected, of which only a few miles had been built. The Lord Lieutenant met the deputation and read a reply to them, stating that the condition of the potato disease was being watched by those whose business it was; that their suggestions would, of course, be submitted to the British Cabinet, who alone could decide such matters, but that there was no immediate pressure on the market.

This was the first of many such attempts by responsible people in Ireland to get something done. The answer was always the same. It would be considered. Commissions of enquiry were appointed by the Government after a while to go over the ground again and again – to take more evidence, to suggest remedies, to report on this, that and the other side of the question, and theorists in political economy revelled in the opportunity to prove that the famine was the result of over-population, or of want of industry, or of true religion, or of any of one hundred and one other causes. This activity did not, however, feed one starving person.

FEVER STALKS WITH FAMINE

In Navan, fever of the relapsing variety had been generally epidemic from 1845 and had become extremely severe by 1847. A Dr Lamprey reports from the districts of Trim and Kilcooly which he describes as the richest in Ireland. So many of the people were engaged in grazing that the failure of the potato crop did not result in starvation. In any case, he says, the failure was not complete in this area. But disease soon became very prevalent, and this is what Dr Lamprey says about the cause:

By far the chief agent in propagating it was the constant practice the people of the western and more stricken counties had of migrating towards the eastern parts of the island. These poor creatures, obliged by their poverty to sleep in ditches and other wretched places, carried the fever, at that time more prevalent in the west and, mixing with the people attending fairs and markets, for the purpose of begging, imparted the disease to them. I have often observed whole families belonging to distant counties lying in fever on the roadside.

FIRST YEAR OF THE FAMINE

Long before the Christmas of 1845, it was obvious that the failure of the potato crop was general throughout Ireland, and that the result must be not just hardship but starvation for a majority of the people. Private charity and good neighbourliness, however, were still able to ward off a little of the effects of the calamity.

The clergy, both Catholic and Protestant, did their best, and the kindness of the poor to the poor saved many a life in that first winter and spring. Some resident landlords and larger tenants were generous. But there are numerous recorded instances of landowners issuing notices that if outstanding rents were not paid promptly immediate eviction would result.

A touching story was reported in *The Freeman's Journal* by one of their correspondents from Tipperary in April 1846: a farmer was picking a pit of potatoes, throwing the bad ones to one side. It was the fourth picking in a fortnight, and in that time the pit had been reduced from sixty barrels to ten. While he was talking to the newspaperman and picking away sadly, a poor woman came up asking for a few potatoes for God's sake. The farmer's wife came out to the pit to get her some, and her husband said, 'Give her no bad ones, Mary. God is good.'

BRITISH REACTION

Refusal to believe that famine existed was the approach of British politicians and of the Prime Minister of the time, Sir Robert Peel, leader of the Tory Party. But the potato disaster soon became a party issue. For a long time an agitation had been going on for Free Trade, but up to this time neither of the two big parties had agreed to the principle.

Up to this time there was a tariff on foreign corn coming into England and, of course, this bolstered the price for the growers, who were the landed gentry. These were still the vast majority of representatives in the House of Commons, and the whole of the House of Lords. But gradually another class of people was entering politics. These were the big manufacturers, the owners of coal mines, the cotton-mill owners of Lancashire, the whole rising class of industrialists whose interest it was to have cheap food available for their poorly paid work-force.

No one suggested that, instead of importing cheap food, wages might be raised to enable a workman to buy English or Irish wheaten-meal for his daily bread. Legislating on wages would have been an unthinkable interference with the Established Order. It was little more than two years (1842) since the first Act of Social Legislation had been passed, declaring that after a certain limited period no woman or girl should be employed in mines or collieries.

Up to then, when the seam of coal was too narrow to allow the trucks to be wheeled, women were harnessed to them with chains and crawled on all fours with their burden to and from the shaft, for fourteen to sixteen hours a day, until they had lost all resemblance to women, or even to human beings.

Women still worked in the iron foundries, and the slavery of little children in the cotton mills was to continue for many years. Statesmen professed the belief that it was wrong to interfere with the freedom of contract between employer and employee, and wrong to feed the hungry who did not work, which did not leave the workman very much freedom in bargaining for higher wages.

PEEL'S RELIEF MEASURES

This digression goes some way to explain, if not to excuse, the official attitude towards the famine. To prevent Irish wheat being sent to England, or to import cheap food, would violate all the theories of English economists. Nevertheless, Peel did order a cargo of Indian corn from America as early as November 1845, and it arrived secretly in Cork, in preparation for future emergencies.

After Christmas, details were issued for the formation of local committees to administer relief schemes. There were so many complications as regards the powers and responsibilities of these committees, so many forms to be filled, so many delays waiting for sanction for each move, that the most willing local workers got disheartened.

Some places were under two local committees, some were under none. The committees were to receive subscriptions, and the government was to give grants equal to two-thirds of the voluntary contributions. Public works were to start, and the committees were to prepare lists of persons deserving employment. Where there were not sufficient shops for the sale of food, the committees might sell food, and they might only give free food to the infirm when the workhouses were full.

All this may seem clear and simple enough, but in practice chaos ensued. Works had to be approved and examined before they were undertaken, and the Board of Works, which had charge of them, employed hordes of new officials. Wages were to be lower than the prevailing rate of wages which, with the increase in the cost of all food, made them totally insufficient. To make it worse, the wages were on a task basis and men who at first were able to earn 10d to 1s per day, became so weak from hunger that they could not, after some weeks do more than 3d or 4d worth of work a day.

Women and girls worked with the men as long as they were able, and when wages did not buy enough food for everybody, necessity decreed that the ones not working in each family were the ones who fasted. There was a scarcity of silver and copper to pay wages, and in many places the shops were miles from the workers and their places of work.

SOME FIGURES

However, in spite of administrative shortcomings, Peel's Government did much to relieve distress, and deaths from actual hunger were few that first year. It did much, that is, by the standards of the time. Isaac Butt, the future leader of the Irish Party, went so far as to say that Peel met the situation, 'with consummate skill and complete success'. Up to August 1846, when the relief works were to end on the coming in of the new potato harvest, the Government had expended over £700,000, about half of it in loans to be paid in short term from local rates, and half in grants.

It must, however, be remembered that since the Act of Union (1801) Ireland was part of the United Kingdom. For taxation purposes the two islands were considered to be equal, yet when it came to expending money Ireland was no longer the 'sister-kingdom'. She was not even a poor relation; she was the beggar at the gates. Many years afterwards, a Royal Commission was forced to admit that through the whole century, Ireland was being over-taxed to the tune of £3million per year.

MEAL AND COERCION

Meanwhile in England, two reformers, Cobden and Bright, had assembled considerable Parliamentary support for Free Trade. Peel, who had been opposed to the principle, changed his mind for reasons that perhaps had to do with keeping his position as Prime Minister. He used the Irish Famine as an excuse for his change of policy, and in the early summer of 1846 the Corn Laws were repealed.

In the same parliamentary session he introduced a Coercion Act for Ireland. It would be a strange thing indeed if, in a starving population, there was no one human enough to break into a corn-store or to attack a bailiff serving notice of eviction on a starving family of little children. Michael Davitt, looking back in anger, said that it must be our greatest shame that our ancestors lay down and died without protest.
The British Government did not think so, and neither did the historian Justin MacCarthy, who wrote:

> While the Corn Bill was yet passing through the House of Commons the Government felt called upon, in consequence of the condition of crime and outrage in Ireland, to introduce a Coercion Bill.

O'Connell and his party were joined in their opposition to the Bill by everyone who resented the Free Trade measure – Whigs because they were the Opposition, and right-wing Conservatives who had broken with Peel.

The result was that the Government suffered defeat on the Irish Coercion Bill just as the Duke of Wellington, Peel's trusted lieutenant, was steering the Corn Laws successfully through the House of Lords. The resulting change to a Liberal government under the leadership of Lord John Russell was not, however, a change for the better.

SECOND YEAR OF THE FAMINE

In the early summer of 1846 anxious eyes watched the growth of the pota-toes in every field and garden and bog and mountain patch throughout the four provinces of Ireland. Not as much as usual had been planted, for seed had been dear and hard to obtain, and hungry people had sometimes eaten at least part of it on the principle that otherwise they would not live to garner what they had sown. If the crop turned out even fairly sound there was hope.

Early in the summer the dreaded spots appeared on the leaves. Before August the stalks were withered, and it was all too clear that this second failure was nationwide. Peel's relief works ended in August as arranged, for they were only destined as a stop-gap until the new crop came in. The new administration, under Lord John Russell, planned a new scheme, generally known as the Labour Rate Scheme, under which the expense of the works would fall on persons of property in the distressed areas.

The changeover to a new scheme resulted in a period of unemployment, new committees, and more red tape. The net result, as far as the now-hopeless people were concerned, was more hunger, more misery, and more deaths.

SILENT SUFFERERS OF MEATH

One day during the second winter of the famine, fifteen inquests were held on the same day in the town of Bantry. There were twenty-five more people dead on the same day, but time did not permit of enquiring into any death that might be, by any possibility, attributed to natural causes.

The first body was that of a man named John Sullivan and, having heard the evidence of death from starvation, the jury considered its verdict and the foreman announced it. Considering, he said, the multitude of deaths which had already taken place, and that the Government had the power to keep the people alive but refused to do so, he and his fellow jurors would bring in no other verdict but one of wilful murder against Lord John Russell.

By April 1847, the number of deaths in Bantry was 4,000. A few doctors and others in West Cork publicised the horrors of the famine as much as they could, and so English and other foreign investigators visited this dis-trict and have recorded details of their experiences.

To a lesser extent we have reports from Mayo and Donegal. But there was very little investigation into conditions in Meath. Officially, there was no famine east of the Shannon and the law for a long time did not allow any free distribution of food there. But an old gentleman, who was born in north Meath some twenty or twenty-five years after the famine, tells me that, if all the truth were known, there was as much suffering there as anywhere in Ireland.

He and others have mentioned to me with horror the name of Spandau, a mansion near Staholmog named after the famous German prison fortress, which it resembled in design. During the famine it was rented as an auxiliary workhouse when the Kells workhouse could hold no more. Holding no more does not just mean that there was one patient in every bed. Reports on workhouses all over the country describe people lying huddled together on dirty straw on stone floors, with one rug serving as a cover for six or seven, some dying of fever, others still healthy, if the word can be used of people emaciated from long undernourishment.

In the auxiliary workhouses conditions were even worse, for there were no beds or bedding to be had for them, and the clothing of the dead was passed on to the living, usually without washing. In Spandau, according to the traditions I have heard, the basements were overrun with rats and the name took on a sinister appropriateness.

CHARITY

It would be easy to go on relating stories of horror, but let us turn to attempts at relief of the horror. The pioneers among relief workers were the Society of Friends, popularly known as the Quakers. In the autumn of 1846 they began to organise for the free distribution of cooked food, with no strings attached. Soup kitchens were set up where the need was greatest, and unobtrusively and methodically they worked, collecting money at home and abroad and recording events exactly as they occurred.

In the course of something over a year, they had collected and expended £200,000. The chief source was what the society's 'transactions' calls 'the munificent bounty of the citizens of the United States'. Meetings were held in all the cities, beginning with Philadelphia. Packages marked 'Ireland' were carried by rail for free. Ships of war approached our shores, eagerly seeking not to destroy life, but to preserve it, their guns having been taken out in order to afford more room for stowage. The *Jamestown*, manned by volunteers, carried 8,000 barrels of flour supplied by the people of Massachusetts, and the captain was given a public reception in Cork at which the renowned Fr Mathew was present.

Another society, The British Association for the Relief of Extreme Distress in Ireland and Scotland, also organised free food distribution, including meals to schoolchildren, chiefly in the west. It is fair to say that the people of England, as distinct from the Government, were generous, and many noblemen came over and worked voluntarily among the starving.

Other countries subscribed too. The Sultan of Turkey sent, as Fr O'Rourke puts it, 'a thousand pounds out of his bankrupt treasury to feed the starving subjects of the richest nation in the world'. The following words occur in the Address of Thanks to him, signed by the noblemen who represented the Government:

> It has pleased Providence ... to visit the poor inhabitants (of this country) with privations such as have seldom fallen to the lot of any civilised nation to endure. In this emergency the people of Ireland had no other alternative but to appeal to the kindness and munificence of other countries ... to save them and their families from famine and death.

A comment on this blasphemous blaming of Providence was made by William Bennett of the Society of Friends:

> ... some millions of our own Christian nation living in a state and condition low and degraded to a degree unheard of before in any civilised community; driven periodically to the borders of starvation, and now reduced to an exigency ... under which thousands ... are dying like cattle off the face of the earth from want and its kindred horrors! Is this to be regarded in the light of a Divine dispensation and punishment? Before we can arrive at such a conclusion, we must be satisfied that human agency and legislation, individual oppressions and social relationships have had no hand in it.

PAYING THE 'COIR'

Just a hundred years after the famine, a free and prosperous Ireland was sending food parcels to our heavily rationed neighbours across the Irish Sea.

We were collecting food and clothing for the afflicted peoples of war-worn Europe. When later calamity struck the people of Turkey, our Government, recalling the Sultan's generous gesture in 1847, sent them, through the Red Cross, a contribution commensurate with the gratitude of our hearts. We help the afflicted everywhere in the world, for we have inherited empathy for people, wherever they are, who are suffering.

UNJUST PAY CLERKS

Then there was the unjust pay clerk in the Public Works. Sometimes the money for paying the men did not come in time, and men might have to wait for a week or a fortnight or more for the miserable sixpence or eight-pence or tenpence a day due to them. Inquests here and there showed that people had died of starvation while a fortnight's wages was owing to them.

Sometimes the clerks gave a note to a hungry man on which he could buy meal on credit from the local shop or government store, but many of them charged interest on the loan, and amassed considerable sums on these accumulated halfpennies of the poor. There were shopkeepers, too, who gave credit until the pay came and charged extra for this accommodation. From *gaimbe*, the Irish word for interest, such people came to be called in English gombeen men, and up to our own time that name has been used contemp-tuously for wealthy shopkeepers whose fortunes were built up in this way during the famine.

VERY LITTLE MONEY

County Meath was probably better supplied with shops than places more remote from Dublin. There were villages in the west of Ireland that were merely collections of cabins, and what shops there were dealt chiefly in liquor, tobacco and snuff.

Poor people in pre-famine times handled very little money. They ate the produce of their small holdings; they still did a little spinning for their own use, though Yorkshire and Lancashire were rapidly making their work unprof-itable for market purposes; they got their light from rush candles; they often paid the shoemaker and the blacksmith in kind so that there was no need for a large amount of silver and copper in the country. Answers to questions in a Poor Law Inquiry in Oldcastle in 1834 gave the following information:

> The country farmer seldom pays in money, but by conacres, grass of a cow, rent of house, etc. Labourers employed by the townspeople are paid in money. There are twenty licensed public houses and there are probably as many more unlicensed houses for the sale of poteen. There was a great deal of illicit distillation last year, and it still prevails, but not to the same extent, being checked by the Revenue Police.

MATTER OF BUSINESS

In passing, it might be well to say that while there was a great deal of drinking during the period, illicit distilling was a matter of business. It was the most profitable way of disposing of grain, and therefore a great help in meeting rent and other cash expenses. Naturally the poteen-maker was tempted to sample his own wares, and drunkenness was common, but most of the poteen was sold secretly to the upper classes, often with the connivance of the revenue officers.

During the famine, starving men were known to spend their last coppers on drink rather than food and no one with imagination enough to place himself in their position would be disposed to blame them. So a real scarcity of coin in the country added to the general chaos in administering relief.

A greater evil was the stinginess of local Poor Law Guardians who, in order to keep down the rates, applied a very severe means test to all applicants for relief, and refused, when the relief was given in meal, to allow more than one pound per adult per day and half a pound per child under twelve.

WHOLESALE EVICTIONS

The greatest of all the calamities that added to the distress was the policy of wholesale evictions. It is hard to get actual figures for each parish, but old people will tell you about twenty houses here and forty there levelled in one day. In one Poor Law district (not in Meath) we have a record of 1,000 houses levelled in six months, and 6,000 further notices to quit served.

From the landlords' point of view the cottiers were a liability. Under the Poor Law Acts, the landlord had to pay the rates on holdings of less than £4 valuation. This was very little trouble before the famine, when rates were very low, but all the relief, so wastefully given, had to be paid for out of rates, and imposed a considerable burden. To help them out, a clause was inserted in a new Bill, excluding from relief anyone who held more than a quarter-acre of land.

With the quarter-acre supporting nothing but the rotten stalks of the potatoes, many a family was forced by hunger to surrender their holding and go to the workhouse. When outdoor relief was finally permitted, some guardians of the landlord class insisted that a family must go to the work-house for a period in order to qualify for outdoor relief afterwards. But when the family came back they found their cabin levelled.

This happened to many who were above the quarter-acre class. Some refused to leave their homes, preferring to starve, but they were forcibly ejected for non-payment of rent.

PASSAGE MONEY

In some cases landlords, anxious to clear their land but shrinking from what amounted to the murder of their tenants, paid the passage to America or Australia for at least some of those clamouring to go. This was not a new idea. In the Oldcastle document already quoted, we are told that in the three years up to the end of 1834, forty-three persons from the parish had taken passage to Northern Canada, some of them being assisted privately by their landlord, I.L.W. Naper, Esq. The emigration rate of course increased enormously during the famine years, and we must admit that in the circumstances of the time men like Naper were doing what they believed to be good and generous.

AN EVICTION

Since I began writing here about the famine, I met a lady who had many traditions of the time. Some concerned the landlord I have mentioned. He was a powerful, big, redheaded man, and his tenants called him Seán Rua. (Note that in that part of Irish-speaking Meath the Irish name applied to the landlord was a term of contempt.)

He was one of the worst evictors in the country, and his last public appearance was at the clearance of a whole row of little cabins on one of his estates.

My informant could not give me the date, but it must have been long after the famine, for I have documents in his handwriting up to the year 1865.

Evictions, as I have already explained, had been going on since the small freeholders were disenfranchised in 1832; they were accelerated by the Repeal of the Corn Laws in 1846, and went on without ceasing until the Land Act of 1880 gave tenants their first security.

Whatever the date, this is the story. The whole row of little houses was being knocked down by the crowbars of the bailiff's men, while Seán Rua and his agent sat on a wall opposite and looked on without emotion. The carriage was parked down the road a bit, with the coachman ready to drive his master home. The escort would follow on a side-car.

BOY'S OUTCRY

The poor householders gathered their little belongings and put them on the roadside; some had beds and maybe old dressers; others had no more than the pot and the pan and the tongs with the few kitchen vessels. There was hurry. The crowbar brigade had a lot to do, and the gentleman wanted to be home to dinner. Fires were trampled out, and roofs were stripped. Above the weeping of the women there was a sudden, loud outcry.

It came from a boy who was perhaps the only able-bodied member of one of the families. He was making a last journey into his cabin when the roof was knocked in and the crowbars threw down the mud wall, covering up all that was left inside. The pot, the good iron pot, was buried in the debris. The boy shouted hysterically – all the bitterness of a childhood of starvation, all the want of security that he had been brought up in, was concentrated in this final blow.

His screams have come down through the memories of three generations – a kind of dramatic climax to a scene in which the horror had become dull. Fr F___ walked out from the town to give what comfort he could to his poor homeless parishioners. As he moved among them, Seán Rua turned to his companion. 'I don't feel well,' he said. 'That black devil has done for me.' He got into his carriage and was driven home. It was his last eviction. I don't know what the doctor called the malady that took him off. He was an old man in any case. But his sense of guilt gave him the superstitious fear that it was the priest's curse that had done for him.

FAMINE IN LOCAL FOLKLORE

Most of what I have written about the famine in Meath has been concerned with the Kells district. I am glad therefore, to quote now from a letter I have just received from a reader in another part of the county. My informant knew a man from Grangegeeth born in 1842. He was five years old in Black '47 and his longest memory was of his mother peeling the potatoes for the colcannon on the Hallowe'en of that or the previous year. They were all black and rotten, except for a tiny bit in the centre.

It is strange that I have heard the same story from many parts of the country. It appears to suggest that the potatoes were not fit for use at all; that the people were living on meal or whatever they could get, but that the tradition of the colcannon for Hallow Eve was so strong that it didn't seem right not to have at least a ceremonial bit, even if it meant, as another old person told me, going through a whole basket of potatoes so that everyone in the house could have a taste.

As to the alternative food available, we have to remember that very few vegetables were cultivated in Ireland at the time, and only the more progressive of the well-off farmers grew turnips for cattle feeding. One of those who did was a gentleman named Blackburne of Tankardstown, and it is remembered to his credit that he gave a half-hundredweight of Swede turnips to every poor family who came for them.

The five-year-old boy accompanied his father to bring home the precious food. But he said, 'the big hunger of the year was over when the wild vetches were ripe, as the children could eat their fill of them'. Before that his mother warned him to eat nothing but sorrel. We know that people boiled nettles with the Indian meal, which would be safe enough, but there are accounts of the use of *pressaugh* (charlock) and other weeds which caused dysentery when eaten in any quantity.

END OF THE WEAVERS

The man whose memories I am quoting bore a name long associated with the textile industry. His people came from Fennor, south of Slane, but the family fell on evil days when the Irish linen industry was wiped out with the advent of cheap English cotton cloth.

There was a village of twenty families living at Newtown Cross, near the chapel of Grangegeeth. They were all engaged in the linen industry and there was a scutching mill there. The famine wiped out most of them, and as they died, they were carried down to the old churchyard in Grangegeeth, wrapped in sheets without coffins.

An old poet in Grangegeeth made a poem about a true famine incident involving a young man who died in the workhouse and who came to Grangegeeth to be buried, 'in his match-box white charity coffin.' The first shovelful of earth that was flung in broke through the coffin and the dead man revived and sat up. He was a bellows maker, and he lived into better times to work again at his trade. How much of history is packed into that short paragraph, which I have copied almost word for word from the letter before me.

The story is not at all improbable. We have horrible stories from eyewitnesses of the callousness of the men employed at the workhouses to bear the daily burden of bodies on carts to the burial place. To save time and labour they were known to coffin the dying with the dead. The only wonder is that the man was brought a distance to his family burial ground. It is likely that some relative was left able to claim him, for the usual practice was to bury all victims in a common pit, often in the very back garden of the workhouse itself.

Older readers will recall the efforts of the late Mr Sean MacNamidhe to have the unmarked graves of famine victims at the back of Navan County Hospital enclosed and blessed and saved from desecration.

FAMINE CLEARANCES

In collecting local information about the clearances, it is difficult to get exact dates for incidents remembered in oral tradition. We hear, for example, of a hundred people leaving Kildalkey on the same day. The estate from which they had been evicted was well on the Athboy side of the village, but they all walked to Trim rather than to Athboy, as the railway fare to Dublin was sixpence cheaper from there. This detail helps us to put the incident into post-famine days, when the railways had been built.

Another story I have heard is dated and corroborated in the footnotes to Oliver MacDonagh's essay on emigration in *The Great Famine*. It is remembered that all the poor of the townland of Glack (parish of Ballivor) were cleared out and given their fare to America. Now this townland was part of the estate of the Earl of Darnley, who owned much of the land around Athboy, Ballivor and adjoining districts. It appears he also had property in Kilkenny, for in the work above-mentioned it is noted that a select committee reported that, 'several Kilkenny landlords, like Lord Darnley ... had sent tenants out from their estates' before the famine, and that Miley, a Dublin shipping agent, said in 1847 that he 'was engaged for several years' in clearing estates by emigration. Another note says that during 1847 many landlords were accused of 'brutal extermination' (by the colonial authorities in Canada) and among them were Lords de Vesci, Midleton, and Darnley.

INHUMAN CONDITIONS

On the side of the landlords it must be said that they had inherited impoverished and over-populated estates, and that no one man could have remedied in one lifetime the accumulated evils of generations of misgovernment and mismanagement. When the famine became acute, it might be argued that it was better to send the people out of the country than have them die of hunger at home. But the conditions under which they were sent cannot be defended.

The Canadian authorities, who would have welcomed able-bodied men, condemned the 'inhuman callousness' of throwing upon their shores the old and helpless, in rags and fever-stricken, with no provision whatever for their first days in the new country.

We must always remember with gratitude that, however much they protested, the people of Canada did all they could for their unwelcome charges, and many of the orphan children were adopted, particularly by the French-Canadians.

CONCERTED EFFORT

Much could have been done by concerted effort. Very early in the famine a committee called together a huge gathering of landowners to unite without 'politics, parties or prejudices' and plan to meet the emergency, praying for Divine Providence to bless their efforts. There were peers and Members of Parliament, including O'Connell and William Smith O'Brien. They made many practical suggestions for the keeping of food in the country, and for public works and other measures. All of these were rejected by the

Government. I mention the committee here again to quote one of its recommendations dealing with emigration:

> ...a scheme of systematic colonisation would, in our opinion, provide the means of subsistence to a large portion of our destitute population, would benefit the colonies by supplying them with labour, would increase the supply of food throughout the world and would largely extend the market for home manufactures.

Of course, they asked the Government to provide the 'pecuniary aid' for such a scheme, and they added that the provision for emigration should extend to those 'who cannot be supported in this country by the exercise of independent labour'. This was the whole point. Rid the country of the aged and infirm who were either encumbering the estates or living in the poor houses at the expense of the ratepayers.

FURTHER PETITION

The Government did not take up the policy of free emigration, so a further petition was launched, over the signatures of eighty important 'Irishmen', for the removal of a million and a half emigrants to Canada. They were to be settled in communities each served by a Catholic priest (to be exported with them) and have schools and a church provided, as well as roads, bridges, and mills. A copy of the document was sent to Right Revd Dr Maginn, Coadjutor Bishop of Derry, and this is an extract from his reply:

> In sober earnestness, gentlemen ... why have the barefaced impudence to ask me to consent to the expatriation of millions of my coreligionists and fellow-countrymen? You, who have made the most beautiful island under the sun a land of skulls or of ghastly spectres – you are anxious, I presume, to get a Catholic Bishop to abet your wholesale system of extermination, to head in pontificals the convoy of your exiles, and thereby give the sanction of religion to your atrocious scheme.

A Protestant gentleman, Mr Thomas Mulock, thus commented in a public letter:

And is it come to this, O ye lords and gentlemen! Representatives of the Irish party, land owners who stand in no relation of aristocracy or leadership … succour or solace to millions of the people who famish on the territorial possessions from which you derive your titles, your importance, your influence and your wealth.

The scheme never came to anything. Starvation drove the people out without state aid, and as the first emigrants got work, the passage money began arriving to bring their brothers and sisters and even parents away from their miserable and pestilential country.

MONEY SENT HOME

A Commission on Emigration in 1870 found that during the twenty-three preceding years, a total of sixteen million pounds had been sent through North American banks – that is an average of £700,000 a year.

Half of this was in the form of pre-paid passages, enough to defray the cost of about 85,000 steerage passages a year. To this amount must be added whatever was sent through private channels and an average of about £13,000 a year from emigrants in Australia.

Fr O'Rourke, writing in 1874, comments definitively on these figures:

There, then, is one more testimony that the Irish race lacks neither industry nor perseverance. For the lengthened period of three and twenty years, something like a million pounds a year have been transmitted to their relatives and friends by the Irish in America … Examine it; weigh it; study it; in whatever way we look at this astounding fact, whether we regard the magnitude of the sum, or the intense, undying, all-pervading affection which it represents, it stands alone in the history of the world.

MEDICAL HISTORY OF THE FAMINE

The decline in population in Meath during the famine years is estimated at between 10 per cent and 20 per cent. This figure is based on census returns for 1841 and 1851 and is lower than the average for the whole country. But patches of North Meath lost over 30 per cent of their people to hunger, disease, and emigration in those ten dreadful years.

Studies of the famine diseases based on the records kept by doctors at the time have been carried out. But these records are of necessity incomplete. Doctors were overworked and an appalling number fell victim to the general infections around them. Though diagnostic and postmortem facilities were scarce, it is clear that the two most common diseases were typhus and relapsing fever.

The former was almost endemic in Ireland, as in most other countries of Europe long before, and was known to spread most rapidly where standards of personal cleanliness were low. In those days even the upper classes were dirty by modern standards; in the homes of the poor, always overcrowded and lacking sufficient bedding and clothing, conditions can be imagined.

In the country, it was not so bad; fresh straw could be got easily enough and there was plenty of water and fresh air. In the towns, where one fountain in an alley supplied a whole warren of tenements, where straw had to be bought and where sanitation depended on an open sewer in the middle of the street, the dirt must have been dreadful. Nowhere in Ireland, however, was it as bad as in the growing industrial districts of England, and most of the typhus in Ireland came in through the cross-channel ports.

Even in July 1847, when one would have thought that Ireland must be the most fever-stricken territory in the world, the English privy council ordered that all steam and sailing vessels (mail-packet excepted) arriving in any port in Ireland with deck passengers from England hoist the yellow flag and proceed to the quarantine station, to be detained there until inspected and passed by a medical officer.

SOME FAMINE DISEASES

The typhus sufferer displays a state of stupor resembling drunkenness (the word *typhos* meaning mist). There is also great pain, headache, and delirium which last for about fourteen days, at the end of which, in those days, the majority of patients succumbed. The dark colour of the skin in typhus gave rise to the country name *fiabhras dubh* (black fever).

In what was known to doctors as relapsing fever, the skin turned yellow and so the common name was *fiabhras buidhe* (yellow fever). It was accompanied by violent rigor, severe sickness and vomiting, and when the attack abated after five or six days the patient was completely exhausted. After another week, a second attack came on, following the same course, and there might be several such relapses before the patient recovered – if he did recover. In some parts of the country reports indicate that relapsing fever caused more deaths than typhus; in others the contrary was the case.

Scurvy was unknown in country districts before the famine. It is a disease caused by lack of fresh fruit and vegetables, and was always rife on sailing ships on long voyages where these foods could not, in those days, be stored. When, in Ireland, the potatoes failed and were replaced by Indian meal, scurvy appeared with drastic and painful consequences.

Then there was dysentery, caused by bad food; which became epidemic and was frequently fatal. Prolonged hunger led to the terrible famine dropsy, described by Revd Dr Traill in these awful words, 'the aged, who, with the young – neglected, perhaps, amidst the widespread destitution – are almost without exception swollen and ripening for the grave'.

OFFICIAL REACTIONS

What means were there to cope with this universal complication of diseases? Almost a century earlier county infirmaries were being established. The Meath County Infirmary in Navan bears the date 1754, engraved over the door facing Academy Street, with the text, 'I was sick and you visited me.' It was later made a condition of these infirmaries that the surgeons appointed to them should have a certificate of competency from an examining board in Dublin.

In the early years of the nineteenth century, there were four bodies which could confer qualifications: Trinity College, the College of Physicians for Medicine, the College of Surgeons for Surgery, and the Apothecaries Hall for licence as an Apothecary. Co-operation between these bodies or between the doctors themselves was scant, though there were several very great men among them, including, in the famine period Graves, Stokes, and Corrigan.

The stethoscope was still a novelty, so was the microscope; germicides were unknown and bleeding was still considered the best cure for a variety of ailments.

When the workhouses were built, just before the famine, provision was made for fever hospitals where none already existed in the locality. (In Dublin, in 1801, Steevens was the only hospital with provision for fever patients.)

With the increase of typhus in the first year of the famine, a Temporary Fever Act was passed, under which a central Board of Health could order the local boards of guardians to set up temporary hospitals with attendants, medical supplies and nourishment for patients, but like the Relief Works this Act went out of force in August 1846, when it was expected that the new potato crop would remove hunger and all its attendant evils.

The doctors were all discharged, and when the 1846 blight brought the calamity to a peak, there was no special provision to meet it. Six months later the board was appointed again and did its best to catch up with the avalanche of disease by hiring buildings, borrowing army tents, recruiting doctors and obtaining medical supplies. They often had to coerce the local authorities into incurring expense and so valuable time was lost. I have already described the overcrowding in the workhouses.

It was just as bad in the fever hospitals – no time to wash bedding or clothes which were given to new admissions straight from the bodies of the dead; not enough food, and not even time to bury the dead with decency.

Of the doctors appointed, one in thirteen died of the fever; many, many more suffered severe attacks. The mortality rate among voluntary helpers and clergy of all denominations was equally high, and no praise can be great enough for these devoted people who gave their lives for the helpless poor.

THE FINAL YEARS

It would be tedious to describe the ravages of disease which persisted into 1850 in any greater detail. In the last years, cholera entered the country from Scotland by way of Belfast, and it is this disease that was most often mentioned by old people I knew who remembered the famine. As I have said, parts of Meath were among the more fortunate places, but Cavan was very badly hit, as was County Laois.

Most of Louth and Westmeath escaped the worst horrors of both famine and fever, though in all counties there were districts that suffered heavily. Naturally, the survivors blamed the government and the landlords, and they were justified in so far as the social conditions of the time predisposed the spread of contagion. But once the disease got a grip, nothing could stop it, due to the state of medical knowledge at the time. From the terrible experience here and in other countries grew the study of epidemic diseases and the enormous advance in methods for coping with them.

IRISH IN AMERICA

The vast majority of famine emigrants eventually settled in the United States. Of the thousands who landed in Canada in the early years, the majority managed, in the face of all restrictions, to cross the land frontier into the Eastern States, and reach Boston, New York, Philadelphia or some other of the great cities near the Atlantic coast.

It is difficult to explain this preference, for there was much more prejudice against them in the States than in Canada or anywhere else in the world, except Scotland. This prejudice indeed extended to all foreign immigrants; the native descendants of the Pilgrim Fathers were extremely conservative, very proud and independent, great believers in freedom for themselves, but not at all willing to admit the equality of 'lesser breeds', whether black or white.

The fact that the Irish were Catholic compounded matters, and there were many riots in which churches and convents were burned and numbers killed in street fighting. The poverty of the Irish was disgusting to the middle-class mentality of the average American of those days. They felt, too, that Britain was using their shores to dump the offal of her own misgovernment, and they were reluctant to take in hordes of paupers and potential criminals. The working man feared that such an influx would lower the rate of wages and perhaps lead to unemployment among the American workforce.

THE SHANTY TOWNS

The general feeling among the first famine emigrants was that America was 'the land of the free', and that if work was hard, wages were good. No criticism of the host country appears in the literature of the period, 'They say there's bread and work for all, And the sun shines always there.' But then the authors of such poems were not emigrants, and knew hardship only at second hand. It would be illuminating to come on a few letters home from America, dated in the eighteen-fifties.

What we do know is that the Irish kept to themselves in the new world. There were already Irish groups in most cities and towns, and new arrivals tried to get to where their neighbours were. We hear later of a Donegal colony in Kansas, a Monaghan colony in Ohio and so on. But the majority did not venture so far inland.

Hardly any sought work on the land. They lacked the capital to take up allotments of land of their own, and their experience at home made them dread the thought of working for farmers anywhere. Besides, there was a feeling of safety in numbers, and in the cities they had a priest, a church, and a school.

As a result, shanty towns grew up – the Irish slums of the growing cities – 'shanty' being a corruption of the Irish *sean-tí*, an old or poor house, a cabin. The actual levels of poverty, crime, drunkenness, and disease were exaggerated by the hostile Americans.

In self-defence the Irish united politically, and voted as a bloc, with growing influence in local and national elections. In this way they won certain rights for themselves, and incidentally for all American labourers. They were – and the Irish in America still are – supporters of the Democrats. But the more opposition forced them into such activity the more opposition to them increased: it is hard to say which was cause and which was effect.

EXILES OF THE FORTY-EIGHT

A decade later, the Civil War in America called for volunteers for the Army; the Irish were among the most loyal and distinguished of soldiers, and the wonderful exploits of the Fighting 69th did much to end prejudice against the Irish, and to help put them on an equal footing with their fellow citizens.

Everyone has heard of General Phil Sheridan who left Cavan an infant in his mother's arms, and all but made the White House. In my notes on John Boyle O'Reilly I mentioned many distinguished Meath men of a slightly later date. There is one, however, in the famine period who deserves mention, if only to show that a few others besides the distressed Catholics found a home in the Western Republic.

Charles Graham Halpine was born in Oldcastle in 1829. His father, the Protestant rector there, was an active journalist and editor of the Dublin *Evening Mail* for a time. The boy graduated at Trinity College just when the patriotic movement known as Young Ireland was inspiring the young intellectuals, Catholic and Protestant alike. It was the time of Gavan Duffy, Mitchell, Meagher and Smith-O'Brien. It was also the time of the famine.

We know how these leaders, fine though their ideals were, failed to confront the disaster, and how some, like Mitchell, were arrested and transported. Others, Halpine among them, grew disheartened and chose exile. He worked as a journalist in America until the outbreak of the Civil War, and then threw himself heart and soul behind the Northern struggle to end slavery.

He joined the Fighting 69th as a lieutenant, and rose rapidly to the rank of adjutant-general. In that capacity, he drew up an order for the enrolment of the first negro regiment, and as a consequence was outlawed by the Southerners – which meant that if captured he was to be executed without trial. He braved the storm, however, and lived to be an active leader of the Democratic Party in which he worked to stem the corruption of Tammany Hall.

He wrote many poems under the appropriate *nom de plume* of Private Miles O'Reilly, some of which are rather stage Irish by modern standards:

> O'Ryan was a man of might whin
> Ireland was a nation,
> But poaching was his heart's delight
> And constant occupation.

O'Ryan treats St Patrick to a jug of mountain dew and a 'rattlin' hare, and as a reward is transported to the haunts of the Great Bear, the Lion, and the Bull:

> So to conclude my song aright
> For fear I'd tire your patience,
> You'll see O'Ryan any night
> Amid the constellations.

One could hardly claim he had imbibed fully the poetic spirit of Davis and Mangan, but he was a brave man and worthy of remembrance.

THE PASSING OF THE GAEL

The great exodus continued from generation to generation, but let no one think that it was a love of adventure, a restless roving spirit that urged Irish boys and girls to leave home. Eithne Carbery has given the reason in burning words:

> The whip of hunger scourged them from the glens and quiet moors;
> But there's a hunger of the heart that plenty never cures;
> And they shall pine to walk again the rough road that is yours.
>
> They are going, going, going and we cannot bid them stay;
> The fields are now the strangers where the stranger's cattle stray
> Oh! Cathleen Ni Houlihan, Your way's a thorny way.

The farewell party on the eve of an emigrant's departure was called an 'American wake' because the parting was permanent. Arthur Griffith, sixty years after the famine, still had cause to write:

> There is no mother so mournful as the Irish mother. Who that has seen the German or French woman grow old with her lusty sons and daughters around her, happy in the evening of her days, and recalled the silent cottages and cabins of western and southern Ireland where the old women sit thinking of the children who have gone from them, has not cursed the Government under which his country exists.

THE FAMINE IN FOLKLORE

The last section of *The Great Famine* is devoted to accounts of the period from oral tradition. It will be remembered by many that some twenty-five years ago, the Irish Folklore Commission, in conjunction with the Department of Education, attempted to make a nationwide collection of all surviving tradition. A book of questions was prepared dealing with a wide range of subjects: ancient crafts, ghosts, games, wakes, bonfires, cures, memories of '98, the famine, the Land League, etc.

Copies of this book were sent to every national school, and the teachers, taking a section each week, got their pupils to find out as much as they could from their parents and neighbours. The children's written records in each school were copied into one big notebook which, when complete, was sent to the Folklore Commission. This collection, the largest in Europe, is still being classified by the small staff of the Commission, and is always available to students who wish to obtain information on any detail of oral tradition.

From this source chiefly comes the last section of *The Great Famine*. Each point made is annotated with the name of the county from which the story came, though as a rule the exact district is not mentioned. Here is a County Meath incident:

One time during the famine a number of carts of corn were going along the road to be shipped. They were guarded by two armed soldiers. A number of men came with scythes and pitchforks to raid the carts. The soldiers called on them to halt, but they came on. One of the soldiers fired over their heads; the other fired to kill, and one of the attackers fell seriously wounded.

Before the soldiers had time to reload, however, the men succeeded in carrying off some of the sacks, and made off, taking their wounded comrade with them. It is possible the soldiers were not too anxious for further battle, for at close range a crowd of angry men with pitchforks would be more than a match for two men with guns. So the convoy passed on to seek reinforcements at the next town. The men, to make their burden lighter, cut each wheat sack in two.

The wounded man was brought to his home, where he died very shortly afterwards. When he was being buried, a troop of police and military attended the funeral, questioned the relatives, and were about to open the coffin in order to see if the corpse was that of the wounded man, when someone in the crowd said 'Fever'. That dread word was enough to ensure that the funeral went its way unmolested, and several hungry families enjoyed their bread in peace.

OTHER LOCAL ACCOUNTS

There are several stories of sheep stealing. One from Westmeath tells of a man who used to skin the sheep on a tombstone in the local graveyard in the dead of night. Another tells of one who always went back and left the skins in the field so that the herd would not be blamed when the sheep were missing. A story from Donegal tells of skins buried in a bog and found fifty years later by turf cutters.

STEALING TURNIPS

Other memories of famine food tell of how the meal or the mill-topping was made into 'sowans' and 'flummery'. Here again I would be glad to record any local details of the making and use of these. The reader quoted above has confirmed the statement from the Folklore Commission records, that people were afraid to eat turnips except boiled with a little meal and that the Indian meal distributed was augmented in this way.

Turnips at that time were only grown by those who kept a lot of livestock, and poor people were not accustomed to them. A reader tells me how the poor people from the Mell in Drogheda went out one night to a field some distance from the town with bags and sacks which they filled with turnips. As they made their way back to the gate, they saw the former owner of the field following them, a man they knew to be long dead. His ghostly hands pulled the sacks from their backs, and they fled in terror. Almost identical stories may be heard in many places: poor starving people believing they were doing wrong in stealing; their imaginations all the stronger for the weakness of their bodies.

THE GREAT DIVIDE

Many of the old people who supplied the information to the children for the school collections dwelt on the change the famine had brought in the old customs, in neighbourliness, in amusements – patterns and céilidhs and sports – in the love of poetry and music. It would appear that pre-famine Ireland was an earthly paradise. I do not think that this is strictly true.

I have shown from written records that there was much poverty, disease, and emigration in the twenty years before the famine, and all of us know that seventy or eighty years ago there were still plenty of good old customs surviving. There was still a place in the corner for the travelling man, or the poor woman; neighbours helped one another at turf or hay or harvest; no one was without a drop of milk while his neighbour had a cow. But the fact that the famine is regarded as a watershed is a measure of the magnitude, not only of the calamity itself, but of its effect on the national psyche.

This powerful impact accounts, I believe, for the popularity of Goldsmith's

Deserted Village, which was allowed into the schoolbooks of our fathers' day. They may not have known that it was written a century earlier, so apt to them was the passage, which ends:

These, far departing, seek a kindlier shore
And rural mirth and manners are no more.

NINE

AN tATHAIR O'GROWNEY

THE LANGUAGE ALIVE IN BOHERMEEN

Before the recent unveiling of the O'Growney memorial at Athboy, I read again that wonderful book compiled by the late Agnes O'Farrelly at the time the remains of Fr O'Growney were brought home from California. I also read again the inspiring story of O'Growney and the Irish revival in the 1942 number of the *Wolfe Tone Annual*.

But after the ceremony in Athboy I met four people with additional information, never published in any book; Mr Owen Gaffney of Girley told me that his mother assured him that the young O'Growney was a constant visitor at her father's house from his childhood. (Her father was his uncle.) At that time there were Irish speakers in the district, and Mrs Gaffney remembers at least two of them quite well – Jimmy King, and Ownie Simons of Liskevin. A few days later I had a letter from Very Revd Henry Gerrard, P.P., North Preston, and a regular contributor to *Ríocht na Midhe*. With his permission I quote it in full:

> I find a note of 1878 (in a family diary): 'Captains FitzGerald and Kearney called; they had been conversing in the ancient tongue with a countryman in Bohermeen.' They were the Duke's henchmen, heirs to estates in the south and proficient in Gaelic. This same year young Eugene O'Growney, Maynooth student, heard his father's workmen converse in Gaelic and he determined to learn it. What old lore has been lost since the Bohermeen meeting of the Munster aristocrats and the Bohermeen countryman! The

living tongue must have been so different to our book Gaelic! Eugene O'Growney, some three miles away, wondering could he ever learn it. I heard it spoken myself in Bohermeen in the 'nineties'.

How true and how sad it is that such precious lore has been lost. To return to Fr O'Growney for a moment, I heard that day of many other relatives of his who are not mentioned in any book. If his biography is to be written it would be necessary to have all these little facts from which to build up his background so that we should see what a great man he was in the context of the time and place in which he grew up. There are other Meath men almost forgotten in their own parishes, like James Martin, the poet of Millbrook, who died in 1860, and his collaborator, Michael Clarke, who died in Nobber in 1847. For now I only mention a scrap of a ballad by an unknown author, commemorating John Doorley, a leader of the North Kildare insurgents in 1798. It begins:

Come all ye true-bred Irishmen, wherever you may be,
I hope you'll pay attention and listen unto me.
When I was young and innocent I lived near Tullamore
Til I became a lieutenant in the United Corps,

It then describes how at Naas he and his men captured 3,000 stands of arms and his further exploits until later when the cause was almost lost:

To Timahoe I next did go;
I had no men but nine,
When horse and foot came powdering down
John Doorley for to find.

Unfortunately, I have not the end of the ballad, but the story is still fairly well known in south Meath. Doorley slept his last night under a bush at Clongiffen (Longwood parish, near Moyvalley). It is still called Doorley's Bush. He crossed the River Blackwater to escape his captors, but the water got into his powder flask, and when he fired his pistol it missed, and he threw it into the water. He was captured and, of course, hanged. The pistol was found in 1904 at the very spot pointed out traditionally. I do not know who has it now but I hope that that story, and a hundred others like it, is being told at the firesides of Meath and being put down in writing to be read by our children and our children's children.

FR O'GROWNEY

In 1854, the townland of Ballyfallon in the parish of Athboy, containing 650 statute acres, was in the possession of a Mr William Martley. It appears to have been part of the huge estate of the Earl of Darnley, descendant of the Bligh of Cromwell's army who had served his master well during the campaign, and who was with him on the Hill of Ward at the massacre of the Plunketts, Lords of Rathmore. Tradition recounts that Cromwell granted Bligh all the land he could see looking down on, and beyond, the town of Athboy, to where the Hill of Kilmer, between Ballivor and Killyon, met the horizon to the southward.

In Griffith's Valuation of 1854, Darnley is given as the immediate lessor of most of the townlands in this great expanse of country, which means that the tenant farmers on the estate were mere tenants-at-will with neither fixity of tenure nor right of sale. In some instances, however, he seems to have leased a whole townland to a single tenant, retaining in fee only pieces of woodland noted as such in Griffith's lists.

In Ballyfallon there is an unusual case: Mr Martley had the whole townland, and Lord Darnley had taken a five-acre lot without any buildings from him. Mr Martley, whoever he was, did not live in or farm the place. It was all sublet to Abraham Colles, who occupied the big house (£40 valuation) and 631 acres of land. Colles further sublet thirteen acres with a fair-sized house (£5 10s 0d valuation) to the Revd Wm. Hutchinson, probably the local rector of the time, and he also sublet six cabins without land. Lastly, there was a house, bigger than the cabins, with two roods and twenty perches of land, occupied by a man named Owen Growney. A few years later, on 25 August 1863, in this humble dwelling, the child who was destined to be the apostle of high and holy revolution, the inspiration of a New Ireland: Fr Eoghan O'Growney was born.

THE FORGOTTEN CABINS

I have led up to O'Growney's story by quoting the record for the townland of Newtown or Ballyfallon, partly to show the complicated interests that had to be supported by the labour of the poor a century ago, but also for another reason. Twenty years ago I was a member of the committee formed to erect a monument to O'Growney for the fiftieth anniversary of his death. A middle-aged woman came to me with a subscription, large for her means, because, she said, her grandfather was a neighbour of the Growneys in Ballyfallon before they were all cleared out. If she told me the surname I do not now remember it, but in case there are any more of the families of these dispersed and afflicted people who have survived somewhere, somehow, here, in tribute to them, are the names of the six cabin tenants: Michael Welsh, Thomas Carroll, James Cunningham, Owen Stanley, Michael Leonard and James Fitzgerald.

O'Growney's biographers record that while he was still young the family moved to the neighbouring townland of Drisoge. It may be significant that Drisoge, a townland of 441 statute acres, was also part of the Darnley estate and was divided into three holdings: one, nine acres of plantation, was retained by the earl; a farm of 29 acres with a house was occupied by a Thomas Maguire, and the remainder of the townland was held by the same Abraham Colles, the sub tenant of Ballyfallon. On this there was a herd's house with farm buildings. It seems reasonable to suppose from this that the elder Growney was a herd for Colles on the Ballyfallon land, and at the time of the clearances was transferred in the same capacity to Drissoge.

In the ensuing years, by dint of hard work and saving habits, they were able to become tenants of a portion of land, and to educate one of their sons for the priesthood.

LEABHAR AN TATHAIR EOGHAN

At the time of Fr O'Growney's funeral in 1903, a commemorative book was prepared by Professor Agnes O'Farrelly, a learned pioneer of the Irish revival, and a native of Cavan. It is on this book I must chiefly rely for what I have to tell of the patriot priest. It contains a drawing of the site of the O'Growney homestead – a bare piece of roadway, a stonewall fence, and some young evergreens, and this is the description in Agnes O'Farrelly's words:

The home where O'Growney was born, and where the mother's influence was first breathed upon him, has passed away as though it had never been.

On a foggy day in late October I saw the site of the house in company with Michael MacKenna. The fence by the roadside has been made out of the walls of the house, and a fir plantation grows where the house once stood, and back into the angle of the garden. The long dank grass was drooping from the constant rain, and the moss on the stones looked black and dismal and slimy. It was all inexpressibly sad and dreary, and only by an effort could one call up the picture of the bright homestead in the long ago, the sweet mother and the thoughtful child, unnoticed in the group of children – the house that was in truth the birthplace of the revival that warms this grey old land.

When the O'Growney statue was being unveiled in Athboy some years ago, the spot described so well above was pointed out by some of the older people in Athboy, and a temporary noticeboard was erected for the day. It was proposed to have a permanent signpost or plaque put up later, and this was recommended more than once by the Monuments Committee of the County Council, and the request was passed on to Bord Fáilte Éireann.

Nothing more was heard about it since, but I have learned lately that Bord Fáilte Éireann does not erect signs on any site connected with persons or events of such recent date. The idea is that local people should be interested enough in their own recent history to do the work themselves. I imagine that, if the O'Growney Commemoration Committee had been aware of this at the time they would have managed the few necessary pounds, considering how hard they worked to collect the very sizeable sum the monument itself cost. In a very few years no one who is able to point out the spot will be left.

A CHANGING WORLD

The young O'Growney grew up in a world of clearances and consolidations, of the miseries of the displaced poor and the comparative prosperity of those who were left. The first ten years of his life saw the rise and fall of Fenianism, the period of the American Civil War, and events nearer home – the shooting of a land agent, the maiming of a grazier's cattle, the sad procession of fifty or a hundred people walking the road to Dublin to save the rail fare, the few shillings extra to help them on their way to Liverpool or America.

The poor, in their dumb resentment, had no champion but 'Captain Moonlight', the personification of all the secret societies that tyranny called into being. The rich were complacent in their condemnation of 'outrages', believing that legal redress should be sought by people with grievances, that they should play the game according to the rules laid down by gentlemen, and not resort to cowardly and murderous attacks from behind stone walls.

The common people were acutely aware of the distinction between 'law' and 'justice', and knew that in the unequal contest for the right to live they must use what weapons they had. So 'Captain Moonlight' continued his operations, and in self-defence some prospective evictors removed all their roadside walls and hedges and replaced them with sunk fences. You can see them here and there today as you drive through Meath and appreciate the fine views of the countryside which they allow. Their original purpose is perhaps best forgotten.

O'GROWNEY AS A SCHOOLBOY

Little is known of the early life of Fr O'Growney. Michael MacKenna, a neighbour, wrote in 1902:

> He attracted but little notice, at least during his schooldays, in Athboy; he was a good, steady, sensible boy, but very few thought there was anything very brilliant about him. Although very intimate with his father, I saw very little of him at this time, except to meet him and see him going to or returning from school.

He was enrolled at the old national school in Athboy at the age of five and presumably remained at school until sent to the Diocesan Seminary in Navan at the age of fifteen. These years had seen the rise and apparent fall of Fenianism, and the foundation of the Land League. In every Irish farmhouse there must have been talk of Stephens and Donovan Rossa, of the Manchester Martyrs, of the Meath Fenian convict John Boyle O'Reilly.

Later it would have been of Davitt and Captain Boycott, and of the young landlord who was taking the lead in Irish politics – Charles Stewart Parnell. What the boy thought of all these things we shall never know. It may be significant that, years later, when he got the idea of translating popular English ballads into Irish, he began with *God Save Ireland*, T.D. Sullivan's song of Allen, Larkin and O'Brien, the national anthem of struggling, distracted Ireland.

A STRANGE LANGUAGE

One incident of his boyhood years, which O'Growney himself told many times in later life, concerns the Irish language. An old man, a labourer working with the O'Growneys, addressed an Irish salutation to the boy, which he did not understand. He did not even know there was such a thing as an Irish language. He asked questions about it. Did people ever really speak any language except English? The old man laughed at him, but the boy, by dint of questioning, made the astounding discovery that there were people still alive in the parish whose first language was Irish. Later he got to know and learn from them.

This story has been questioned by some old people I have discussed it with. A near relative of the O'Growneys told me that the boy used to go almost every Sunday to Smiths of Kilskyre, the home place of Mrs O'Growney (she was Margaret Smith) and that in the neighbouring townland of Liskevin there were numbers of native Irish speakers, of not more than middle age. In fact a lady from Girley wrote to me a few weeks ago to say that she knew native Irish speakers in that district as late as 1914.

There is even evidence that O'Growney's own father could understand a little Irish. But all these facts are not as contradictory as they appear. The old people who knew Irish no longer spoke it, even among themselves; the language had long fallen into disrepute among all who had any pretensions to 'respectability'; by 1870 it was part of an almost forgotten past, remote as the mounds on the Hill-of-Ward or the cairns on Sliabh na Caillighe.

BRIAN O'HIGGINS ON THE PERIOD

Brian O'Higgins, in the course of a lecture on Fr O'Growney in 1913, provides a comprehensive background:

There were old people in Athboy and its neighbourhood who knew the language, as there were in all parts of Meath and all over the country, but it was no longer spoken, and the so-called national schools, then thirty years in existence, had done their deadly work of Anglicisation. In defiance of the terrible Penal Laws of the eighteenth century the people of Ireland had clung to their native language, and right down to the English-made Famine of 1847 it was spoken generally almost throughout the entire country.

Here in Meath, where an intensive war against the native speech had been going on unabated for seven hundred years – since the time the Normans had built their castles from the Shannon to the eastern sea – the Irish language lived longer than in many a place in which one might think it could be more successfully defended. Even after that murderous uprooting and extermination of the people in Black '47, there were Gaelic poets as well as Irish speakers in Meath, and some of them, poor and unknown, carried on their blessed work almost up to the time of O'Growney's birth. He heard no Irish spoken in his childhood, but there were scores of Gaelic words in daily use among the people, names of things mostly for which no English had been learned. The disastrous break had come generations before when Daniel O'Connell, a native speaker, frowned on the Irish language, welcomed the Anglicising schools, and declared it was better for the country and for education and culture (God bless the mark!) that everyone should give up the fight of centuries and adopt English as their everyday speech.

Young Eugene O'Growney must have heard the terms 'cannrán', 'gíostra', 'geilimín' and 'arcán' applied to children by indignant, worried mothers when reproving them for their boldness or headstrong ways. He must often have heard some man described as having a 'straos' or a 'can' on him from ear to ear. He must have heard of the 'bacán' of a gate, the 'buailtín' of a flail, the 'doirnín' of a scythe, the 'droman' of a horse's traces, the 'taoibhín' that was put on a broken boot or shoe. He must have heard someone say that he was going out to cut a 'seas' of hay from the rick, or to clear away the 'spadach' from the top of the high bank on the bog, or to shake out the 'deannach' from a meal bag.

These and scores of other Irish words were in daily use, passing as English by those who used them – sometimes indeed used fifty times a day by anti-Irish Seoinini who prided themselves on being speakers of polite English, and who looked down with ignorant contempt on anyone so low and vulgar as to make use of an Irish phrase that had survived the extermination of a treasure more priceless than gems or gold.

O'GROWNEY'S STUDENT DAYS

Eugene O'Growney entered St Finian's Seminary in Navan at the age of fifteen with the intention of studying for the priesthood. In those days few boys, apart from the sons of the very wealthy, ever went to a secondary school except at the call of a religious vocation. The O'Growneys were far from wealthy and there were other children, but they were proud to provide for the education of their gifted boy: his mild manner, dreamy-looking countenance and studious habits seemed to show that God had already marked him for His own.

At first he stayed with his cousins, the Darcys of Dunderry, and attended the seminary as a day pupil, in company with one of the boys of the house. Sometimes they walked the four-odd miles; sometimes they went on horseback, for the bicycle was as yet unknown in the country. In the class was young Denis Flynn, who was later ordained with him and became Monsignor Flynn, parish priest of Kells.

Monsignor Flynn tells us that O'Growney was much ahead of his class in Greek, Latin, and the other scholastic subjects; that he read very widely, and yet found time to continue the study of Irish. The language was not part of the course of studies, and it is likely that the professors would consider it a waste of valuable time if they'd known.

There were a few Irish speakers in Dunderry parish too, and when Eugene had his home lessons completed, he used to go to the house of a poor old woman nearby to sit on the stool in the chimney-corner and ask questions to learn new words and phrases.

'He was the mildest and humblest of boys,' wrote Monsignor O'Flynn, and:

> ... though naturally very retiring, he could amuse all of us with a fund of humour ... in giving his experiences or recounting some anecdote picked up in his reading. He was a most even-tempered boy, and I think I scarcely ever saw him perturbed except when something was said by way of joke or otherwise to disparage his leanings towards the Irish language.

It is likely that much was said to perturb him by way of joke or otherwise, and it required no little courage for the country boy to persevere.

ANOTHER SIDELIGHT

It was about this time that, according to Michael MacKenna, a horse trainer named Johnny Gantly called to O'Growney senior, and in the boy's presence, commenced a conversation in Irish. It may have been holiday time, or just before his entry into the seminary. Gantly was fluent, and on seeing the boy's interest, he went to some trouble to help him.

MacKenna says that it was on this occasion the boy became really enamoured of the language, and saw in a flash of inspiration that there could be no worthwhile national movement without the language as 'its soul and grace', that, in MacKenna's words:

> ... if the people of Ireland would not re-learn their native language, and cultivate their arts, their music and their literature, they would inevitably get further and further away from Irish thought and ways, and in the end they would not even know they had a country of their own to love, honour and defend.

We are not told where Gantly the horse trainer came from. It may be only a coincidence that a few years later it is recorded that horse dealers from the Munster estates of the Duke of Leinster came to Gibbstown House, and discussed the points of horses, in Irish, with the stable boys, all local lads from the parish of Bohermeen. This is told in a family diary now in the possession of Very Revd Henry Gerrard, P.P., Leatown, Lancashire.

After a time, O'Growney entered the seminary as a boarder. Although his health was beginning to give cause for anxiety, he continued his studies and was ready to enter Maynooth in 1882 at the age of nineteen.

The Chair of Irish in Maynooth was vacant in 1882: it had been vacant for four years and was to remain so for another nine until Fr O'Growney himself was appointed professor. The first occupant of the chair was a Meath man, the scholarly Fr Paul O'Brien, who was professor up to 1820. The last permanent occupant was a Fr Tully from the Diocese of Tuam. He held the chair from 1828 to 1876, during the years when the Irish language was falling into neglect and disrepute. He lacked the enthusiasm that might have inspired a sense of duty in a generation of young priests to their native language, but in this he was not different from his contemporaries, clerical and lay, among the learned and influential.

For a couple of years after Fr Tully's death, the young Dr Michael Logue, afterwards Cardinal Primate, was professor, but then he was given the Chair of Theology, and Irish was left to a postgraduate student who acted as lecturer during his own year of study in the Dunboyne Establishment.

This changing from year to year was naturally unsatisfactory, but, to make matters worse, students could only attend lectures during one year, and except for those from Irish-speaking dioceses the attendance, even for this one year, was voluntary. There were, in this course, lectures for beginners and lectures for more advanced students. Only the very few, who were really enthusiastic, joined the advanced class. In Fr O'Growney's year there were only three 'volunteers' – himself and two disciples, Michael Hogan and Laurence Kieran, who as priests were his lifelong friends and whose tributes will be quoted later.

From his first day in Maynooth, O'Growney found his own opportunities for study. There were students in the college from Connemara, Kerry, and Donegal, and he managed to have a couple of these as his companions in the evening walks and to draw from them the rich treasures of their native speech, while firing them with some of his own enthusiasm.

During the holidays he wrote in Irish to these friends, and one letter at least is preserved from 1883, when he was only twenty. He began spending his holidays in the Aran Islands, and during term he snatched every minute he could spare for visits to the college library where he found another rich vein of linguistic treasure in dusty old books and manuscripts.

During the holidays in 1884, the Society of Antiquarians visited the Hill of Ward. Among the speakers was Michael Cusack, who had been instrumental in founding the Gaelic Athletic Association a couple of years before. He spoke in Irish, and there in the front of the crowd was the young clerical student, notebook in hand, listening eagerly and noting down any new word or phrase.

How much Cusack said is not recorded; in fact there is no official note of the visit in the society's records at all. But Michael MacKenna afterwards published an essay (in English) which O'Growney wrote and sent to him some time previously on the history of the Hill of Ward – the ancient Tlachtgha.

It is a remarkably fine essay for a boy with little time for historical research, and gives evidence of considerable study. When, a few years ago, our own Meath Archaeological Society visited Tlachtgha, we recalled and made use of Fr O'Growney's work, and there was little need to go further.

As a senior in Maynooth, O'Growney founded a Gaelic Society among the students, and, as might be expected, his chief supporters were men from the Archdiocese of Tuam, educated under the influence of the great Dr John MacHale, then an old man.

In his last year before ordination, he was sent to the seminary in Navan as a prefect where he taught some of the junior boys, superintended studies and made himself generally useful. It was always a brilliant student who was chosen for this work, and O'Growney, though he had no ambition to shine in examinations, was recognised as brilliant.

He did his theological studies well and conscientiously, and devoted his spare time to what he already felt to be his second vocation – the revival of the Irish language and all that it stood for. 'Second vocation' is perhaps not the right term – true nationality was to him a part of the virtue of piety, part of the love of mankind, in God and for God.

Among the juniors in Navan that year was a boy named Michael Conlan. Those of us who had the privilege of knowing him as the venerable parish priest of Athboy realise how much his love of Irish language, history, and tradition was the result of Fr O'Growney's influence. On any question of Irish scholarship he would quote *An tAthair Eoin* and that finished the argument.

FR O'GROWNEY'S LIFE AND TIMES

The card commemorating Father O'Growney's ordination in Maynooth in 1889 was in Irish, a rare thing in those days. He ministered for a short time in Mullingar, and then went as curate to Ballynacargy, where he laboured for two years. He was much loved by all, especially the poor, for his gentle charity, and we have the words of a contemporary that the parish priest, Fr Peter Murtagh, 'simply worshipped him.'

We know very little about these two years, apart from his correspondence which shows that he was as preoccupied as ever with the idea of the Gaelic Revival. In a letter to Eoin MacNeill he writes, 'My time for Irish is limited to intervals snatched from a very busy life – one in which, from the very nature of things, no real method can be adopted.'

Then a whisper went round that the Chair of Irish in Maynooth was to be re-established. Fr O'Growney believed that the move was initiated by the President, Monsignor Browne, who had been very sympathetic to the little Gaelic groups among the students. Fr O'Growney was anxious to be a candidate for the sake of the good he could do, but in a private letter he admitted that he would be far happier to remain a curate.

He had been planning an article on the national language for the *Irish Ecclesiastical Record*, but changed his mind, lest anyone should think he was courting the favourable attention of the College Trustees. This was characteristic of his humility but it had no effect on the decision. Fr O'Growney was the obvious person for the post; he was elected unanimously and entered on the arduous and not very rewarding duties of Professor of Irish in 1891.

Three years later, failing health dictated a long vacation in a warmer climate. He lived and worked for five years in California, but gradually he realised that he would never again see Ireland. He died in 1899, and four years later his mortal remains were laid to rest in Maynooth College.

A LINGUIST AND MORE

In this brief survey there may seem to be nothing to distinguish Fr O'Growney from many other good and holy men. The quiet, delicate, and soft-spoken young priest can hardly have appeared to the majority of his contemporaries as the founder of a new revolutionary movement. But he himself was conscious of what he was doing. Though he was a linguist, his interest in the Irish language was more than that of a linguist. During his college days, he and a friend subscribed to a modern Greek newspaper which they understood quite well from their knowledge of classical Greek. He had a fair knowledge of German and mastered Scots Gaelic and Welsh.

He believed that the foundation of true national freedom must always be freedom of mind and spirit. However desirable political or economic freedom might be, if the way of life and thought was dictated by English ideas, and through English channels, even independence would be an empty triumph.

It was not a new doctrine. Many patriots had professed it, notably Thomas Davis, forty years before O'Growney's time. But O'Growney put the doctrine in practice. He learned the Irish language and took practical steps to encourage others to learn it and to make the learning easier for them.

One was the publication of his *Simple Lessons in Irish*, the work by which he became best known in Ireland and America during the first years of the Gaelic League.

We must therefore, return to Fr O'Growney's work in conjunction with that of other pioneers of those years.

THE NEED FOR IDEALS

No movement is the work of one man. It grows perhaps out of the need of a generation. When there is a period of materialism men's minds and souls crave something which perhaps they cannot name – something they are not even conscious of. Then, one here and there catches his dream and discovers his voice and the movement begins. Finally, the personality of a leader gives it a form and a name.

So it was with the Gaelic League, founded in 1893. In my opinion, at no time in our history were standards so low, ideals so far abandoned, public life so full of self-seeking.

The sixties had been years of heroic – almost suicidal – endeavour on the part of the Fenians to win the complete freedom of an Irish Republic. Men were transported, tortured in English prisons, condemned as anarchists. It may be that they were no more than a handful in each parish, but they had awakened a spirit in the common people, and if they had the luck of even a little success they would have every small farmer and labourer in Ireland with them.

I have already told this story in my notes on John Boyle O'Reilly. A young contemporary of O'Reilly, sentenced to seven years in an English jail, began to think over Irish affairs and ponder on the reason why Fenianism had apparently failed. He had left Ireland as a baby when his family was evicted from their small holding in Mayo. As a child labourer in an English mill he had lost an arm. As a boy he had joined the Fenians in England. Now he had time in his solitary cell to look back and to look forward.

He concluded that martyrdom would be useless in loosening England's grip on Ireland because it implied open warfare against vastly superior forces. A more effective strategy would be to reform the system of land ownership, and then, in more prosperous times, to strike again for national independence. The boy's name was Michael Davitt.

I shall not dwell on the details of the Land War at this point. Suffice it to say that by about 1880, when the young O'Growney was entering Maynooth, the grip of the landlords was being broken through the concerted efforts of Davitt and Parnell, the young leader of a regenerated Irish Parliamentary Party. Meath's part in the struggle will be worth detailing at a later stage.

ANGLICISATION

Looking back over eighty years we observe a curious result of the victory, and one which neither Davitt nor Parnell could have been expected to foresee.

Farmers, big and small, now had security of tenure and their rents could not be raised. The hard savings of the years of slavery could now be taken out of hiding. Farmers built better farmhouses, added substantial sheds, dressed and ate better.

It was only to be expected that some of the richest of them should adopt the manners and attitudes of their former masters. They asserted themselves by their contempt for the lower orders and anything that suggested poverty, and in a word, became as anglicised as possible.

There were exceptions, of course, but I think on the whole this judgement is not unfair. (I have heard that a similar phenomenon is noticeable in England where better-off workers tend to become Conservative in politics.)

At the same time the movement for Home Rule was forging ahead with apparent success. It would have meant more opportunity economically for the middle and upper classes. Then in 1890, the bombshell dropped. Parnell fell from his position of Uncrowned King of Ireland and the party was split. In the bitter struggle that followed, all sense of proportion and fair play seemed lost. The society I have tried to describe, lacking ideals, was rife with the pursuit of personal gain and petty triumph.

I have no desire to write at any length on this tragic period. At the very moment when materialism was at is height, ten young and almost unknown men held a meeting in Dublin to form a society for the revival of Irish as a spoken language. They elected Douglas Hyde, son of a Protestant minister from Roscommon, as their president, and Eoin MacNeill as their secretary.

Fr O'Growney had long been the driving force of the movement and now assented to becoming its reluctant vice-president. The frail young priest, with his little Irish book for a banner, had started on the road that was to lead to an April morning in 1916, and I believe he knew it. In the words of an earlier Irish poet:

One man with a dream at pleasure
May go forth and conquer a crown;
And three, with a new song's measure,
May trample a kingdom down.

CELTIC SCHOLARS

A few years ago we celebrated the centenary of the Catholic University founded in Dublin under the Rectorship of Dr John Henry Newman, later Cardinal Newman. He was an Englishman, a convert to the Catholic Church, and had no particular interest in Ireland or her aspirations to political freedom.

His chief concern was that Catholics should have a university of their own, and Dublin seemed the most suitable city of the then United Kingdom in which to make the foundation. We would hardly expect from him any particular interest in the revival of the Irish language.

Newman was one of the greatest scholars and philosophers of the century, and it was inconceivable to him that the national language of any country should be neglected in its chief educational institution. He insisted on the establishment of a chair of Celtic studies, and for first professor the choice was Eugene O'Curry. O'Curry had collaborated with John O'Donovan as a young man in research into Gaelic literature, place names, and related matters, and in his new position he presented the fruits of his labours in a series of special lectures on Irish literature. O'Curry as to write afterwards:

Little did I think, on the occasion of my first timid appearance in the chair that the efforts of my feeble pen would pass beyond the walls within which those lectures were delivered. There was, however, among my varying audience one constant attendant, whose presence was both embarrassing and encouraging to me. At the conclusion of the course, this great scholar and pious priest (for to whom can I allude but our late illustrious Rector, the Revd Dr Newman) astonished me by announcing to me, on the part of the University, that my poor lectures were deemed worthy to be published at its expense.

Thirty-five years later, in the *Irish Ecclesiastical Record* (1890), Fr O'Growney pointed out that one of the objects of the publication was, as clearly stated by O'Curry himself:

> ... to convince the Irish Catholic public, and more especially the educated class, that to them, first of all, belonged the duty of becoming acquainted with, and learning to appreciate at their proper value, the language and litera- ture of their ancestors. Has that end been reached?

CATHOLIC TRADITION

Fr O'Growney answers his own question with a sad negative, and thereby shows us his own high motives in the work to which he had turned his hand. The Irish language embodies, he says, the greatest Catholic literature of the world, but the study of it is 'chiefly in the hands of foreigners, and almost exclusively in the hands of non-Catholics'. He praises the great toil and labour expended on the O'Curry collection of manuscripts by Dr Atkinson of Trinity College – an Englishman and a Protestant – and goes on:

> Two centuries ago, a Tipperary priest, a fugitive in the Glen of Aherlow, with a price on his head, composed valuable and beautiful works – some asceti- cal, others historical [the priest was Keating]. After that lapse of time the most important of these have just been set forth, not by a priest, nor by an Irishman, nor by a Catholic, but by the same Dr Atkinson.

He goes on to cite the work of great continental scholars in the study and publication of Irish manuscripts: Kuno Meyer, Zimmer, de Jubainville and a host of others whose names are known to Celtic students everywhere. To these illustrious names he adds the name of Dr Whitley Stokes, one of a distinguished Anglo-Irish family; but there is hardly a dozen true natives, and none of them is a person 'of eminence'.

In looking back, O'Growney observes that the greatest men of the past valued the language and saw in its revival the work of true patriotism. Flood, Grattan's contemporary, left his large fortune for the encouragement of Irish, and:

> … witness Archbishop MacHale, a great and consistent patriot, who during his life did all he possibly could to encourage his people to use their native language, and who undertook the translation into Irish of a considerable portion of the Holy Scriptures, of Moore's Melodies, and even of half the 'Iliad'.

Fr O'Growney's language is very mild. He grants 'that the richest and sub-tlest Catholic minds are engrossed with professional studies and duties, with political questions, with great social problems'. The thrust is very delicate, and the irony rapier-sharp.

UNKNOWN PATRIOTS

There were humble people working quietly: young priests whose ambitions did not rise to great literary heights, but whose everyday speech was as beautiful as the language of Keating himself. There were the country national teachers who devoted their well-earned leisure time to writing, as well as they can teach themselves to do, some of that great body of folklore handed down orally from one generation to another, which is yet to be met with in those parts of Ireland where the vernacular is the language chiefly used. Many teachers taught Irish as an extra subject, but they were forbidden to teach it to any class lower than fifth, when youth, the proper time for learning a language, is to a great extent passed. This teaching had to be outside normal school hours. In all Ireland that year (1890) only 274 students passed in Irish in the Intermediate Examinations; of these 234 came from the Christian Brothers' schools, leaving forty to all the seminaries and colleges of the country.

It was to the unpretentious people, that Fr O'Growney turned now in his great effort. It is good to remember, however, that the inspiration of his *Simple Lessons* was His Grace, the Archbishop of Dublin, Most Revd Dr William Walsh.

SIMPLE LESSONS IN IRISH

I have before me, as I write, the five parts of the *Simple Lessons* bound lovingly together by the schoolboy who bought the first part in 1901, and followed up his studies so well that in three years he had mastered the whole series. The original publication date was 1894, and in the seven years Part I had run into the thirty-second edition, and 150,000 copies had been sold. That is a more eloquent testimony than words can provide to the immediate popular appeal of the Gaelic League, whose first publication this was.

In these days when books in Irish are so numerous and of such diverse content, it is a shock to find that O'Growney had to give a phonetic pronunciation for every word – he was writing for people without a teacher and without any previous knowledge whatsoever of even the appearance of the written characters. His scientifically sound approach produced results.

The first three parts are Fr O'Growney's unaided work – Part IV has an introduction by Eoin MacNeill, dated 1897, explaining that, 'the state of Fr O'Growney's health has prevented the completion of the series by him'. Part V (1900) is all MacNeill's, for by that time Fr O'Growney was in his grave in California.

O'GROWNEY THE WRITER

Fr O'Growney was too busy a man to devote himself to writing for writing's sake. He did not aspire to fame as an essayist, poet or novelist – indeed he did not aspire to fame at all; he saw something to be done and, quietly and humbly, set about doing it. But in the course of his short life he did write various essays and newspaper articles in connection with his work, and some of them were collected by Agnes O'Farrelly in *Leabhar an tAthair Eoghan*.

The best of them are in the Irish language: a long article on the Aran Islands, where he spent much of his spare time in his student days, an appreciation of Dr Nulty, Bishop of Meath, and, more importantly, a retelling in modern Irish of old Irish sagas. In his time no one, except a few Celtic scholars, had ever heard of the Voyage of Maelduin or the Sorrows of the Children of Uisne – hardly even of Lis or Maeve. These stories are now, of course, part of the material of literature for all Irish schoolchildren, and the inspiration of poets not only in Irish but in the general stream of European literature. It is not possible to quote here from these works, but later I may give some passages in translation.

Fr O'Growney also wrote in English when he wished to reach a wider public. Most of this work is done with the same serious purpose and does not lend itself to quotation. One should read his long paper on Irish family names in its entirety, which appeared in the *Irish Ecclesiastical Record* during the summer of 1898. I do not think that the subject has been treated as well since.

The following year he wrote an article for the Christmas number of the *Weekly Freeman*, a paper that was very helpful to the Gaelic League in those days, publishing a weekly column in the Irish language for many years. This article shows the very human sentiments of the man rather than the erudition of the scholar. The fact that the article appeared posthumously gives it a special appeal and I make no apology for reproducing part of it here:

A Sod of Turf
In San Francisco, one day not very long ago, I was in conversation with a good old Irish woman. She was telling me that all her people were either dead or settled at a great distance from her, and had neglected to write for years, as frequently and inexplicably happens.

'But wait a bit', she said in her native Gaelic, 'I have something to show you', and she left the room, returning a moment later with 'the something' carefully wrapped up in soft tissue paper, tied with a green ribbon. It was a sod of turf from Ireland: 'and I'll have it buried with me in the coffin'.

Some might find material for a coarse joke in this remark, but to a Celt there was something touching in this clinging to a sod from green Tyrone. When all near and dear on this earth had left her, at least she had this humble souvenir of the bright heath over which she had skipped some fifty years ago in her young strength and light-heartedness.

It was none of your sods of *spodda* or soft brown or yellow light porous and spongy stuff, such as wily bog men impose on unwary housekeepers; nor was it the 'mud-turf' or 'hand turf' made into artificial sods from the dregs of the bog, but a hard, brick-like, coal-black sod, cut by the sharp 'slane' from the bottom of the 'high bank' – one of those sods our mothers looked for when some deed of cookery was to be done, and when they sent one of us out to the clamp to bring in 'a lock of *keerauns*'.

Yes, this was the 'keeraun', or rather the very father of keerauns, (a word I had not thought of for years), those small black sods, or pieces of sods, which, when heated, become fiery, red *keers* on glowing coals. I remember we used to give the same Gaelic name to a berry such as the scarlet berry of the mountain ash or rowan tree. Perhaps the glowing red coal suggested the scarlet berry; but I leave that to the scholars.

Turf cutting on a bleak bog was hard work, but the recompense came with winter, around the clear turf fire in the hearth, under the great chimney. The fireside is even more of an attraction when at nightfall the floor of the kitchen is newly swept, and the stools are drawn up near the fire to await the expected neighbours who came 'a kailey'.

In olden days, the 'kailey' was the rural substitute for newspaper, club and parliament. Some of the *habitués* came every night over a mile to take their places under the wide chimney, through which those sitting nearest the hop could look up and see the stars; that is to say if they could see anything through the paraphernalia hanging in the chimney space, everything from 'flitches' of bacon hung up to dry to blackthorn sticks, which, after having been straightened, oiled, and otherwise prepared, were placed in the sooty chimney to season and take a good, black colour. Hence the phrase, 'I have a waffle in the chimney for him', a phrase ominous with meaning for 'him'.

The great landmark fireside stories were 'The Year o' the Short Oats' (1826); 'The Night o' the Big Wind' (1839); 'The Year of O'Connell's Meeting on Tara' (1843); 'The Famine' (1847), and 'The Time of the Fenians' (1867), and others dealing with great local elections, and the various phases of the Home Rule movement.

The legends of Patrick, Brigid and Columcille were handed down, and every rath and wood, every hill and glen, every ruined shrine and holy well, every castled crag and inland lake had its own legendary lore. Giants and pygmies, the gifts of the seventh son, and the fate and fortunes of the third brother, the strength and wisdom of the friendly horse, fox, eagle and salmon that the hero calls upon in his hour of need, are not surpassed or indeed equalled in the early romance of any country.

One could listen in the turf-fire light to those eerie tales of the 'borderland', in which not only the orthodox everyday, or everynight, ghost appears, but the more misty fetch or second-sight, the death watch, the pooka, or going deeper into the unsubstantial world of spirits, one could hear of the various ranks and degrees of the fairy world, from the historic *bean-sidhe* or 'woman of the mound' to the spirits of Hallow Eve or the rarer 'leprechaun' or *gankaun*.

And so the sod of turf has brought us back to a distant land, to the thatched rooftree of our old home, to the brown bog and the green pasture, just above the river where we fished for the pinkeens. If I close my eyes I can still count the stepping stones, but I open them on another land, the Tír na nÓg of many of our race, for I see before me the deep blue of the Pacific and the sunset through the Golden Gate of San Francisco.

AMERICAN REACTIONS TO O'CROWNEY'S DEATH

Soon after going to America, Fr O'Growney, in a letter to Dr Douglas Hyde, President of the Gaelic League, which they had founded together only two years before, said he hoped to be able to come home in the summer, quoting the proverb *grásta Dé agus bás in Éireann*, and adding that he would not like to die anywhere except among his own in Ireland. He often expressed similar sentiments during his illness, but when it became certain that his end was near, he no longer mentioned being buried at home. He was too humble a man to dream that he would be so honoured as to have a public funeral across thousands of miles of land and sea. He never saw himself as a great man – he was a worker in a cause that needed workers, and his only regret was that he was able to do so little. So he died with only one close friend near him – Mr Laurence Brannick, a student of his Maynooth class, now settled in Western America. Many Irish, clergy and laity, came to his funeral, and the sermon was preached by a Maynooth man, Fr Barron. But in a matter of days the Irish societies in America were discussing resolutions like this one at the Boston Philo-Celtic Society, 'Superintendent Galligan gave notice of motion to appropriate a sum from the funds of the Society to defray the expenses of sending the remains of Fr O'Growney to a final resting place in his native land.'

Boston was, it will be remembered, the city in which John Boyle O'Reilly had settled after his famous escape from the convict settlement in Australia; he had been editor of the influential *Pilot* until his death only nine years previously, and his successor (Roche) had carried on the tradition. Fr

O'Growney had contributed articles to *Pilot*, as he did to many other great American papers, during his years of exile. Ford, editor of *The Irish World*, published letters advocating:

> ... the sacred duty to bring to Holy Ireland – the land for whose honour and language he martyred his young life – the precious bones of Fr O'Growney, whose memory, as long as Gaelic lives, will never be forgotten at the Irish fireside, or at the fair or market, on mountain or moor.

Soon, a Gaelic League convention in Chicago started a fund for the purpose, and when, after certain unforeseen delays, the final arrangements were made at another Gaelic League convention in Philadelphia in 1902, the man put in charge was Revd P.C. Yorke, State President of the Gaelic League in California, and one-time class-fellow of the young O'Growney in Maynooth. They had been close friends since those early days when they had spoken Irish at recreation round the college walks, or met in the holidays at the firesides of the Aran Islands.

One could go on listing famous names in the America of the time which appear in notices of the various meetings, but one quotation speaks volumes, 'A Month's Mind Memorial Mass was celebrated at St James' Church, New York, for Rev. Father O'Growney... A eulogy was pronounced by Revd Michael P. Mahon of Cambridge (Mass.). The eulogy was given in Irish...' It was not a conventional eulogy. The speaker broke into such obviously heartfelt phrases as 'O, *a chairde, ba mhór, ba bhreágh an fear é.*'

AT HOME IN IRELAND

Ireland heard the news of Father O'Growney's death in a four-word cablegram in Irish from Laurence Brannick to the headquarters of the Gaelic League. From there telegrams went out to prominent Gaelic Leaguers all over the country. Agnes O'Farrelly recalls the telegram boy coming to her home in Cavan through the October sunshine, and her grief not only for the loss of a fellow-worker but for one beloved 'for his own earnest self'. She goes on to record the universal feeling of loss for, 'The climber dead on the hillside/ Before the work is done.'

All over Ireland special Gaelic League branch meetings were called, but nowhere perhaps was there such personal mourning as at the branch in the great Abbey of Mount Mellary:

> The Reverend Director told how close had been the friendship between himself and Father O'Growney, how frequent their exchange of letters and what interest Father O'Growney had always taken in that branch. To him, Mellary with its crowd of monks, its seven times daily chanted office, its daily Solemn mass, its noble library, its great school ... reflected the vanished glory of Clonard, or Bangor, or Lismore or Clonmacnoise. Around its walls, when he paid his first visit to the monastery he had heard with delight our native speech in ordinary daily use. In its church for the first time in the south, he had heard its moving accents delivered from the pulpit, and marked its power on the hearts of an Irish congregation. His heart dilated with joy and pride. He found that Irish was not then taught in the school, he pleaded that it should be, and his earnestness and enthusiasm were irresistible. When finally, after he had left Ireland, he learned that the classes were at work, and that a branch of the League had been regularly constituted, he lost no time in showing how much he was gratified and how highly he valued the example set to the other schools of Ireland. From that day to the day of his death, and it might be said even afterwards, for his last letter arrived when it was known he was no more on earth, he maintained the warmest interest in the work of the branch, and cherished the highest hope in its influence.

Tomás Concannon, one of the big names in the Gaelic revival, had visited O'Growney during his illness in America, and had cheered him with first-hand information about the progress of the work at home. Now, as an organiser for the Gaelic League, he is quoted in *An Claidheamh Soluis*, the Gaelic League's paper, in the course of an appreciation:

> The influence of a life like Father O'Growney's springs afresh even from the grave. Our organiser tells of a teacher in the west, who, reading of Father O'Growney's noble and self-sacrificing labours, with tears in his eyes, threw the paper on the table and vowed that he himself, henceforth, would do his part for the revival of the language.

Four years later, at the time of the funeral to Maynooth, Miss O'Farrelly writes:

Four years ago at the time of Father O'Growney's death, the language was a very faint influence in the country. From the moment he died it would seem as if he watched over the cause and made it prosper, sending back his blessing to the little office in O'Connell Street, and to the Irish men and women who worked with him.

THE O'GROWNEY FUNERAL

On the morning of Wednesday, 2 September 1903, the grave of Fr O'Growney in Los Angeles was opened in the presence of Laurence Brannick and several other friends. From that moment until the final re-interment in Maynooth at the end of the month, we have a complete account of the funeral in *Leabhar an tAthair Eoghan*, compiled at the time by Agnes O'Farrelly.

I propose to recall only the names of Meath people concerned, except in the case of nationally – and sometimes internationally – known figures. There was John Devoy, the Fenian veteran whose life is part of our history; it comes as a surprise to find on the next page the name of Fionán MacCullom whose reminiscences are still a familiar and welcome feature on Radio Éireann. And at Cobh we meet Dr Mannix, vice-president of Maynooth College, now the revered Cardinal Mannix of Melbourne.

IN CALIFORNIA

The body was placed in a casket of enamelled steel, ornamented with gold and bearing the name engraved in Irish on a gold plate. Inside were documents in Latin, Irish and English, certifying to the identity of the body. There was a lying-in-state in the Cathedral, and Solemn Requiem Mass, at which the Bishop of Los Angeles presided. Pallbearers were from the heads of various Irish organisations – the Ancient Order of Hibernians, the Knights of Robert Emmet, the Irish Volunteers, as well as the Gaelic League and the Knights of Columbus.

It was the same story in San Francisco, where the body reposed for almost a week. At Solemn Office, chanted in the evening, the church was crowded – there were the leaders of all the Irish Societies, and there were the poor, the dock workers and their wives and children, and when the Rosary was said in Irish, 'it was noticed that few in the church were unable to respond'.

The sermon at the Solemn Mass was preached by Fr Yorke, 'Thousands and tens of thousands are watching this funeral to-day with wet eyes, and are saying from sad hearts, "*Beannacht De len' anam*"... His career was short, but it was like the blast of a trumpet among the hills.'

Fr Yorke went on to speak of patriotism as a sacred virtue, and gave a brief but extraordinarily satisfying summary of the history of Ireland. In spite of conquest, nationality had survived down to almost the memory of his hearers, and nationality, he said, 'is to a country what personality is to an individual'. But since Catholic Emancipation:

> ... a certain public life grew up in the island, which had its roots not in the past of the old nation ... Catholic laymen found that careers were opened to them under the English law and they used the English speech and the English parliamentary methods. The people, seeing their leaders whom they loved using these English ways, began to imitate them, and finally to despise those who clung to the old speech and the old customs of the Irish nation. The establishment of the national schools, the great famine, the emigration to America, the improved methods of communication, all conspired to a result which you now see, the disappearance of the ancient Irish nation, with its language, literature, music and customs, and the assimilation of the people of Ireland to England and America...
>
> This is the sublime service that Eugene O'Growney rendered his people: he saw, and was able to make others see, that the whole existence of the Irish race is bound up with the Irish language. A language is the soul of a people, and when a language dies the soul of the people dies with it. There might be a free Ireland, there might be a prosperous Ireland, there might be an Ireland Catholic from sea to sea, but it would not be an Irish-Ireland whose progenitors were the missionaries of Europe, but rather an English colony come to its full estate. He did not live to realise that he had turned the tide. When he was ordained, no sane man in Ireland believed that the Irish language would survive the first half of this century. Only fifteen years have passed by, and now he goes home to be received in state by marching thousands of disciples in a land where the old tongue is heard on the lips of children in thousands of schools, from Aran of the Saints to the Gates of Dublin.

It is a wonderful oration which I wish I could give in full. But even the extract I have chosen should provide food for thought. Perhaps the personality of a Eugene O'Growney or a Peter Yorke is needed to reteach the simple lesson that men like these taught so well, not only in their words but in their noble and saintly lives.

THE O'GROWNEY FUNERAL

The year 1903 was one of great national activity. In the summer a monument was erected in Dowth cemetery to John Boyle O'Reilly. A mile-long procession marched from Drogheda to the music of bands from almost every village in east Meath and north Dublin. There were contingents from all the football and hurling clubs, including the Major MacBride Club from Dublin. Major MacBride had fought for the Boers against England only a couple of years before, and was regarded as a hero by all in whom the Fenian tradition was even vaguely alive.

Even more significant was the Emmet centenary commemoration in September. Huge crowds marched through the streets of Dublin to the site of the scaffold in Thomas Street where Emmet uttered the immortal words, 'When my country takes her place among the nations of the earth, then, and not till then, let my epitaph be written.' The marching men and women were certainly not planning an insurrection, but there was a spiritual exaltation in their hearts that made them aware of themselves as a people on the march.

The following week came the O'Growney funeral. Young Ireland, Irish-Ireland, bore the coffin of the dead Gaelic Leaguer in triumph through the streets of Dublin. His ideals gave direction to the march of the nation.

After Mass in the Pro-Cathedral the coffin was carried to the hearse by fourteen young men picked from the Athboy, Kilskyre and Dunshaughlin hurling clubs. The Lord Mayor and several members of the Corporation were present, the representatives of the Gaelic League from all over Ireland, and the clergy of Meath and Dublin.

Marching to the Broadstone Station, the Athboy Hurling Club led the way, carrying draped camáns. The Meath branches of the Gaelic League came next, Athboy and Rathmore leading. The Navan branch followed under Fr Farrell, later parish priest of Ballivor, whom the account before me describes as, 'a forceful worker, both in the language and the industrial revival'. Then Kells, Trim, Oldcastle, Dunboyne, Stackallen, Warrenstown and Dunshaughlin branches, 'the rearguard of Meath being brought up by the Mullingar men'.

The procession was four miles long, and the route was arranged by O'Connell Bridge, Dame Street and Capel Street in anticipation of the great numbers who would march. All the way along, the streets were thronged with people, watching the contingents with their banners in Irish, their hurleys, their bands: all, as the papers of the following day reported, 'impressive in orderliness as well as in dimensions'.

IN MAYNOOTH

The special train that carried the remains from the Broadstone to Maynooth had carriages for about 500 people – the relatives and those immediately connected with the ceremonies. But train after train had been coming into Maynooth all day, while the people of Meath and Kildare had been arriving on bicycles and horse cars or on foot. The college staff was on the platform to receive the remains, and the students in their white surplices were waiting in long ranks outside to join the procession.

Again the Meath men had the honour of carrying the coffin to the hearse. The unusual throng made the horses restive, but even so when out in the street they were halted again: a train was heard coming along the line, and no one was to be denied the chance of sharing in the great tribute. It was a gesture that Fr O'Growney would have understood and appreciated.

The long line of priests and acolytes followed the great cross, borne by a Meath student, Patrick Smith of Kilskyre, later parish priest of Kilcloon. His tall figure is easily recognisable in the faded photograph of the procession in my copy of the O'Growney book. After the clergy came the hurlers with lowered camáns, then the hearse drawn by black horses: by the side of the hearse were Dr Douglas Hyde and Eoin MacNeill, the relatives, Dr Heneberry and the other American delegates. Then came the Gaelic League branches, GAA and other organisations, the general public thronging the road so that it was hard to move along.

People still alive who were present have told me the crowd was such that it was hard to see anything, but all could hear the solemn *Miserere* rising and falling as the coffin was borne to a bier in the grounds of the college for the final ceremonies. A *Caoineadh* – a song of mourning – was sung in Irish, and the remains were then borne into the college chapel where the Office for the Dead was sung.

PARALLELS

On one occasion, Dr John MacHale, Archbishop of Tuam, was invited to distribute the prizes to the students in Maynooth College. It was long before O'Growney's time, in the period when the Chair of Irish was vacant, and the language was not regarded as worthy of serious study. In his address, the great prelate commented on the high standard the prize winners had reached in the study of classical languages and of modern English and French. However, he said, in their own country, and still alive among many of them, was a language as ancient as Greek and as graceful as any European tongue.

Among the students that day was a young man entered in the college register as Peter O'Leary. He was from the Irish-speaking part of West Cork, but he had never thought of the language of the poor at home in the context of scholarship or literature until MacHale's words enlightened him. Years later, when Fr O'Growney was writing his little books for beginners, there was ready to hand for the new generation, from the pen of An tAthair Peadar O'Laoghaire, a body of modern Irish literature comparable with the best of its kind in any language.

He took the living speech of the people – *caint na ndaoine* – and used it as his medium of literary expression, a method adopted by many of the greatest writers of this century, in both Irish and English. Custom may have staled the beauty of *Seadna* to those who had to do it as a school text; it should be read again in adult life, for it has that rare charm which makes a classic of one book in ten thousand.

A YOUNGER SCHOLAR

There is a strange parallel in the story of Fr O'Leary. In the year of the O'Growney funeral, Fr Peter Yorke visited Maynooth. It will be remembered that Fr Yorke had been a class-fellow of Fr O'Growney's but had gone for ordination to America, and worked there all his life. He had received Fr O'Growney on his arrival in America, had visited him as often as his duties allowed, and he had preached his funeral sermon in San Francisco.

Fr Yorke addressed the students on the urgent duty of rescuing the language and all the treasures of Christian tradition it contained. The first generation of Maynooth priests had, he said, allowed the language to decline; it behoved the generation of that day to repair the loss. Among the junior students was a boy of eighteen from Ballinea, Mullingar. His name was Paul Walsh. He had entered Maynooth the previous September and the prize lists show that he led his class in mathematics, logic, metaphysics and ethics, and won prizes in French, English and Italian. He was third in his class in Irish.

Fr Yorke's words had the same effect on him as Archbishop MacHale's had on the young O'Leary a generation previously. Like O'Leary and O'Growney, he devoted himself to Irish from that day forth, and his name ceased to appear on the prize lists. Naturally he did not neglect his theological studies, but he made no effort to gain particular distinction. Such, however, was his genius that in his final year he led his class in the degree of Bachelor of Divinity.

It should not be necessary to recall the personality of Fr Paul Walsh to readers of this paper. He is well remembered in the various parishes in which he ministered: Dunsany, Kilcloon, Stamullen, Eglish and Multyfarnham where he was parish priest from 1932 until his death eight years later, at the age of fifty-five.

What may not be known is the place he holds as a scholar. His writings are not of the kind to make a popular appeal: they are the fruits of such research as no other Irishman in this century had the genius and the will to undertake; they will continue to be sources of reference for Celtic scholars for a very long time to come. The *Place Names of Westmeath* is probably well known in his native county, but he has done much on the biographies and genealogies of the O'Neills, O'Donnells, Maelseachlainns and other Irish chiefs. His last work was a new edition of the *Annals of the Four Masters*. Colm O'Lochlainn has edited much of Fr Paul's work in recent years, and it is from *Irish Men of Learning* that I have taken the story of Fr Yorke. In this edition, Colm O'Lochlainn has very fittingly added a chapter on the author himself, to Fr Paul's study of Mac Firbhísigh, O'Cleirígh and the other scholars of a thousand years. He is at home among them.

A MAN CALLED PEARSE

One could go on and on citing the names and works of great men who were influenced by O'Growney and the movement of which he was the embodiment. But one more incident must be told. It is an incident described by Desmond Ryan which occurred when he was newly arrived in Navan in 1904.

His father had come from London to take up the editorship of *The Irish Peasant*. The boy, then entering his teens, had been in contact from infancy with every side of the Irish Revival among the Irish in London – literary, social and revolutionary. Afterwards he was a pupil of St Enda's, fought with Pearse in the GPO, and wrote the first biography of the leader, under the title *The Man Called Pearse*. In the passage I am about to quote, he tells of the first time he saw Pearse, about the year 1907:

> In County Meath, on the rain-soaked Hill of Ward, he mounts the platform in defiance of all the fierce showers which washed previous speakers to a dumb and damp retreat ... Pearse appears on the platform bareheaded. He waves an umbrella aside imperiously that some one would hold over him, and soon the rain-soaked audience are in the grip of that flaming sincerity which we know today moved even the judges at his court-martial. Pearse soars and lifts us from the sopping green and dull soil of Meath. The gathering is to commemorate the life and work of Father Eugene O'Growney, one of the most famous of the language revivalists from whose simple text-books students throughout Ireland just then first grappled with Irish, landing salmons and stools and the time of day and bread and oxen, and that very Asses' bridge of Irish: the three forms of the verb 'to be'. Father O'Growney had died in exile, alone and ailing, a burning flame quenched in the end by that Irish plague which has quenched so many bright flames: consumption. In exile he had written to his old friend, Patrick Pearse, then editor of the Gaelic League official organ, and a traveller into every Irish-speaking district in the land on foot and a wheel, a gleaner of plant-names, and bird-names and place-names, and many lists of these Father O'Growney had sent him, just before death comes ... when the exiled priest knows he will never see Ireland again, and turns to a wall in far San Francisco and weeps. Such was the tale Pearse told, on a rainy day in Meath.

I have heard that these lists of names which Fr O'Growney sent to Pearse lay around in the offices of the Gaelic League and finally got lost. We have, however, in print some lists of Meath words gathered by Fr O'Growney from Irish speakers in his native district. They are of immense interest today.

TEN

JOHN BOYLE O'REILLY

HIS EARLY YEARS IN BRITISH JOURNALISM

John Boyle O'Reilly was born at Dowth in 1844, the second of a family of
eight children. While he was still an infant the Great Famine swept the land,
but nowhere in his memoirs does he suggest that he remembers any hunger.
No doubt his father's salary as teacher in the Netterville school was enough
to keep the family from starvation. In one district for which records have been
published, teachers' salaries at the time ranged from £11 to £28 per annum, but
the endowment at Netterville may have added a bit of cash and kind, and, at a
time when a labourer's wages were 8d to 10d a day, this meant frugal comfort.

The eldest of the family, William, was articled as an apprentice to *The
Drogheda Argus* at a fee of £50. After some months he fell ill and it appeared
he would never be strong enough to go back to work. So John, at the age
of eleven, took his place and began to learn the printer's trade. At first he
was paid half-a-crown a week, but as time went on he seems to have been
so quick and so willing to take a hand at any part of the office work that he
often earned more. By the end of his fourth year the owner of the paper died,
and for some reason the successor did not keep on the young apprentice. It
may be that the young John didn't want to stay. In any event, he left and went
to live with an aunt in Preston, Lancashire, whose husband was captain of a
ship plying over and back to Drogheda in the grain trade. There was still a big
export of corn from Meath and Louth through the port of Drogheda, though
it was declining as a result of the clearances which were turning the land into
cattle ranches and driving the tillers of the soil to the emigrant ships.

The boy spent four more years in Preston, working on *The Guardian* and having the time of his life. He learned shorthand and got in on the reporting side of the business. Being a handsome, brilliant youth with pleasant manners, he was soon one of the most popular young men in the town. He was in a rowing club, in the boxing club, in amateur theatricals, in all the fun and games of a small but thriving town. He even joined the Territorials and was very much pleased with amateur soldiering.

He wrote bits of poetry in his spare time – topical verses of no great merit – and if anything deeper and more lyrical was taking shape in his inner mind, its only visible expression was in the depths of his fine dark eyes. All in all, he was a happy young man with a fine career before him in English journalism, a lucky young man to have got away from the misery and hopelessness of his native land.

That is how things looked in 1863 when he was approaching the age of nineteen. Within three years he was to be sentenced to death as a Fenian. The bare facts are these. His father asked him to come home and take a position on an Irish newspaper; he came home and did not continue as a journalist but joined the British Army; soon he was the trusted lieutenant of John Devoy, with the dangerous task of swearing British soldiers into the Fenian Brotherhood.

To understand this apparent change of heart it is necessary to recall the circumstances in which the Irish Republican Brotherhood swept the country, to the terror of the then almighty British Empire; how that movement turned plain men into men willing to sacrifice their lives. For as long as anyone alive a hundred years ago could remember, there had been poverty, oppression and injustice. Through hunger and eviction, people had been told that their part was to bear all in patience and to pray that some day the hearts of their rulers might be moved, not to justice, but to mercy and benevolence. It was not an easy doctrine; as one of the Gaelic poets said, 'Ní hé an boctanas is measa liom ach an tarcaisne a leannan é' (It's not poverty I think the worst, but the insult that follows it).

The one period when hopes began to rise was when, under pressure from Davis, Mitchell and the other Young Irelanders, the ageing O'Connell organised a mass rally for the repeal of the Union. At the monster meeting on the Hill of Tara in 1843, the multitudes who heard the voice of the great orator believed that the time was coming when they would be asked to rise.

Within three or four years they were tragically disillusioned. Famine – artificial famine – was stalking the land, and no voice was raised to tell the young men that self-preservation was the first law of nature, or that it was their duty to take the abundant harvest growing on their tyrants' fields rather than see their wives and children dying of hunger.

Michael Davitt, looking back in anger, writes:

> It is related that John O'Connell, MP, eldest son of the Liberator, read aloud in Conciliation Hall, Dublin, a letter he had received from a Bishop in West Cork in 1847, in which this sentence occurred: 'The famine is spreading with fearful rapidity, and scores of people are dying of starvation and fever, but then tenants are bravely paying their rents.'
>
> Whereupon John O'Connell exclaimed in proud tones: I thank God I live among a people who would rather die of hunger than defraud their landlords of the rent. It is not, unfortunately, on record that the author of this atrocious sentiment was forthwith kicked from the hall into the sink of the Liffey.

Davitt had reason to be bitter. Born about the same time as O'Reilly, his earliest memory was of coffinless graves by the roadside in his native Mayo. He was only five when his own family was evicted from their little cabin, and all his childhood in Lancashire he heard over and over again, from his Gaelic-speaking parents, tales of hunger and disease and eviction that had swept away almost a quarter of the population of Ireland. It appeared that the native population might be all cleared out during the coming decade, leaving the land to a class of tenants who would appreciate the blessings of British civilisation.

But things did not happen that way. The wholesale emigration produced a new race – the American-Irish – breathing the fresh air of freedom for the first time, and feeling hatred in their hearts for the tyranny that had murdered their kin and exiled themselves.

Half of the new revolutionary movement grew up among these Irish; the other half was made up of the young at home who, remembering the degradation of the famine, knew that if there was something their countrymen needed even more than bread it was freedom, the God-given right of men to be men. A generation sick of asking on bended knee for miserable concessions, and being refused and insulted, heard the new secret call as a clarion call to arm and fight for an Irish Republic.

Almost overnight there were Fenian centres in every parish in Ireland, and in every English city where Irishmen were working in factory or mine. There were sworn Fenians in the very heart of the garrison. When Stephens was arrested and lodged behind a series of double locks in Richmond Jail there were enough Fenians in the prison service to spirit him out, and all the efforts of Dublin Castle failed to get the faintest clue to the mystery.

It is said that it was in Preston that O'Reilly first heard of Fenianism, and that is very likely, for it was very much an Irish town. It may be that because of his particular talents he was chosen and sworn to undertake the dangerous task of joining a British regiment and preaching the gospel of nationalism to the Irish soldiers there. At all events, Private John O'Reilly of the Tenth Hussars chose the road that was to lead through prison cell and convict settlement to an honoured place on the roll of those who served the cause of liberty.

LIFE WITH THE TENTH HUSSARS

It is a reflection on the poverty and degradation of post-Famine Ireland that, of the rank and file British army soldiers in 1863, one third were Irishmen. Yet the private soldier was looked upon as an outcast even by the poorest people. Recruiting was done at fairs and markets and often young men in an advanced stage of intoxication 'took the shilling' from a beribboned sergeant in the public house, to find next day that there was no turning back. Army life was brutal, flogging was an accepted means of discipline, and among the officers were many who, even west of Suez, could boast of breaking 'every one of the Ten Commandments between Reveille and Lights Out'.

But the Tenth Hussars were, at least, physically a cut above the average. There were good men as well as good soldiers among John Boyle O'Reilly's comrades at Island Bridge barracks. He was a model soldier himself and a great favourite with officers and men. Though he had enlisted for the express purpose of recruiting for the Fenians, he enjoyed being a soldier, and tells how, riding through Dublin in the gay trappings of a cavalryman, he used to admire himself and his steed in the plate-glass windows of the shops. He tells us, too, how with boyish recklessness he stitched national emblems to the underside of his saddlecloth, and on the lining of his military cloak. In barracks he was the principal organiser of concerts, often singing treasonable songs, and so winning men gradually to the cause of Irish freedom.

For two years O'Reilly went no further than this. Then in September 1865, he happened to be one of the party detailed for guard in the courtroom where the trial of O'Donovan Rossa, who had been arrested with Luby and O'Leary in the offices of their newspaper *The Irish People*, was taking place. Years afterwards, when they met in America, the fact that Rossa recognised his former guard testifies to the fact that O'Reilly was already known to him as a Fenian.

But I like to think that the young man's faith was strengthened and purified by seeing and hearing the man at whose grave Pearse was to pay tribute on the eve of the 1916 Rising:

> He was splendid in the Gaelic strength and clarity and truth. He, almost alone in his day, visioned Ireland as we of today would surely have her – not free merely but Gaelic as well; not Gaelic merely, but free as well.

The following month, when Rossa was incarcerated in an English prison, John Devoy, on whose shoulders fell much of the organising work, made contact with O'Reilly through one Harry Byrne, a veterinary surgeon from Drogheda.

Within three months, O'Reilly had sworn eighty of the hundred Irishmen at Island Bridge into the Fenians. The inevitable happened. His activities were discovered by a spy, and he was arrested and tried for treason. He was sentenced to death but the sentence was commuted to twenty years' penal servitude. I shall have to tell about the life of the prisons and the convict settlements, but first there is a small incident worth mentioning – it is the story of *The Old School Clock*.

Awaiting trial, the young prisoner amused himself composing verses, and when he knew he was to be removed from Arbour Hill prison he managed to conceal the scraps of paper on which they were written in one of the ventilators. Then he managed somehow to convey a message to a fellow-prisoner whom he knew to have been arrested in error and to be certain of release. He asked this man to take the poems with him and have them sent to his father, but the prisoner apparently could not find O'Reilly senior, and instead, gave the pages to Sir Vere Foster, with whom he may have been acquainted. This Sir Vere was a philanthropist and had travelled to America in a coffin ship as an emigrant in order to get first-hand information on the infamous exploitation of the Irish poor after the famine.

Sir Vere was also interested in education and was then planning a series of headline copybooks which older readers will remember from their school-days. When he read O'Reilly's poem on *The Old School Clock* he thought it so suitable for children's reading he had it printed on the back of the copybooks with a picture of the two clocks described. One was a wag-o'-the-wall which was hung in the school room at Netterville in the poet's childhood:

'Twas a quaint old clock with a quaint old face,
And great iron weights and chain;
And it stopped when it liked, and before it struck
It creaked as if 'twere in pain.

But the children, who most likely had no clocks at home, gazed at it with admiring eyes, and pondered and guessed at the wonderful things that were inside the old school clock. It frowned at the truant who came late and smiled again when it was time to go home, 'that genial good humoured old clock'. But then:

Well, years have passed and my mind was filled,
With the world, its cares and ways,
When again I stood in that little school
Where I passed my boyhood days.

My old friend was gone! And there hung a thing
That my sorrow seemed to mock,
As I gazed with a tear and a softened heart
At a new-fashioned Yankee clock.

And the poet goes on to reflect on, 'the way of the world, old friends pass away, and fresh faces arise in their stead'. Not great poetry, perhaps, but just the simple, pleasant, touching words and thoughts to appeal to schoolboys and remain with them through life as a nostalgic echo of their youth. That was what Vere Foster thought. But the Board of National Education refused to sanction the work of a Fenian, and the copybooks had to have a new cover design.

A few years after, when O'Reilly's spectacular prison escape had made his name famous in three continents, Sir Vere Foster met him in Boston, and recorded their meeting thus:

On my arrival I called on the proprietor of 'The Pilot'. He said: 'Tomorrow I shall send a young man from this office to call on you and I will print a paragraph which may be the means of bringing your old friends about you.' Next morning a handsome young man of good address called on me at my hotel, and after some conversation I asked him his name. 'John Boyle O'Reilly', said he. 'Are you the author of a little poem called The Old School Clock?' 'I am', he replied. He didn't know that the poem had been found, and a copy of it given, as he had desired, to his parents, whom I had hunted up in Dublin, and at length found lodging in the same street as myself, or that the poem had been published. I had but one copy with me, which he was delighted to possess. He entertained me at dinner, and showed me all over the city.

It is not clear whether the poet's parents were living permanently in Dublin when Sir Vere Foster discovered them, or were only staying there to be near their son during his trial. Both were dead within five years, and are buried in Glasnevin cemetery. Their eldest son was a Fenian prisoner for a time and died shortly afterwards. About the younger members of the family I have no information. I have not seen the O'Reilly's grave in Glasnevin, but Roche (the patriot's biographer) says that these words were part of the inscription on the father's coffin-plate:

Deceased was father of John Boyle O'Reilly, a good Irish soldier. Convicted by English court-martial, and self-amnestied by escaping from Western Australia to America. May the brave son live long, and may the noble father rest in peace. 1871.

BARBAROUS TREATMENT IN PRISON

I have not described the trial of John Boyle O'Reilly, which took place in the Royal Barracks on the eve of his twenty-second birthday in 1866. As he was a soldier he was tried by military court, but where Fenians were concerned the type of court mattered little. Even where actual evidence was wanting, the verdict was certain. In O'Reilly's case it was death, but commuted to life imprisonment. Sharing in the crime, and in the punishment, were some half-dozen other soldiers. Two of them, McCarthy and Chambers, were his friends, and together they were marched in chains through the streets of Dublin *en route* for Pentonville, the first of the English prisons O'Reilly was to know during the next year.

We are familiar today with terrible descriptions of prison tortures in faraway places, and young readers may imagine that such things could not happen in a Christian country. John Mitchell in his *Jail Journal* has described the horrors of Millbank. He confesses that while he could and did endure physical torture, the solitary confinement at Millbank almost broke his spirit. O'Reilly had eight months of it. The cell was just big enough to take three paces in one direction, turn, and take three back. But the rules prohibited walking in the cells. One hour a day walking alone in the yard and the scrubbing of the cell at dawn was the only exercise allowed. For the rest, sitting or standing was allowed but movement was forbidden.

Dartmoor was even worse; the iron cells were seven feet by four and a little over seven feet high. Ventilation was from a corridor by a space at the bottom of the door. During the summer, prisoners worked under an open shed on the brink of the prison cess-pool, pounding up rotting bones, the refuse of the prison. In winter they dug drains through the moor, standing in more than a foot of water, in trenches two feet wide and ten feet deep, heaving the wet peat to the top, to be carried in armfuls and spread out for drying.

Some years later, when letters from O'Donovan Rossa got into the newspapers of many countries, William Gladstone was forced to appoint a Commission of Inquiry. It was revealed that the Fenian prisoners were singled out for special treatment, under which some went mad, some died in prison, and some were released broken in mind and body. In three years Rossa was 123 days on bread-and-water punishment, 231 days on penal diet in a darkened cell, 28 days in the absolutely dark cell, and, in all, 39 days in handcuffs. These facts are from the verbatim report of the Commission, and those who wish to read more about the subject should get the *Wolfe Tone Annual* 1954, in which Brian O'Higgins tells the story of Rossa and the Fenian movement.

But O'Reilly's fine physical condition and deep religious convictions got him through, and the experience only increased his love and sympathy for all mankind. Criminals, he found, were human, too.

Luckily for him, after a year he was sent with more than sixty other Irish political prisoners to the penal settlement at Fremantle in Australia. There was another barbarous journey in chains to the port of embarkation, but on board the prisoners met with quite unexpected kindness from the ship's crew and were not forced to live with the 300 ordinary criminal convicts on board.

There was a chaplain on the vessel, Fr Delaney, and he obtained for them paper and pens which they used to produce a weekly manuscript magazine entitled *The Wild Goose*, of which O'Reilly was editor. Seven weekly numbers had appeared before the long voyage round the Cape was completed, and the prisoners had their first sight of their new home.

The summer landscape of Western Australia was overshadowed by the penal prison on the hill. But at least there was fresh air and fewer locks and fetters. The prison chaplain, Fr Lynch, was the first free man to speak to O'Reilly as a fellow human being. The prisoners were chiefly engaged in the making of roads through bush still occupied by natives. Years later, O'Reilly was to write, 'I found that these creatures were men and women like the rest of us, the difference between those poor black boys and the men of the Somerset Club was only external.'

But the bush meant starvation to a convict without tools or weapons, or knowledge of bush craft. There were native trackers in the pay of the prison authorities. No one could escape. Those who had attempted it had, sooner or later, come back in chains to suffer added years of punishment in the hardest grade of servitude. It could even mean the death penalty, though that might be easier than what O'Reilly describes:

> The toil accurst;
> The scorching days and the nights in tears,
> The riveted rings for years and years.

But the young Irishman was determined to attempt the impossible. He had made two attempts to escape from English prisons, but the memory of these failures and the resulting punishments did not deter him now. He was twenty-three and life was sweet. Long afterwards he wrote, in a wonderful and very terrible poem called *The Mutiny of the Chains*, of men who attempted escape and failed:

> They saw what the heart of man must see,
> That the uttermost blessing is liberty.

This was his own feeling, and he discussed it with the only person he could trust, Fr McCabe, parish priest of the vast region round Bunbury where the prisoners worked. This priest, it is hardly necessary to say, was an Irishman, but I do not know what part of the country he came from. He had already given fifteen years of his life in the service of these miserable thousands of outcasts, the dregs of human society, and O'Reilly tells us that he was, in the lives of all of them, whatever their religion, the only reminder that God was love and not tyranny.

Fr McCabe told him plainly that, if he wanted to die, suicide would be easier than the thousands of miles of bush and desert. But like almost everyone else who encountered him, the good priest saw that this boy was different from the other convicts, and finally agreed to help him on the condition that O'Reilly would wait and make no move until he heard from Fr McCabe again.

Months passed before the daring escape was planned and successfully accomplished. Before telling the story I give one incident that occurred during the period of waiting. O'Reilly, on account of his education and good conduct, was chosen as a helper to the wardens; he kept accounts, looked after stores and was sent at intervals on messages to section headquarters. On his first visit there the officer in charge warned him that this did not mean any special privileges, on the contrary, any breach of regulations on his part would be all the more severely dealt with.

One day on his journey he delayed a couple of minutes to help an old prisoner of the tree-felling party whose strength was not equal to his task. As a result, though he hurried, he found the overseer waiting, watch in hand and was told he was on the penalty list for six months. A few days later, when he came back on another message, the overseer had in his hand a black-edged letter, addressed in the handwriting of O'Reilly senior. The boy, fearing bad news, stretched out a hand to take it, but the overseer, who, of course, had read it, tossed it back in the box, saying that he would get it in six months. It was the news of his mother's death.

Years afterwards, when he told the story, he refused to mention the official's name, saying one should rather pity than blame a man capable of such a deed.

ESCAPE FROM AUSTRALIAN PRISON

On a night in February 1869, a notice was posted up in all public places in Western Australia, and copies were sent to all British colonies and ports of call:

1868
44   *24*

Absconder

John Boyle O'Reilly, registered no. 9843, Imperial convict; arrived in the
convict ship, 'Hougoumont' in 1868, sentenced to 20 years, July 1866. Healthy
appearance; present age, 25 years; 5ft 7½ins. High; black hair, brown eyes, oval
visage, dark complexion; an Irishman. Absconded from Convict Road Party,
Bunbury, on 18th February, 1869.

It was not until nine months later that the escaped convict set foot on
American soil, but long before that a letter he had managed to send to his
father on the night of his great venture found its way into the Dublin newspapers. The full story was not told for many years – not until those who had
assisted in Australia were beyond the reach of legal vengeance. But the very
absence of detail made the story all the more mysterious – it was the sensation of a lifetime and the world press made the most of it.

O'Reilly had waited as patiently as he could for word from his friend Fr
McCabe. Then one day, as he was making his usual journey up the convict
road, he heard someone calling him from a strip of land that was being
cleared on contract by non-convict labour. A man approached him, the
only living person within sight, and introduced himself as Maguire, a friend
of Fr McCabe. O'Reilly was wary and feared a trap but a note in the priest's
handwriting convinced him. Maguire told him that some whalers were due
to call at Bunbury some two months later and that a passage would be
arranged for him on one of them.

The two months passed slowly, and again Maguire hailed the convict.
This time he had every detail of the plan of escape worked out and com-
municated it clearly in the very few minutes there was for talk.

That night, when the other convicts had retired, O'Reilly changed into
a pair of civilian, or non-stamped, boots which he had procured, and stole
through the bush by the exact route agreed upon. Hardly had he gone a
hundred yards when he heard a step behind him. It was a convict named
Kelly, an ordinary criminal, serving a life sentence. O'Reilly's feeling, after
all the planning and waiting, was that he was in this man's power. But the
convict held out his hand, 'I saw you talking to Maguire and I knew you
meant it … God speed you! I'll put them on the wrong scent tomorrow.'

It was hardly dark that southern summer night as the fugitive made his
way for miles through the woods, but by good luck he was unobserved and
found Maguire with a friend as arranged. They were mounted and had a

spare horse for O'Reilly. They rode for hours through byways to a place where other friends were waiting to take the horses, while they continued on foot to a spot near the sea. There a row-boat was ready and by sunrise they were out of sight of land, and pulling the forty miles across Geographe Bay to the place where the whaler *Vigilant* was to keep a look-out for them the following day. This plan was necessary lest tracker dogs should pursue them overland to the near shore of the bay.

By some oversight they had no food, and by the time they arrived at the further shore O'Reilly was almost in a state of collapse from hunger, and still more, from thirst, for the heat of the day was intense. The others went to the house of an old English settler named Johnson and, without revealing their secret, managed to bring back some food and a bottle of water. O'Reilly, however, had already solved the problem for himself. He had noticed that the natives found the freshly killed meat of the possum was drink as well as food, and, weak as he was, he tracked a possum to its hole in a tree, climbed up, pulled it out by the tail and cracked its head against the tree.

Next morning the *Vigilant* was in sight and the party rowed out in high spirits. But though the ship seemed very close, and though they waved and shouted, she coasted around for a while and then sailed off. This was a bitter blow to all of them. What was to be done now to keep the fugitive alive and safe until other arrangements could be made? There was nothing for it but to tell the whole story to Johnson, and this they did. The decent old Englishman agreed to send down a supply of food to O'Reilly's hiding place every day until the others should return or communicate with him. And so he did, his young son being the messenger.

Waiting was hard, and O'Reilly could not believe that the *Vigilant* would sail without him. So, on learning from young Johnson that his father kept a little old boat some miles along the coast, he walked along until he found it. Having stuffed the cracks with bark, he ventured out on the open sea, and pulled all night and until almost noon the next day. Then he sighted the ship again. So near did it come that he could see the men on deck and hear their voices, but, as he afterwards learned, they failed to see him in his little boat, and finally turned away, while in despair he watched their sails disappear over the far horizon.

A week later, Maguire and his friend M_____ came back, with the good news that Fr McCabe had arranged another whaler, the *Gazelle,* to pick him up next day. To make sure, the priest had given £10 to the master Captain

Gifford, though it was quite unnecessary, and later, at parting, Gifford insisted on O'Reilly taking it and more to help him on his way. There was one snag, however. Another convict had found out the secret, and threatened to inform if he was not taken along too. This would have ruined all who were helping in the escape, including Captain Gifford, so there was Bowman with Maguire and M_____, and he, too, was in the boat that pushed off from the shore of Australia next morning, with a parting blessing from old Johnson and his son.

Soon, from the deck of the *Gazelle*, the friendly hand of Henry Hathaway, the mate, was reaching down to welcome O'Reilly, a free man, into the company of cheering shipmates. 'God Bless you', said Maguire, 'and don't mention our names till all is over.' And when the account was published in America years afterwards the good Maguire was dead, but M_____ was still in Australia and so his identity was not revealed.

Hathaway and O'Reilly became fast friends, and as we shall tell later they both figured in an even more sensational rescue operation years afterwards. But during these first weeks, O'Reilly, with the intoxication of new-found freedom, insisted on working at the whaling with the others and had at least one narrow escape from a killer whale. His experience provided material for a fine, long poem, *The Amber Whale*. In an atmosphere reminiscent of *The Ancient Mariner*:

With his head right dead to windward then as straight and as swift he sped
As a hungry shark for a swimming prey; and bending over his head.
Like a mighty plume, went his bloody spout, Ah shipmates, that was a sight
Worth a life at sea to witness! In his wake the sea was white
As you've seen it after a steamer's screw, churning up like foaming yeast;
And the boats went hissing along at the rate of twenty knots at least.

But more terrible than the killer whale was the police boat that came alongside when the *Gazelle* pulled into the British island of Roderique for water. The story of the narrow escape is too good not to tell.

HAIR-BREADTH ESCAPE FROM CAPTURE

The *Gazelle* spent two months whaling in the southern seas. One member of the crew was known officially as Brown, though every man on board knew he was John Boyle O'Reilly, Irish Fenian, escaped from the penal settlement at Bunbury, Western Australia. The real Brown had died some months before on the outward voyage. There was another stranger on board too, the convict Bowman, who had discovered O'Reilly's secret plans and demanded to be taken also. This man was as unpopular on board as O'Reilly was popular. It may be that the sailors were prejudiced against him from the outset, but even the tolerant O'Reilly has no word of excuse to offer for him.

At the end of two months the *Gazelle* called for a supply of fresh water to the little British island of Roderique in the Indian Ocean. News of O'Reilly's escape had already reached the British authorities on the island, though it is not likely that the name of the ship was known. A boat bearing the governor himself and a police escort came alongside the *Gazelle* to carry out a routine search. 'Have you a man on board named John Boyle O'Reilly?' the search party demanded.

As Captain Gifford had gone ashore, it was Hathaway the first mate, who answered that he knew no one of that name. The Governor gave the official description of convict number 9843, and Hathaway replied that it did seem to fit a man named Brown who had died on board in the straits of Sundra two months previously. The description must not have been a very good one, for while this conversation was going on the object of it was standing not two yards away, showing just the amount of curiosity that might be expected of a sailor in the circumstances.

The Governor was not so easily satisfied and ordered Hathaway to have the whole crew lined up for inspection, but failed to recognise anyone answering to the description. A young sailor who had suffered much bullying from Bowman indicated him by a slight jerk of his thumb and the police took Bowman away for examination. As he went down the gangway Bowman looked straight at O'Reilly and said, 'Goodbye, shipmate', but for the moment no one pretended to notice and the boat headed for harbour.

It was obvious to O'Reilly what Bowman meant to do. He would try to bargain to have his own punishment commuted in return for information leading to the arrest of the more important fugitive. For O'Reilly it would be the chain gang, and rather than face that he told Hathaway he would borrow a revolver from the cabin and sell his life dearly. But Hathaway had a plan.

An hour later, as it was growing dark, O'Reilly was wandering about the almost deserted deck. Hathaway was talking to the man on watch and naturally they discussed the events of the evening. 'We must keep an eye on him,' said Hathaway. 'He is desperate and may try to do away with himself.'

The words were scarcely out of his mouth when there was a loud splash. Men rushed to the spot and shouts of 'Man Overboard!' were raised. Four lifeboats were launched and for an hour they searched. One man said he saw the white face of a man under the water and was sure that it was O'Reilly, but they failed to catch any further glimpse of the body. Hathaway was in the last of the boats to return. He found the second mate sobbing aloud, 'The poor fellow is gone!' The men in the other boat found his hat floating.

It was a night of mourning on board. In the morning Captain Gifford saw from the shore that the flag of the *Gazelle* was at half-mast, and he hurried out to learn the sad news. Immediately following was the police boat, with the Governor and convict Bowman. But there could be no doubt that the grief of the whole crew was genuine. The man whom Bowman had come to identify was no longer there. His sodden hat lay on the hatchway.

By evening the ship was outside the territorial waters of Roderique. Hathaway left the captain on deck to go below for a cigar and when he returned a few minutes later he was not alone. The second man strolled up to the captain, who was absently looking out to sea, and, as Hathaway tells the story:

> I went to the side of the ship, and stood there, smoking and pretending to be scanning the horizon. I saw the Captain give one look at him – a kind of scared look. He thought it was his ghost. Then he rung O'Reilly's hand and burst out crying like a baby. Pretty soon he looked at me. I never said a word. 'Did that fellow have anything to do with it?', says he.

Explanations followed, as the whole crew gathered around, hysterical with joy. They were shown a small cupboard under the steps of the companion-way, where a man could just squeeze in with difficulty. It would not attract anyone's attention as a possible hiding place, so small did the visible side of it appear. As for the splash, that was the ship's grindstone. O'Reilly had thrown it overboard with his hat and had just time to disappear before the splash brought the first of the crew to the spot. Only O'Reilly himself and Hathaway were in on the secret to prevent anyone inadvertently betraying their comrade.

It was thought wise for O'Reilly to leave the ship before the next port of call. A Boston ship was hailed, and the captain, who alone was told the whole story, willingly gave 'John Soule' a passage to Liverpool. At Liverpool the captain and an English gentleman passenger named Bailey, found a safe retreat for O'Reilly until they booked passage for him on another ship bound for Philadelphia.

At sunset on the second day out, the coast of Ireland was just visible on the horizon. O'Reilly described that moment in a lecture in Boston some months later, 'Home, friends, all that I loved in the world was there, almost beside me – there under the sun, and I, for loving them, a hunted, outlawed fugitive, an escaped convict, was sailing away from all I treasured, perhaps forever.'

And forever it was to be. Though other Fenians were amnestied, the escaped convict was never permitted to enter the Queen's dominions. Not for him the consolation he described in a poem about a friend:

> He returned and died in the place he loved,
> Where a child he played
> With those who have knelt by his grave and prayed.

TRIUMPHAL WELCOME IN UNITED STATES

25 years / Ala

John Boyle O'Reilly landed in America in November 1869; two years from the day he left England in the convict ship bound for Australia. He was now in a free country where, as far as he was aware, no one knew him or had any interest in him. Imagine his surprise to find that news of his escape had reached Ireland by means of the letter he had written to his father on his last night in the penal colony, and that the Fenians in America were waiting to give him a triumphal welcome.

He was invited to lecture in various places, and, had he been a different man, could have lived on his reputation. But he preferred to work for his bread and serve his country and mankind with the talents he had and at the trade he knew best. Soon he got work on *The Boston Pilot*, a paper founded some years before by a Cavan man named Donahoe.

One of his first assignments was to accompany the Fenian force on their attempted invasion of Canada. The affair was a fiasco. The young reporter was shrewd enough to see that the time for physical force was past. He had the courage to speak his mind and criticise the many dissentions he had observed among the American-Irish.

Later the same year, he lashed out at the Orange versus Catholic scenes that occurred in America every St Patrick's Day and every 12 July. An Orange parade marching through the Catholic part of the city to the music of 'The Boyne Water' and with cries of 'Croppies lie down' was attacked with sticks and stones. The Orangemen responded, and in the melee that followed four people were killed and several wounded.

The following week in *The Pilot* O'Reilly wrote:

> We talk of patriotism and independence! What evidence is this? What are we today in the eyes of Americans? Aliens from a petty island in the Atlantic, boasting of our patriotism and fraternity, and showing at the same moment the deadly hatred that rankles against our brethren and fellow-countrymen.

This early leading article struck the keynote of O'Reilly's journalism. Later, as editor of the paper, he was to employ his influential pen repeatedly in the cause of tolerance. He preached to his fellow Irish-Americans the doctrine of self-respect, the need to avoid the 'poor Irish' mentality and falling prey to every demagogue who proclaimed himself a friend of the Irish:

> Are we debarred from equality? Have we not got the ballot? Have we not got reason enough to judge as American citizens what American citizen we should vote for? The idea of allowing every new candidate for office, every raw youth from the country, every cunning fellow who aspires to anything, between the offices of President of the United States and that of policeman, to bid for the Irish vote by setting it out in large letters, 'He's a friend to an Irishman', is simply an insult, and it should be resented accordingly.

Similarly he attacked those Irish who sponsored and performed in stage-Irish shows. The fact that he had a record of personal courage and sacrifice left him above reproach when he took an unpopular side in any controversy. For instance, he did not agree with the more extreme Fenians in their opposition to parliamentary efforts for Home Rule.

The people at home, he said, know best what kind of movement suits the circumstances. He took a similar attitude towards the Land League, though

247

it appears that his personal view was that political freedom should be the first aim and that economic reform would follow. This is the kind of question to which it is hardly possible to give a definite answer, and O'Reilly was not the man to claim that all the right was on one side.

The question of the Land League, of course, did not arise during these first years. O'Reilly was a free man in America before the young Davitt was sentenced to his seven years of penal servitude. While in prison he thought out the whole question for himself. When, on his release, he secured the co-operation of Parnell for the New Departure, it was difficult to induce American Fenians to give up their opposition to moral-force politics.

Devoy, O'Reilly, and Patrick Ford of *The Irish World* employed their efforts to rescue the revolutionary body in America from what Davitt dubbed, 'the grotesque harlequinade of saloon conspiracy which was rapidly killing, with the deadly weapon of public ridicule, what was left of the force and hope which had once centred in the name of Fenianism'.

A meeting was arranged in Boston as part of a campaign in the United States, and here are Davitt's own words, written long afterwards:

> The late Mr John Boyle O'Reilly was the chief inspiration of the meeting. Like Devoy and myself he had been in penal servitude for Fenianism, and had experienced the feeling common to all thinking men who find themselves thus contemptuously disposed of by the enemy – the feeling of bitter chagrin that you are suffering more for an intention than for an action. There was no satisfaction to be found in a consoling thought or knowledge that we had displaced a solitary brick in the edifice of English rule in Ireland. A new movement was essential if Irish revolutionists were ever to accomplish anything beyond wasting themselves in barren conspiracy and in English convict cells ... no man entered more heartily into the idea of the new policy than O'Reilly, who was then on the threshold of his literary fame in the United States. He was probably as loveable a character as nature in her happiest moods ever moulded out of Celtic materials; handsome and brave, gifted in rarest qualities of mind and heart, broad-minded and intensely sympathetic, progressive and independent in thought, with an enlightened and tolerant disposition in religion and politics more in keeping with a poetic soul than with an ordinary human temperament. He was a personification of all the manly virtues. No one could know him without becoming his friend, and it was impossible to be his enemy once you experienced the spell of his affectionate personality.

Davitt's words show the impression O'Reilly made on a man who was anything but impressionable, and whose judgements of his friends and enemies was always shrewd, fair and well balanced. We can thus understand how O'Reilly became the most popular man in literary circles in Boston. He was a founder member of the Papyrus Club, whose members were all persons interested in literature, and one of the first celebrities to be entertained by them was Henry Morton Stanley, the famous African explorer and a fellow journalist. The genial company of this gay young Papyrus man was in strange contrast to the solitary confinement and the chain-gang society O'Reilly had known. There he passed the happiest hours of his life, relaxed from politics, world catastrophes and the rush to press that is the day-to-day lot of an editor.

EDITOR AND PART-OWNER OF THE BOSTON PILOT

The Boston Pilot was the most influential Catholic paper in America. Like most middle-class newspapers, it had a magazine section and did book reviewing and comment on current literary affairs. In the course of his work for this section of the paper, John Boyle O'Reilly came across a little story in a juvenile magazine, which appealed to him as having an unusual quality for such a publication.

Enquiries about the author led him to one 'Agnes Smiley', the pen-name of an American born to Irish parents. Her father was Murphy from Fermanagh and her Donegal mother's surname was Smiley. Within a short time they were engaged, and as soon as O'Reilly had repaid his debts to the good seamen and saved a little money, they were married.

That was in 1872, three years after his arrival in America. There were four children of this marriage, all girls, and though Mrs O'Reilly later became a semi-invalid, their home life was exceedingly happy. Of financial worries there were none. As early as 1874 he wrote to his aunt in Preston that his salary was $3,000 a year – £2 per day – besides what he made from contributions to the leading literary magazines in the country. They could afford long vacation trips and later bought a place on Boston harbour, where they built a beautiful house and designed a charming landscape garden.

In 1872, *The Pilot* offices were burned in the disastrous fire which swept the city of Boston. The owner lost everything, and owing to the immensity of the losses all over the city the insurance companies failed to pay compensation. With the general depression it became obvious that the paper would have to close down. The owner, Mr Patrick Donohoe, was getting old. He had founded the paper more than thirty years previously, and had brought it to a position of eminence, but now the load of debt was more than he could carry.

So in 1876, *The Pilot* was sold to Most Revd Dr Williams, Archbishop of Boston, and John Boyle O'Reilly. The new purchasers promised to pay £15,000 due to poor creditors, and within ten years they had carried out this voluntary obligation. With O'Reilly as editor and part-owner, the paper went from strength to strength. Dr Dwyer Joyce was already a contributor, and many young poets who afterwards achieved fame had their first acceptance from the Irish editor, accompanied by words of encouragement.

The earliest works of Katherine Tynan, T.W. Rolleston, W.B. Yeats and Lady Gregory appeared in *The Pilot*. Lady Wilde, already famous as Speranza of the *The Nation*, contributed poems. Her more famous son, Oscar Wilde, at the height of his brilliant career, wrote to O'Reilly, 'I esteem it a great honour that the first American paper I appeared in should be your admirable *Pilot*.'

Many American poets, too, paid tribute to his aid and encouragement of their first efforts. But to all of them, he himself was the greatest poet of all. He continued to write poetry through all the years of his heavy editorial duties, and maturity of expression did not dull the lyrical quality of his early work. It is a pity his collected poems are not readily available to Irish readers, for the few short quotations I give here convey no idea of their wide range. There are love poems and humorous poems, long narrative poems, elegies and commemoration odes, but I think O'Reilly is at his best when he strikes out in indignation at tyranny and injustice:

Emperors, stand to the bar! Chancellors halt at the barracks!
Landlords, and Lawlords and Tradelords,
the spectres you conjured have risen,
Communists, Socialists, Nihilists, Rent-rebels, Strikers – behold!
They are fruit of the seed you have sown – God has prospered your planting.
They come
From the earth, like the army of death.
You have sowed the teeth of the dragon!

Hark to the bay of the leader!
You shall hear the roar of the pack
As sure as the stream goes seaward.
The crust of the orator beneath you
Shall crack and crumble and sink, with your laws and rules
That grind the rent from the tiller's blood for drones to spend
That hold the teeming planet as a garden plot for a thousand.

We can see in these lines, part of a poem entitled 'Reaping the Whirlwind' an echo of Davitt's burning indictments of Irish landlordism. But with tyranny in Ireland he couples tyranny everywhere, the horrors of industrial America with millions of workers living and dying in slavery that the owners might accumulate fabulous fortunes. He foresaw what has happened in our own time, the organisation of the working classes and the fight of subject peoples for the right to live. He had faith in the future of the North-American negroes and felt that the discrimination against them was the greatest blot on a country that called itself the 'Land of the Free'. In a speech to the assembly of the coloured men of Massachusetts he describes a 'coloured people's waiting room' at a railway station, wretched and overcrowded in which mothers with little children sat on the dirty floor, while next door the white people had cheerful rooms, carefully attended and comfortable. He goes on:

Every hour I saw things that made me feel that something was the matter either with God or humanity in the South; and I said going away, 'If ever the coloured question comes up again as long as I live, I shall be counted with the black men.' The American Negro is like new metal dug out of the mine. He stands at this late day on the threshold of history, with everything to learn, and less to unlearn than any civilised man in the world. In his heart he carries the traditions of Africa … At worst, he has only a century or so of degrading civilised tradition and habit to forget and unlearn … He is the only graceful, musical, colour-loving American. He is the most spiritual of Americans; for him religion is to be believed, accepted as the very voice of God, and not invented, contrived, reasoned about, shaded, and made fashionably lucrative and marketable as it is made by too many white Americans. The Negro can be a great man if he will avoid modelling himself on the whites. No race ever became illustrious on borrowed ideas, or the imitated qualities of another race. This is the meaning of race distinction, that it should help us to see God's beauty in the world in various ways.

These were brave words in an age when black men had few champions, and when racial prejudice was unbelievably bitter. What we see of this evil in the world today, revolting as it is, is but a shadow of what it was a century ago; and then, as now, Irishmen, perhaps by reason of their own long experience of injustice, were strong on the side of the under-privileged. O'Reilly was but an eloquent spokesman for the best of his race at home and abroad.

But there was only one prejudice above which O'Reilly did not rise; he was totally opposed to votes for women. His arguments are interesting, now that we have experience of the nominal equality of the sexes:

> Women might change the world on paper; but the men would run it just the same. Women are at once the guardians and the well-springs of the world's faith, morality, and tenderness; and if ever they are degraded to a common-place level with men, this fine essential quality will be impaired, and their weakness will have to beg and follow, where now it guides and controls.

DREAMER AND MAN OF ACTION

Revd J.A. Anderson, an Augustinian priest from Drogheda, once visited John Boyle O'Reilly in Boston. They became fast friends, and after Fr Anderson returned home they corresponded. In one letter O'Reilly referred to all the places around Drogheda they had talked about during the visit:

> I may never go to Drogheda, but I send my love to the fields and trees along the Boyne, from Drogheda to Slane. Sometime, for my sake, go out to Dowth, alone, and go up on the moat, and look across the Boyne, over to Rosnaree, to the Hill of Tara; and turn eyes all around from Tara to Newgrange, and Knowth and Slane and Mellifont and Oldbridge, and you will see there the pictures that I carry forever in my brain and heart, vivid as the last day I looked on them. If you go into the old graveyard at Dowth you may find my initials on the wall of the old church. I remember cutting J.B. O'R. on a stone, with a nail thirty years ago. I should like to be buried just under that spot, and please God, perhaps I may be … God bless you. Fidelity to the old cause has its pains, but it has its rewards too, the love and trust of Irishmen everywhere. You have learned this and you have got it.

252

O'Reilly never got his wish. In life and death he was an exile. Once, when he was invited to deliver an oration in Ottawa, the Canadian authorities unofficially assured him as an American citizen of protection from arrest. O'Reilly asked officially through the American Minister what the attitude of the British Home Secretary was. The reply was that O'Reilly would be treated as any other convict guilty of 'prison breach'. Some of the Irish members in the House of Commons – T.P. O'Connor, Tom Sexton and Tim Harrington were the chief speakers – brought the matter up, and in the course of a long and lively debate, the Home Secretary said he had never heard of O'Reilly before. T.P. O'Connor said he must be the only educated gentleman in the world who did not know Mr O'Reilly, 'one of the best known, most respected and most eminent citizens of the United States'.

Mr Harrington had intended including O'Reilly's name with that of Stephens in a petition for amnesty, but he telegraphed asking to have his name withdrawn. He wanted no favours from the British Government.

Yet he was haunted by dreams of his youth on the banks of the Boyne, and his letter to Fr Anderson embodies the same thoughts as his poem, 'The Cry of the Dreamer'. There is also perhaps in the poem an echo of his affection for another dreamer, John O'Mahoney, head of the Fenians in America, who died in poverty in New York about this time. Of him O'Reilly wrote, 'The life of a good and pure man – a life held in his hand and daily offered up with pagan simplicity for one unselfish object – for his country – can never do that country aught but good.'

In case there are any readers who do not know the lovely nostalgic poem, I venture to give it in full:

THE CRY OF THE DREAMER

I am tired of planning and toiling
In the crowded hives of men;
Heart-weary of building and spoiling,

And spoiling and building again.
And I long for the dear old river,
Where I dreamed my youth away;
For a dreamer lives forever,
And a toiler dies in a day.

I am sick of the showy seeming
Of a life that is half a lie;
Of the faces lined with scheming
In the throng that hurries by.
From the sleepless thoughts' endeavour,
I would go where the children play;
For the dreamer lives forever,
And thinker dies in a day.

I can feel no pride, but pity
For the burdens the rich endure;
There is nothing sweet in the city
But the patient lives of the poor.
Oh, the little hands too skilful,
And the child-mind choked with weeds!
The daughter's heart grown wilful,
And the father's heart that bleeds!

No, no! from the street's rude bustle,
From trophies of mart and stage,
I would fly to the woods' low rustle
And the meadows' kindly page.
Let me dream as of old by the river,
And be loved for the dream away;
For a dreamer lives forever,
And a toiler dies in a day.

But dreamer though he might be, O'Reilly crowded more action into his short life than most people. Space only permits me to tell of the daring rescue of six prisoners from Australia, planned by O'Reilly and an equally devoted group of Fenians. Devoy proposed buying and fitting up a ship for the rescue, and slowly and secretly the necessary $20,000 was collected among the not very wealthy thousands of Clan na Gael in America. On the suggestion of O'Reilly, the ship was a whaling vessel, and made a genuine whaling cruise in the Southern Seas before landing at Fremantle.

Chief advisor in the fitting out of the ship and engaging a crew was Hathaway, O'Reilly's rescuer of the *Gazelle*, now chief of police in New

Bedford, Massachusetts. There was only one Irishman among the crew, and only the captain knew the true purpose of the cruise. The brave John Breslin, who had years earlier carried out the rescue of James Stephens from Richmond Jail, undertook the trickiest part of the whole project. He went to Australia and posed as a wealthy 'Mr Collins', studying the markets with a view to investment. He got to know the Governor and had ample opportunity, as an interested American, to see the prisoners. Opportunity was found to communicate details of the plan to one of the prisoners, and every move was timed to the second.

When Captain Anthony of the whaler *Catalpa* landed, a coded telegram set the wheels in motion. The prisoners slipped from the working parties as they were leaving the prison at 7.30a.m. Horse-drawn cars, waiting in seclusion nearby, were driven away at breakneck speed by 'Mr Collins' and his friend (Desmond by name) to the jetty where a rowboat from the whaler was tied up, ostensibly to be fitted with a new anchor. It was a two and a half hour drive, but the mounted police who set out in pursuit within minutes of the escape arrived to find the boat almost two miles out, making for the *Catalpa,* invisible below the horizon.

The danger was not yet passed. All day and all night, in the teeth of a gale, oarsmen put their backs into the oars. Breslin, Desmond and the six prisoners took turns to relieve them. In the morning they sighted the ship, which bore down to meet them. But another craft, the coastguard boat, was making sail to intercept them. The *Catalpa*, reaching the row boat first, saved valuable seconds by lowering grappling hooks to hoist the men aboard.

The officer in command of the coastguard boat called on the captain to heave-to and deliver up the prisoners whom he could see on board. But on the order of 'Mr Collins' the captain refused, arms were distributed, and the mate, pointing to the American flag, determined to sink rather than surrender.

The coastguard's threat to fire proved empty. The *Catalpa's* sails filled and the police launch, in danger of being rammed, steered hastily back and returned to land. Some time later, when the prisoners had arrived safely in America, and the world was laughing at the discomfiture of the British, a confidential letter, requesting help in recapturing the prisoners, was delivered to The Officer in Charge, Police Department, New Bedford, where it provoked a chuckle from Henry C. Hathaway.

TRAGIC END TO A BRILLIANT CAREER

The expression 'he touched nothing he did not adorn' has often been used with kindly exaggeration in biographical sketches of famous men. It might be applied with literal truth in reference to John Boyle O'Reilly. A few examples will suffice to outline his many activities in the public life of his day.

A national monument was erected to the Pilgrim Fathers at Plymouth, Massachusetts. The descendants of the Pilgrims, the Puritan New Englanders, dominated American thought. They were noted for their intolerance and narrow exclusiveness, but it was their boast that they 'broke no contract' and 'owned no slave'. It says much for them and for O'Reilly that he was invited to write the Dedication Ode for the unveiling of the monument. In the poem he described how they had left home and come to a new land so that they might be free; how their splendid example was America's guiding light and should lead the country towards still truer use of freedom:

Oh, may our records be
Like theirs, a glory symboled in a stone,
To speak as this speaks, of our labours done;
They had no model, but they left us one.

On the day after the ceremony, O'Reilly boarded the harbour steamer as usual to come to his office. The crowd of passengers was reading the morning papers, with the account of the proceedings, when he appeared. With one accord they stood up and cheered. America had crowned the Irish felon as her Poet Laureate.

In 1880, Parnell visited America to make an appeal for the starving people of Ireland, following a bad potato harvest. Delegates from all over the United States met the leader in New York, and next day, the Meath men were to present him with a special address of welcome, as the representative of their own county in Parliament. In preparation for this, a committee of Meath men met, under the chairmanship of John D. Nolan.

After some time the chairman called for silence, took the floor and declared:

Fellow Meath men, I notice that Mr John Boyle O'Reilly has entered the room. He is a native of county Meath, a fervent Irishman, an author of recognised ability, who has passed not only into the literature of America but of the world. He is a representative Irishman in every sense of the word and I move that he be selected to deliver this address to Mr Parnell.

The motion was carried with applause, a fine tribute to a man of only thirty-five years of age. I have tried to find out more about John D. Nolan, who must have been a Meath man of standing, and a friend has suggested he was a relative of Dr Nolan of Athboy.

Now we come to O'Reilly's sudden and tragic end. It was August 1890, when the political scene in Ireland was darkened by the beginning of the Parnell split, which saddened patriotic Irishmen at home and abroad. O'Reilly felt it very keenly, though, as we shall tell, he was not to see the death of the Chief or the most sordid part of that wretched conflict.

He had acted as judge at the games of the National Irish Athletic Association, being an athlete himself and an able amateur boxer. He was preparing the following week a special number of the *Pilot* devoted to the veterans of the Grand Army of the American war, for whom special celebrations were in progress in Boston. Preoccupied and exhausted, he went home one night to find his wife ill and depressed. She had long been a semi-invalid and he had always been kind and devoted to her. He went for her doctor and asked him to give her some more of her sleeping draught.

Later that night when she still could not sleep he went for the doctor again. Then he went to his study adjoining the bedroom to work.

Some time later Mrs O'Reilly woke and, wondering why he was working so late, went to the study where she found her husband dozing on the couch. 'Yes, my dear,' he said, 'I did not feel sleepy so I have taken some of your medicine, and I feel so tired now that I think I'll sleep here.' These were the last words he spoke.

That morning, failing to rouse him, his wife called one of their daughters and sent her for the doctor. But all efforts were in vain. Within an hour O'Reilly was dead. He had not known that the new medicine the doctor had given his wife that night was stronger than what she had been using formerly.

Rarely has the death of a private citizen caused such widespread and genuine grief. It was not confined to the Irish or the Americans, but to lovers of truth and justice regardless of creed or colour. Cardinal Gibbons, the head of the Catholic Church in America, expressed the feelings of many, 'His death is a public calamity, not only a loss to the country but a loss to the Church and to humanity in general.'

More than thirty pages in Roche's biography are devoted to the description of the funeral ceremonies, the panegyrics, and the appreciations from all over the world. At a public meeting of the citizens of Boston, Edwin G. Walker, the coloured lawyer and orator, spoke in the name of his race:

> John Boyle O'Reilly sent, through the columns of a newspaper that he edited in this city, words in our behalf that were Christian and anathemas that were just. Not only that, but he went on to the platform and in bold and defiant language he denounced the murderers of our people and advised us to strike the tyrants back.

The Irish members of parliament convened a special meeting to pay tribute to him, but at his funeral the pallbearers were Fenians, Diarmuid O'Donovan Rossa among them. And there was his old friend and rescuer, Henry Hathaway, by the graveside, best loved perhaps among the hosts of friends he had made in the New World.

He is buried in Holyhood Cemetery, under a giant weathered boulder, a majestic memorial worthy of the man. Within a year his friend and successor James Jeffrey Roche had written his biography. With it is printed his complete poems and speeches, edited by Mrs O'Reilly, with an introduction by Cardinal Gibbons. It is to this fine book that I owe most of the information given here.

MONUMENT IN DOWTH CEMETERY

O'Reilly was succeeded as editor of the *Pilot* by his friend James J. Roche, who at once set about the biography from which I take most of the facts given here. It speaks volumes for Roche's energy and ability that the biography, with a foreword by Cardinal Gibbons, was published within a matter of months.

The beloved Boston patriot was not forgotten in death. The Meath men got together some years later and subscribed for a monument to his memory. I am indebted to Dr Philip O'Connell for a description of it. Dr O'Connell will, I am sure, be known to most of my readers as the historian of the diocese of Kilmore and a brilliant research worker in the field of medieval history. He comes from Virginia, near enough to Meath to give

him a special interest in all our doings, and has accompanied our archaeological society on many outings, and has written much for our journal on
the history of Kells and district. Dr O'Connell wrote to me to say how glad
he was that the story of John B. O'Reilly was being retold and he described
to me a visit he made to Boston. I quote:

> In the aristocratic Back Bay section of Boston, and beside the entrance to
> Fenway Park, rises the splendid monument to O'Reilly by David Chester
> French. It consists of a great granite block with delicate Celtic bordering. The
> background has the bust of the poet, showing determination and courage.
> On one side is depicted Patriotism and on the other Courage, while above is
> Erin twining a wreath of laurel. There is a warrior in ancient Irish dress and
> a winged figure holding a lyre. It is a triumph of the sculptor's art. Passing
> into the Park to see a baseball match, I halted my party and gave a cheer for
> Dowth.

With money left over from the subscription to the Boston monument, the
Meath men decided to erect another monument in Dowth cemetery. I do
not know if it is a replica on a smaller scale of the Boston one, but at least it
is not unlike what Dr O'Connell describes. I was kindly permitted to turn
up the files of the *Drogheda Independent* for an account of the unveiling in
their issue of 18 July 1903.

A mile-long procession walked out from the Mall in Drogheda, headed
by the Mayor, Mr John McGuinness, and the Corporation in their robes of
office. There were fife and drum bands and brass and reed bands from the
whole district between Drogheda and Dublin – Rush, Malahide, Skerries,
St Patrick's, Drumcondra. Trades and societies marched under their respec-
tive banners, the Labourers' Society of Drogheda, the Bakers, the Brick
and Stonemasons and many more. And, the report says, there were several
branches of the Gaelic League. The newly resurgent movement had not yet
been founded when O'Reilly died, but in his own way he was one of its
precursors. More significant still was the Major MacBride Club with their
hurleys, the new physical force men following in the footsteps of the old
Fenians.

The unveiling was performed by the aged Fr Anderson who had visited
O'Reilly in Boston many years before, and to whom, in a letter, O'Reilly
had described the spot in the old churchyard of Dowth where he would

like to be buried. Now at least his memory was to be enshrined in that very spot. Fr Anderson had been the friend of the Fenians, the defender of Land Leaguers, and now his heart was in the language movement. He taught Irish classes for the Gaelic League in Dublin, where for some years he was attached to the John Street house of the Augustinian Fathers. Old and ill as he was, he travelled on that day to his native Drogheda to pay his last tribute to his friend. It was to be his last public speech. The very next number of the *Drogheda Independent* announced his death.

Roche's successor as editor of the *Pilot* was a Miss Kathleen Conway. Dr O'Connell tells me she was born in America of Irish parents, and had been trained by O'Reilly himself. She must have been a great admirer of his, for she produced a book in his honour, a copy of which Mrs M.K. McGurl (Meath County Librarian) has kindly lent me. Entitled *Watchwords from John Boyle O'Reilly*, it is a beautifully produced volume containing short extracts from his prose and poetry with charming illustrations. The dedication reads, 'To all to whom the words and deeds of John Boyle O'Reilly have been help and example and inspiration, the message of this book.'

A Cavan man wrote to me that he had recently met a priest home from Western Australia and heard from him that the Boyle O'Reilly tree is still known and pointed out to visitors. While O'Reilly was working in the tree-felling gang preparing the way for a new road through the forest, he was struck by the beauty of one particularly beautiful mahogany tree and pleaded with the overseer to save it. The overseer thought it funny and told his wife the story that evening. She was curious enough to come and see the tree, and the result was that the road was diverted and the tree is still there by the great highway.

ELEVEN

LAND AND BISHOP NULTY

THE LATE BISHOP NULTY

Dr Nulty was not only a great Churchman but an active worker for the redress of the social evils of his time; he was the hope and encouragement of the oppressed tenants in their struggle for the right to live on the land, free from fear of the battering ram and the emigrant ship.

His life, spanning the years 1816 to 1898, reflects the history of Meath in the nineteenth century. For the account I give here, I rely chiefly on a broadcast from Radio Éireann given many years ago, and published later in *The Meath Chronicle*. The speaker was the late Fr Gibbons, brother of the late revered Mother Columba of St Anne's Loreto Convent, Navan. Fr Gibbons had the details of the Bishop's early life from a letter written by an old parish priest, and quoted by courtesy of Revd John Brady, Diocesan Historian.

EARLY DAYS

Thomas Nulty was born at Fennor, Oldcastle, the son of native Irish-speaking parents. He went to a hedge-schoolmaster named Caffrey, who taught in Terry Brady's cow house at Newcastle. As a small boy he was often late for school, and the master, as a punishment, made him write on his slate, 'Tommy is a lazy boy', but when the elder boys laughed at Tommy the old master told them that there was something great in store for the late-comer, such was his talent and capacity for hard work.

I have no further information of this school or its teacher, though it is possible that such is to be found in the report of the Royal Commission on Education published in 1826. Dr Philip O'Connell in his *Schools and Scholars of Breffni* has lists of Cavan schools from this source, and it is not likely there was much difference between Caffrey's school at Newcastle and the one kept by 'lame Jack' in Mountnugent:

> Where 'midst the simple neighbours, who but he
> Could sound the depths of Voster's Rule of Three,
> Engrave a sundial, make a Patrick's Cross,
> And catechise the children after Mass.
> Find the moon's age correct by Doogan's Rule,
> and prove each neighbouring pedagogue a fool.

Mathematics was a much esteemed subject in the hedge-schools of Meath. The teachers, too, prided themselves on their knowledge of the English language, and many of them translated Irish poems and stories, using most extraordinarily long words and involved and pedantic sentences. Fr Gibbons, in his broadcast, quoted an old master as asking the fiddler at the crossroads dance to play 'The Zephyr That Makes The Cereals Tremble' when he meant 'The Wind That Shakes The Barley'. He goes on:

> We could laugh and weep with those old days of the Hidden Ireland. No doubt
> the old heroic tales and most of the conversations were in Irish. For we learn
> that even after he became Bishop and while his mother lived (his father had
> died many years before) whenever he visited his home he would spend hours
> of the night pleasantly conversing with her in Irish, delighted with her stories.

THE POOR SCHOLAR

At the age of eleven, the future Bishop, with his satchel of books on his back, some spare clothes and a little money in case of emergency, left home and journeyed southwards in search of higher learning. At that time the schools of Munster were famous all over Ireland for their teaching of Greek and Latin. These were higher schools than the ordinary parochial ones attended by young children, and though there were some such academies in the northern half of Ireland, it was usual for boys, particularly aspirants to the priesthood, to go to Limerick or Kerry for what we would nowadays call secondary education.

Dr Joyce, who received his own education in a higher class hedge-school, says that many of the students had professions in view, some intended for the priesthood, others seeking to become medical doctors, teachers, surveyors and the like. Among the students, he says, were always half a dozen or more poor scholars from distant parts of Ireland who lived free in the hospitable farmers' houses all round. Such was Tommy Nulty.

As a rule, the people along every road in Ireland gave food and shelter to the poor scholars: it was an honour to do so, for learning was still held in reverence with what Joyce calls 'the instincts of the days of old'. Carlton has described his own experiences on the road, the jaunts he got in empty post-chaises, the meals at roadside inns where he was not allowed to pay a single farthing, the friendly company of fellow travellers. Dr Nulty may well have described his experiences, too, but the only detail quoted by Fr Gibbons is that kind people along the road used to fill his pockets with roasted potatoes.

On the homeward journey, four years later, he used to tell that on his way through Mullingar, tired and thirsty, he saw a girl making butter outside a door and longed for a drink but was too shy to ask for it. The kindly girl, however, noticed the student with his satchel and offered him a noggin of the fresh buttermilk.

It is a pity we know so little of the years 1827 to 1831, the exciting years of Emancipation, but we can guess that by the firesides of Munster the talk varied from the events of the day to the poetry and literature and legend of that still Gaelic province.

PRIEST, PROFESSOR, BISHOP

On his return from Munster, the young Nulty carried out some further study of Classics with a Mr McMahon of Oldcastle, before entering St Finian's, the Diocesan Seminary in Navan. It will be remembered that St Finian's was founded by Dr Plunkett in 1802 and was for many years the only institution of its kind in the northern part of the country. (Carlow was earlier but the Dublin Diocesan Seminary at Clonliffe was half a century later.)

From Navan he progressed to Maynooth and was ordained there in 1846, at the age of thirty. According to Dean Cogan, he had a distinguished academic career, and was appointed for a time to the staff of St Finian's, later serving in Athboy, Trim and Mullingar, and then as president of St Mary's College in Mullingar for seven years.

He appears to have been a scientist ahead of his time, and not only taught physics but applied his knowledge to putting running water into the convent in Navan, and attempting to light the Industrial School in Mullingar by electricity. During his student days he had probably witnessed the experiments of Dr Callan of Maynooth, the inventor of the electric battery, and as Fr Gibbons says, the former hedge-school pupil must have wanted the children of the poor to have every comfort and happiness he could give them.

After a period as parish priest of Trim, Fr Nulty was appointed co-adjutor to Dr Cantwell and, on the death of the latter two years later, he became Bishop of Meath. The year was 1866 and Dr Nulty was just fifty.

So remote from our experience are the days of the Penal Laws and the hedge-schools that it is hard to believe there are many still alive who were confirmed by Dr Nulty. Here is Fr Gibbons:

> It was to the old St Finian's I myself went, and many times I saw the venerable Bishop the guest of honour at our concerts or amateur theatricals, where he always praised our youthful efforts and complimented us on our academic successes. I still remember what mingled feelings of awe and affection were mine, when I had the honour of reading an address from the seminary on the occasion of his golden jubilee in 1896. It was composed by the president, Dr Dooley himself a brilliant product of St. Finian's and Maynooth. I am sure it sounded like wisdom coming out of the mouth of babes, for all I remember of my borrowed eloquence on the occasion is one line: '1846! 1896! What a length of years and how full of works'

DR NULTY ON THE LAND QUESTION

In 1873, the Local Government Board of Ireland was directed by His Excellency the Lord Lieutenant, representative of Her Majesty Queen Victoria, to prepare a return of all the land owners of Ireland with the acreage of all property belonging to each.

It took two years to prepare, and, having been presented to Parliament by command of Her Majesty in 1876, was published in book form, the printer being Alexander Thom of Dublin. It is clearly a most interesting record because it shows the state of land tenure in Ireland on the eve of the Land League and I am very grateful to the Athboy reader who has lent me a copy from which to prepare these notes.

The population of Meath at the previous census in 1871 was 95,558 and the number of inhabited houses was 18,814 – an average of between five and six persons to each family. But of these 18,814 families only 1,324 owned land. Of this 1,324 there were 278 who owned less than an acre, 92 who owned from one to five acres, and roughly a similar number owning from five to ten acres. These figures may need some explanation. How did it come about that nearly 300 people owned patches of land – freehold – of less than five acres? The addresses of these little estates answer the question: The Commons, Navan; The Commons, Duleek; The Red Bog, Dunshaughlin. These three occur again and again. Others are known to me as wasteland: a few that I do not know have such suggestive titles as Moortown. The owners were poor people who had built cabins and reclaimed patches of bog and commons and had thereby acquired squatters' rights.

MEN OF GREAT POSSESSIONS

At the other end of the property scale we find that Lord Athlumney, Somerville, owned 10,213 acres; the Earl of Darnley, Clifton Lodge, Athboy, 21,858 acres; the Marquis of Lansdowne, Berkeley Square, London, 12,995 acres; James Lennox Naper, Loughcrew, 18,863 acres; and that the following had estates of from 5,000 to 10,000 acres: the Earl of Fingall, Killeen Castle; Robert Fowler, Robinstown, Enfield; Viscount Gormanstown; the Marquis of Headford; Christopher A. Nicholson, Balrath, Burry; John Joseph Preston, Bellinter, and the trustees of Edward Bligh.

There are 111 names of people owning from 1,000 to 5,000 acres. Adding up very roughly the property of these 122 landlords, I estimate that they held between them about 400,000 acres of the total 577,893 acres of land in the whole county. About another 100,000 acres consisted of smaller estates, 600 to 1,000 acres, and, of the remainder, the given 'owners' were most probably lease-holders. (There is a note in the report which justifies this conclusion.) These leaseholders were the lucky people to whom landlords granted a lease to hold their farms for at least ninety-nine years, and they include holders of quite small farms – fifteen to thirty acres – though the majority are of the hundred-acre size.

Adding up all these owners of properties, great and small, the result is that, of the 18,814 families in Meath, 17,490 owned nothing. They were tenants-at-will on their farms or in their houses in the towns, or in their cabins by the roadsides. To live on a holding which one's ancestors had farmed for generations was no guarantee that one would continue to live there for a further six months. If the landlord served notice to quit there was no redress, and no compensation for buildings, hedges, drains or any other improvements made by the tenant.

It is true that many landlords were just men who would never exercise their legal right of eviction and who never claimed an excessive rent, but there were exceptions. Besides, many landlords living beyond their means were selling or leasing their estates to new owners – speculators who wanted as much return for their money as possible and who had no scruples whatsoever about rack-renting or evicting tenant farmers, big or little, solvent or insolvent, old or young, sick or well.

MORALITY OF STRIKE WEAPON

Such was the condition in which Dr Nulty found his flock when he became Bishop of Meath in 1866, the same condition on which the young Michael Davitt pondered during his seven years in prison. By the time he was released in 1877 he had made up his mind that the Fenian idea of armed insurrection to secure an Irish Republic was not practicable at that time. Instead he had formed the plan of the Land League – a combination of farmers against unjust land laws, to be carried on by orderly agitation, using the weapon afterwards named the 'Boycott'.

It was in effect the same principle underlying trades unions of a later day, that an injustice to one is an injustice to all; but in those days any combination of farmers or workers was held to be immoral, a crime against the sacred rights of property, and, in a word, nothing short of Communism. As such the Land League was condemned by many conservative Churchmen.

Dr Nulty, like Dr Croke of Cashel, wholeheartedly supported the new movement. In a letter addressed to the clergy and laity of the diocese in April 1881, he wrote:

> If the tenant farmers refuse to pay more than a just rent for their farms, and that no one takes a farm from which a tenant has been evicted for the non-payment of an unjust or exorbitant rent, then our cause is practically gained. The landlords may, no doubt, wreak their vengeance on a few, but the patriotism and generosity of their countrymen will compensate them abundantly for their losses.

CLEAR THINKING

In 1880 a Coercion Act had been passed. Now Gladstone was preparing a new Land Bill, a result of the strength of the Land League, backed by the strong Irish Parliamentary Party led by Parnell. The Bishop placed very little hope in the Bill. He wrote:

> The hereditary legislators (the House of Lords) will, I fear, never surrender the monopoly in the land which they have usurped for centuries past; at least till it has become quite plain to them that they have lost the power of holding it any longer.

The 1881 Bill was better than was expected and marked the beginning of a series of Acts which gave farmers, first, fixity of tenure at fair rent, and secondly the possibility of owning their own lands on a terminable annuity. Some of the credit for the success of the Land League must go to Dr Nulty. The letter from which I have quoted was accompanied by a masterly essay on the whole land question in Ireland. Coming from such an exalted source this logically reasoned exposition of the facts carried great weight with supporters and opponents alike, and still merits study today.

I conclude with one further quotation from Dr Nulty's covering letter, where he expresses his feelings towards the landlord class clearly and directly:

> I do not, of course, address you as your Bishop, for I have no divine commission to enlighten you on your civil rights, or to instruct you in the principles

of land tenure or political economy. You know but too well, and perhaps to your cost, that there are bad landlords in Meath, and worse still in Westmeath … We are, unfortunately, too familiar with all kinds of extermination, from the eviction of a parish priest who was willing and able to pay his rent, to the wholesale clearance of the honest industrious people of an entire district. But we have, thank God, a few good landlords, too. Some of these, like the Earl of Fingall, belong to our own Faith; some, like the late Lord Athlumney, are Protestants, and some among the very best are Tories of the highest type of Conservatism. For my own part I can assure you I entertain no unfriendly feelings for any landlord living. I write of them not as individuals but as a class. But that I heartily dislike the existing system of land tenure, and the frightful extent to which it has been abused by the vast majority of landlords, will be evident to anyone who reads this essay through.

DR NULTY ON THE LAND QUESTION

Some years ago *The Meath Chronicle* republished the full text of Dr Nulty's 'Essay on the Land Question', written in 1881 and dedicated to the clergy and laity of the Diocese of Meath.

In giving some extracts here, I ask readers to bear in mind the temper of the times in which the essay was written. Land was still the greatest source of wealth; the status of 'gentleman' was associated with possession of land; the landed gentry made and administered the laws, therefore no law was so sacred as the law of property, which established that the owner of land had an absolute right to use his property as he pleased, and had no obligations whatever to his employees, his tenants, or the community as a whole.

Kindly people might express the wish that landlords would show mercy to their poor dependents, but few dared to say that there was any obligation on them in law to do so. If the harassed peasantry, tired of waiting for mercy, sought to impose justice by violent means, their action was described by the word 'outrage'.

Dr Nulty begins his essay by saying that the fact that this attitude towards property has the sanction of long-established usage is no reason at all for its continuance, and he makes a comparison with slavery, an evil that had only a short time previously been abolished in America and the British Dominions.

Slavery is found to have existed as a social institution, in almost all nations, civilised as well as barbarous, and in every age of the world, up almost to our own time ... as a settled, established and recognised state in which generation followed generation in unbroken succession, and in which thousands upon thousands of human beings lived and died.

Hardly anyone had the public spirit to question its character or denounce its excesses ... and the degradation in which it held its unhappy victims was universally regarded as nothing worse than a mere sentimental grievance.

On the other hand, the justice of the right of property which a master claimed in his slaves was universally accepted in the light of a first principle of morality. His slaves were either born on his estate and he had the cost of rearing them or he acquired them by inheritance or free gift, or failing these he acquired them by the right of purchase – having paid for them what was regarded as their full pecuniary value. Property in slaves was, therefore, regarded equally as sacred and as inviolable as any other species of property.

So deeply rooted and so universally received was this conviction that the Christian religion itself, though it recognised no distinction between Jew and Gentile, between slave or freeman, cautiously abstained from denouncing slavery itself as an injustice or a wrong. It prudently tolerated this crying evil, because in the state of public feeling then existing ... it was simply impossible to remedy it.

The practical approval, therefore, which the world has bestowed on a social institution that has lasted for centuries, is no proof that it ought to be allowed to live on longer, if, on examination, it be found to be intrinsically unjust and cruel, and mischievous and injurious besides to the general good of mankind.

The system of land tenure in Ireland enjoyed a long and similarly prosperous career, and it, too has created a state of human existence which, in strict truth and justice, can be briefly characterised as the twin sister of slavery. The vast majority of tenant farmers of Ireland are, at the present moment slaves. They are dependent for their peace of mind, for their material comforts, for the privilege of living under the roof beneath which they were born, and for the right of earning their bread on the farms which their fore-fathers enriched with their toil, on the arbitrary and irresponsible will of their landlord.

Abject, absolute and degrading dependence of this kind involves the very essence and is, in fact, the definition of slavery. They toil like galley slaves in the cultivation of their farms only to see, substantially, the whole produce of their labour and capital appropriated by others who have not toiled at all, and who leave them, not what would be allowed for the maintenance of slaves who would be expected to work, but what hardly suffices to keep them, from dying of want.

When grazing on land had been found more remunerative than tillage, and the people consequently became too numerous, the superfluous multitudes were mercilessly cleared off the land by wholesale evictions. Such as had the means left to take themselves away were forced to fly for refuge as exiles into almost every land; and the thousands who could not leave were coolly passed on through hunger and starvation to premature graves.

Let anyone who wishes visit this diocese, and see with his own eyes the vast and boundless extent of the fairest land in Europe that has been ruthlessly depopulated since the commencement of the present century, and which is now abandoned to a loneliness and solitude more depressing than that of the prairie or the wilderness.

Thus has the land system actually exercised the power of life and death on a vast scale, for which there is no parallel even in the dark records of slavery.

His words were a terrible indictment coming, not from the pen of an agitator or even of a popular reformer, but from a venerable Bishop who had, among his Catholic flock, not only the poor and dispossessed but representatives of the powerful interests he so fearlessly condemned. In his sixty-five years of life he had seen the evils of Irish land laws from all aspects – as a boy in his native Oldcastle and as a priest in various parishes of the diocese. He refrains from giving instances of particular horrors: no doubt he felt them to be out of place in the kind of essay he was writing, and in any case they were only too well-known to his readers of 1881.

THE DISPOSSESSED

One story of the clearances on an estate in County Meath tells of the cottiers and very small farmers who were evicted, and an order given that if any of the remaining tenants gave them shelter, they too would be liable to eviction. This was, from the landlord's point of view, a necessary precaution: the poor who could not emigrate were often permitted by small farmers to construct cabins, in lean-to fashion against walls or hedges. In this case, there was, among the evicted, one poor man with a wife and family, who failed to get shelter anywhere.

He conceived the idea of making a home in the one place that surely was beyond human claim to possession – the graveyard. On the inside of the enclosing bank he dug a hole – a burrow like a wild animal's den. He protected the opening with a few sacks and there the family lived through the cold and rain of winter. But even God's Acre was not immune; he was served with an ejectment notice and was brought before the court. It was held that his burrow was a dwelling-house within the meaning of the Act, and notice to quit was served.

The case aroused some notice even in those days; it was reported in the local newspapers at least, for I have seen the cutting, but I cannot say what was the ultimate fate of this family was.

The story of the Rathcore evictions was told in this paper a few years ago by Mr Garret Fox who had it from a man who remembered the incidents he described. There are other eyewitness accounts from other parts of the county which I will not repeat here.

The occasional retaliation is referred to. A liberal gentleman of the time, Mr William O'Connor Morris, writes in 1870:

The poorer classes, forced off from the soil by the operation of influences they cannot understand, and often pinched by distress and want, feel jealous of the rich ... The consequence of this state of things is that deeds of lawlessness and outrages have been too common in this county.

There is a footnote, 'Unhappily, since this was written, several frightful outrages have taken place in Meath.'

RIGHTS IN PROPERTY – DR NULTY'S EXPOSITION

If Michelangelo, in that delirium of artistic frenzy in which he called on his celebrated statue of Moses to speak, had dealt it a blow of his mallet which had actually shattered it to atoms, the world might indeed deplore the destruction of this immortal work as an irreparable loss, but it could not complain that he did it an injustice or a wrong. Michelangelo was master of his own actions, and he was not bound to spend years of labour and toil in producing that incomparable statue to delight and please the world, and even after he had produced it he was not bound to preserve it for its enjoyment: he might do what he liked with his own.

Dr Nulty illustrates very clearly the kind of property to which one has an absolute right. The material from which the statue was made was of negligible value: its worth derived almost entirely from the work of the artist – to that value which he had created he was absolutely entitled. So every man is justly entitled to the fruits of his labour. If a man takes a piece of waste and barren land, and by the work of his hands turns it into a fruitful field, he has created an addition to the property, to which he has an absolute right; he may sell it, bequeath it or will it to anyone he pleases.

It had long been the custom for Irish landlords to allow poor people to settle on waste land and reclaim it by their own toil. When it acquired value a rent was put upon it, not just a token rent commensurate with the original nominal value of the barren land, but a rent on the new value which was almost entirely the fruit of the tenant's labour.

Furthermore, the landlord claimed absolute ownership of the property, and the right to evict the tenant at any time and without showing any cause. In this the law of the time was on the landlord's side, and it was to have the law changed that various Tenant Right Associations had been formed during the nineteenth century. Many great thinkers had stated the case, but none more clearly or logically than Dr Nulty.

RIGHTS ACQUIRED BY LABOUR

'When God first put man on earth, the land needed not the labour of man to produce all that satisfied to the full his wants, wishes and desires.' But with the Fall came the sentence that henceforth the land was no longer fruitful of itself; man must earn his bread by the sweat of his brow. However the land is still God's gift to the people, the inheritance of all, out of which by their labour, they can 'provide themselves with everything they require for their maintenance and support, for their material comfort and enjoyment'.

Dr Nulty develops this idea at some length, making it clear that the land of every country is God's gift to the people of that country – to all of them – and that a system which excludes even the humblest from a share in the common inheritance is, 'an impious resistance to the benevolent will of the Creator'.

The problem for all nations is how to bring the most effective labour to bear upon the common heritage in order to produce the greatest amount of human food, comfort and enjoyment, and how to distribute the aggregate so as to give everyone his fair share.

The principle of private property secures these results and therefore, 'has been regarded by all nations as a necessary social institution'. We may notice that Dr Nulty does not say that the principle of private ownership of land is fundamental or ordained by God – only that it has been found the most effective. He writes:

> The most powerful principle of human action that we know of is self-interest and self-interest is the principle of private property. We labour with untiring energy, earnestness and perseverance when we know that we are working for ourselves, for our own interest and benefit.
>
> Wherever, therefore, the principle of private property in land is carried out to the full extent that its justice and the interests of the community demand the land of that country will be parcelled out in larger or smaller lots among the people, on the plain principle of justice, that the increased fertility which they shall have imparted to the soil shall be their own, and that they shall have a strict right of property in the returns – no matter how abundant – it shall yield to their capital and labour. No man will incur the expenditure (of capital and labour) if others, not himself, are to be benefited by it ... no term of years can produce on men's minds what has been most felicitously called 'the magical effects of perpetuity of tenure'.

TENANT PROPRIETORSHIP

In addition to fixity of tenure for the tenant, Dr Nulty advocated the principle of peasant proprietorship, which was the ultimate aim of the Land League. At the time such a view was regarded as rank Communism, and it must have been a wonderful consolation to Davitt, and the whole movement he led to have a Catholic Bishop make a public statement like this, proving clearly that what they were demanding was strictly in line with Christian principles of social justice.

Dr Nulty lived to see not only fixity of tenure but the full Land League programme recognised by the British Government. In the year of the pamphlet (1881) Parnell pressed hard for a Land Purchase Bill but his efforts were not successful. Four years later, however, Lord Ashbourne included the same proposals in a Bill which became law. Under this Act, tenants who could come to an agreement with their landlords to buy their holdings could borrow the whole purchase price through a new body called the Irish Land Commission, paying in return a yearly sum of 4 per cent for a period of forty-nine years to clear the loan and interest.

The sum allocated under this Act was £5million – not much when spread over all Ireland – but it was a beginning at least and further sums were later allocated. Most of the land was purchased under the Wyndham Act of 1903 in which the repayment period was sixty-nine years and the amount of annuity therefore considerably less.

COMMUNITY'S RIGHT TO CONFISCATE

In these Acts there was no provision for compulsory purchase. The price was made by agreement, and as the tenants was most anxious to own their own land, and as they had been accustomed to high rents, the amount fixed was usually very generous to the landlords. Most of them, no doubt seeing the writing on the wall, were glad to get out while the going was good.

All this was very much in the future when Dr Nulty was writing. It took a very great man to make the revolutionary statement that 'a non-improving landholder has no right to be left in the possession of it at all'. This means that if a man is holding land which he does not work to reasonable capacity, the Government, in the name of the people, has the right to take it from him without any compensation at all. Logically this follows from the distinction between the land itself – God's gift to all His children – and the right of an individual to the fruits of his labour on the land. Dr Nulty writes:

> I have made no distinction between the landlords of a country and the tenant farmers who hold under them, for, in truth, on the question of property in land there is no room for any such distinction. I am quite ready to allow the full benefits of the right of property in land to any landlord or tenant who has created such property; but I cannot allow either to tenant or landlord any other or further rights of property in land than those I have enumerated. Who has right to demand a rent for the natural fertility of these lands (of Meath) 'which no man made?' He who produced it. But He who produced

it is God and in bestowing His gifts He shows no respect of persons. I infer, therefore, that no individual or class of individuals can hold a right of private property in the land of a country; that the people of that country in their corporate capacity are the real owners of the land of their country – holding an indisputable title to it in the fact that they received it as a free gift from its Creator, and as a necessary means of preserving and enjoying the life He has bestowed upon them.

AFTER THE LAND ACTS

The Land League's success gave the people a sense of victory, a victory won after generations of defeat; it meant economic freedom and the right to live and work in peace on their own land. The Land League leaders were venerated and there was no doubt in the popular mind about their ability to achieve Home Rule just as they had achieved the Land Acts. If old Fenians harboured any doubts about the value of a constitutional movement they were not likely to be listened to. Parnell was the Chief whom all were ready to follow to victory.

It is difficult for us today to understand the spell this extraordinary man cast on the people of Ireland, the respect and fear he inspired in England, and the legend he had become in the eyes of the world.

He had the elusive quality which 'personality' only begins to describe. That is why, when the crash came, he was so bitterly hated by those who turned against him. The depths to which both sides in the 'split' allowed themselves to descend are a measure of the heights on which they had set their idol.

Nowhere in Ireland was the conflict as bitter as in Meath, Parnell's own constituency. The general story may be read in one of the many studies of Parnell and it is not my intention to retell it here.

LOT OF THE LABOURER

One aspect of the Land League and Home Rule days that is not often dealt with is the efforts made to improve the lot of the labourers. It is worth quoting from *The Irish Labour Movement* by W. P. Ryan:

In the years of the Land League it never, apparently, entered the consciousness of the general pioneer or observer that the labourers were to be anything but under-men to the end of time. It was forgotten that they, too, were the descendants of the dispossessed Gaels; it was forgotten also to a great degree that they were human, that they and their children had potential capacities, the training of which would make them great co-operative units in a natural State or Commonwealth. They were never regarded as being on the same human plane as the farmers, the professional and the parasitic classes. During the Land League years they were repeatedly the subject of the pity and the promises of the orators; but the assumption always was that, though their lot would be certainly improved, they and theirs would still remain an under-folk, a serving class.

It is true that Parnell secured an Act by which cottages might be built for agricultural labourers, and in every parish we may see one or two of the first cottages. They were a miracle of comfort to the poor people living until then in sooty, one-roomed cabins. But only one in fifteen agricultural labourers got cottages during the first fifteen years of the Act, and there was no provision at all for non-agricultural labourers.

It is a sad fact that the farmers so lately emancipated from the tyranny of the landlords had very little sympathy with the rights of the labourers. They grumbled at giving up half-an-acre as a 'cottage site' because, to quote W.P. Ryan again:

> The man with the cottage and the plot was considered too independent, unwilling to bind himself to one master, or to work when and how the master desired. In short he was in the way of outgrowing the serf habit.

VOICES IN THE WILDERNESS

It is well to remember that in the struggles of the Land League, agricultural labourers and town labourers threw themselves wholeheartedly into the fight, 'helping to make it the greatest example of combination and direct action in Irish history'. Men who had nothing to gain were the loudest to cheer at the Land League meetings; they were also the ones to risk most when there was boycotting to be done or cattle to be driven, or even an obstinate land agent to be dealt with by direct if unofficial methods.

When the farmers got on their feet they were proud to describe themselves as people with a stake in the country and to refer to agitators in later struggles as people with nothing to lose. But history has had its own ironies since then.

Davitt himself would have been a Labour leader if he had lived in the generation of Connolly and Larkin. As it was, he had ideas far in advance of his time, but Parnell and the majority of his parliamentary colleagues had little understanding of or sympathy with such ideas – their background and education was much too conservative.

Readers will recall the work of John Sweetman. It is not to take from his good intentions to note that his solution for the poverty of Irish cottiers was to help them to emigrate *en masse*. That was the solution for over-population in England and many European countries at the time. Let the surplus go to build up the colonies or, in the case of Ireland, let them go to build roads and railways for the United States as she extended her territory westwards over the vast lands of the Red Indians. The idea of developing Ireland's own resources did not seem equally feasible and the few experiments made to establish industries were almost complete failures.

One man of vision in County Meath who deserves to be remembered in this respect is the late James MacCann of Ardsallagh. He was before his time – a voice crying in the wilderness – but the works he initiated and the ideas he promulgated in his writings have since borne fruit in the industrial progress of the town of Navan. I shall briefly round off the life story of Dr Nulty.

LAST DAYS OF A GREAT BISHOP

Dr Nulty's successful advocacy of the tenant farmers' cause brought him many enemies among the powerful ascendancy. He was maligned in the English Press and misrepresented at the Vatican itself. When he visited Rome shortly after the election of Pope Leo XIII he explained the true state of Irish affairs to the Pontiff but, humble as he was, he offered to refrain from further part in the public affairs if such were the Pope's wishes. Leo put his hand on the Bishop's shoulder affectionately and said, 'Scribe, scribe, write on, write on.'

Shortly afterwards, in October 1889, Dr Nulty celebrated his silver jubilee as Bishop. Fr O'Growney gives an account of it in Irish in *The Tuam News*. It must be one of the earliest examples of newspaper reporting in

Irish. In the description of the various receptions, the decoration of the towns and so on, we can feel the triumphant pride of the people in the patriot Churchman who was their beloved Bishop.

Fr O'Growney rejoices that one of the addresses presented to the Bishop was in Irish, the first ever, and that in the Christian Brothers' School in Mullingar an Irish ode was read and Irish songs sung by the boys. (This, it must be remembered, was four years before the founding of the Gaelic League.) It was a year of achievement and of high hopes for greater things to come.

Alas, before the year was out, the Parnell split had happened and the aging Bishop's last years were darkened by the strife that divided his flock, clergy and laity alike, into bitterly opposing camps. He himself opposed Parnell and neither his years nor his works saved him from the consequences. He had welcomed and introduced Parnell to Meath in 1873 and supported him for almost twenty years. Now, the end was tragedy.

Dr Nulty died on Christmas Eve, 1898 – a great man who in his lifetime saw the dark days of fear and famine and lived, as Fr Gibbons put it, 'to see Catholic Ireland rise proudly from the Catacombs'. May he rest in well-earned peace.

THE END OF AN AGE

The passing of Dr Nulty in 1898 marked the end of an epoch in the history of Meath. The death of Fr O'Growney in the following year was not an end but rather a beginning. The new century was to develop a mode of thought, expression and action animated by the spirit of O'Growney; the constitutional movement, which had served so well in the years when Dr Nulty was preaching land reform, lost its force with the fall of Parnell, and never again attracted the youth or the intellect of Ireland.

There are many people better fitted than I am to write the rest – people who could relate at first hand what I am trying to gather here and there from books, from stray conversations and from the letters I am grateful to receive from many readers of *The Meath Chronicle*. In the next couple of articles, therefore, I shall put together a few odds and ends from these sources, and to begin with I shall quote a little more from W.P. Ryan's book *The Irish Labour Movement*, from which I took last week the statistics on labourers' cottages.

PIONEER OF LOCAL INDUSTRY

The Land League, Ryan says, was supposed to have affected a revolution; yet two years after the opening of the new century:

> Mr James McCann, M.P., an economist of the wealthier classes, who had been for years a voice crying in the wilderness, found the whole situation still hopelessly wrong, the Irish peasantry – in whom he included 400,000 small farmers – robbed, over-taxed or forced by evil circumstances to emigrate. In 'Some Pleas for the Preservation of the Irish Peasantry in the Land of the inverted Pyramid' (1902) he insisted as emphatically as Connolly himself, that at bottom, and in its roots, the Irish problem was material and economic.

Mr McCann's argument was that the great increase in bank deposits during the closing years of the century was not, as it was held to be, a sign of growing prosperity among the ordinary people. Their labour and capital were absorbed by middle men and by the heavy burden of indirect taxation so that for two million people life was 'a gamble for existence in a crop of potatoes and turf'. And on the fortunes of these depended the livelihood of tailors, shoemakers, small dealers and others.

James McCann did more than write about the evils of his time. To quote again:

> ... broke up grass lands in Meath, initiated local industries – wood works and a bacon factory – and established *The Irish Peasant* to drive home his ideas for the preservation of the folk whom he saw were the basis, yet the least regarded part of the nation.

It was as editor of *The Irish Peasant* that W.P. Ryan came to Meath. I am sure there are still people who remember him. I met him many years afterwards when, as an elderly man, he was studying for a teacher's certificate in Irish, so that he might, in his scarce spare time, conduct classes in the Gaelic League in London. That was in 1917, when he was, I think, editor of *The Daily Herald*.

Navan people in particular should know of the patriotic work of James McCann of Ardsallagh, and perhaps some one will tell the story more fully than I can do here.

WAR ON STAGE IRISHMAN

Another name that flits through the pages of Meath history is that of Tom Daly. His work for the Gaelic League is mentioned in the O'Growney funeral book and I have already quoted at least one reference to him. Brian O'Higgins, in describing his own youth, says:

> It was in Clonmellon I first met Tom Daly, founder, proprietor and editor of *The Meath Chronicle*. He had a pleasing voice and was a member of a concert party from Kells that had come to entertain us and raise funds for some parochial purpose. The concert party was typical of many such to be found at that time all over Ireland. The members of it blackened their faces indulged in what they thought were nigger jokes, sang coon songs and what was supposed to be Irish humour, manufactured in London and New York for the set purpose of exhibiting Irish Paddy as a buffoon to the rest of the world. There was one stage Irish song that got my blood up. I wrote a parody on it, satirising the whole murky, slavish business and sent it to Tom Daly, never thinking for a moment that he would have the courage to publish it, seeing that he was a member of the concert party himself, and that the functions at which such parties appeared brought him business as a publisher and a printer. But he published it, and wrote me a letter saying that my attitude was the right one, the only one, for self-respecting Irishmen, and inviting me to write as much as I liked in a similar vein for *The Meath Chronicle*. In a few years' time this big, quiet, genial man was in the forefront of the Irish-Ireland struggle in Meath, and the columns of his paper were open to all who wanted to preach the gospel of Irish freedom.

TWELVE

EVERY PLACE NAME HAS A MEANING

A DUTY TO RECORD THEM, EVEN PHONETICALLY

Ptolemy, writing in Greek, in the second century, presents a description of Ireland based on earlier works. He mentions over fifty places, whose names had been learned from early Phoenician sailors, but few of these can now be identified. One easily recognisable name is *Bovinda*, our own River Boyne, and another, *Doonon*, is a form of Dun which is found in Dunderry, Dunshaughlin and a hundred other places through the county. The Greek reference brings home to us the antiquity of our place names, and even a little knowledge of simple Irish root words can set one off on a voyage of discovery in one's own parish.

We may take it that every name has a meaning, and that when it was invented the meaning was intelligible to everyone. The process of naming from a distinguishing feature goes on all the time: the Five Lamps, Carey's Cross, the White Walls, etc. The earliest names are those connected with geographical features: hills, lakes and plains. The most common Irish word for a hill is *cnoc*, anglicised as 'knock' or 'crock', but this name which, according to Joyce, forms the beginning of 1,800 townland names in Ireland, is comparatively rare in the level lands of Meath.

Mullagh, however, which means 'a top' or 'summit', is very common. There is the Mullagh on the Cavan border, for instance, and the Mullagh on the road from Summerhill to Dunboyne. It may be noted, in regard to the latter, that the first generation of English speakers translated it as 'The Hill'. Both names were used, and then a generation which forgot the original meaning called it 'The Hill of the Mullach'. A similar process gives us 'The Naul'. The Irish was *An Aill* (the cliff). The English 'the' was substituted for the Irish *an* but the 'n' got tacked on to the name itself. Naturally *Magh* (a plain) is very common in Meath. It is usually turned into '*Moy*' in English, and as such appears as 'The Moy' for a district near Summerhill; but another form is 'Muff' of the famous battle.

Moynalty, the plain of the herds, is one of our oldest and most beautiful names. Ferguson felt its charm when he made the Fianna warriors say they would bury their beloved queen where she would hear 'the lowing of Moynalty's kine'. The old name of East Meath was *Magh Breagh*, sometimes translated as 'the beautiful plain', but more probably 'the plain of a people called the Brega'. Readers will be able to name a dozen other Moys, and those in North Meath may be interested to know that *Maghera* is another form of the same word. *Magheracloon*, for instance, is 'the plain of the meadow' – a lovely name if we remember that *cloon* is more than a meadow in the modern sense: it is rather a rich sweet pasturage. *Clonmore* is the big meadow; *Clongill*, the meadow of the foreigner; *Clondalee*, the meadow of the two calves.

Here I have named only three or four common roots found in place names because this note is intended merely as an introduction. You will find, of course, the Irish form of the name of every post office printed over the door, and the names of towns and villages on the signposts. Some of them you may understand; some are doubtful, and a few are incorrect, but in every parish there are dozens of names which have never been recorded.

The first book ever written on Irish place names was by Dr P. W. Joyce (1827-1914) in 1869. He drew, of course, on earlier topographical and historical works, particularly on the collections made by John O'Donovan during his travels for the Ordnance Survey. But even Donovan could not progress far beyond the townland names. In recent years, scholars have collected the place names of particular districts, and the Place Names Commission has been working for some years on the names of townlands, particularly in the Gaeltacht counties. As far as I know, little, if any, fieldwork has been done in our county. The interpretation of names is, of course, work for scholars. Recording them phonetically is something we can all do.

If this work is neglected, ancient and interesting names will have dropped out of use before the official collectors get around to us. Many a *Raheen* and *Meel Ditch* will have been bulldozed out of existence, and many a piously named terrace will have consigned to oblivion the Fossachs and Butterstreams and Friarsfields that still border our towns.

THE FASCINATING STUDY OF PLACE NAMES

Tradition has it that before the coming of St Patrick all buildings in Ireland were round in shape. It is recorded in one ancient life of St Patrick that there had been a prophecy that he would bring, among other changes, the custom of building houses with four corners.

All over Ireland we have remains of circular enclosures, called locally forts, raths, raheens or lioses and in the manuscripts the dwellings of chiefs are constantly referred to by these names.

Shelter is one of the most basic needs of human beings, second only to the need for food. Early man made his dwelling place from the material nearest to hand, and chose its site from consideration of safety, proximity to food and water, convenience of access and so on. He may have had, and very likely had, an eye to beauty of surroundings as well, for in all ages every human heart is human.

In a flat country with stretches of bog and marsh, and with slow-flowing rivers subject to winter floods, the high ground was naturally the most suitable place for house or fortress. It is said that at an early period there came a cycle when the climate was hotter than it is since historic times, and that that accounts for the signs of habitation and even of agriculture on the very tops of mountains. In our part of the country there are few heights deserving of the name 'mountain', except perhaps the Loughcrew hills. But all through Meath, on hillsides and ridges, are mounds and rings of various kinds and we feel, perhaps, that we should be able to identify them at sight.

It may console us to know that even the experts cannot date a site with any certainty on the evidence of the eye alone. Circular structures were erected for military, domestic and burial purposes from before the dawn of history, and as late as the eleventh century of the Christian era it is recorded that chiefs built for themselves 'princely palaces of circular form'.

We might perhaps make a rough generalisation. Circular mounds of even symmetrical shape and rounded tops are burial mounds; flat circular plat-forms surrounded by one, two or three rings are dwelling places, and may have been built and occupied at any time from before the dawn of history up to the early Middle Ages. The same applies to *crannógs* or lake dwellings; flat-topped mounds, with usually one steep side and one sloping side, are Norman moats.

We must also remember that various peoples used the same sites successively. The Danes, for instance, established themselves on fortresses already in existence, though they sometimes built new ones. Many Christian churches were built inside raths. The Normans adapted earlier mounds to their own purposes, though they more often built anew.

The commonest names for enclosures are *rath*, *liós*, and *dún*. Originally, each name described a different kin of structure. It would appear that the *dún* was a strong fortress, and the *liós* the domestic enclosure surrounded by ramparts, in which the whole village was situated, while the *raths* were the dwellings of kings and chieftains. The royal residences on Tara, for instance, include *Rath Cormac*, *Rath na Rí*, *Rath Maeve* and *Rath Gráinne*; but at present the names have become confounded and are not in themselves evidence of the exact origin or purpose of a particular structure.

Mr L. Price has computed the number of townlands in Ireland whose names begin with *Rath* as 1,085; with *Lios* as 1,274, and with *Dun* as 450. In the modern County Meath, the numbers are 55, 10 and 14 and for Westmeath, 56, 22 and 12. That is, in ancient Meath there is more than the average number of strong fortresses. The term *liós* is more common in the North of Ireland than elsewhere.

These figures do not include the townlands where the name of the earthwork comes at the end, like Balrath, a very common Meath place name, meaning either 'the townland of the rath' or 'the road (*bealach*) of the rath'. The hill of Down is 'the Hill of the Dun' and Whiteleas in the parish of Stamullen looks like a compound of *liós*.

Ratharney is said to be a very ancient name derived from Athairne, its builder, while Ratoath gets its name from a Danish chief, Todh, a thousand years later. Dunboyne is said to be named, not from the River Boyne, but from a chieftain named Baoithin who had his fortress there. Dunshaughlin is not a *dún* at all, but a *domhnach* or great church, founded by Seachlán, a near kinsman of St Patrick. Lisnabo, near Kingscourt, is not named after any great man, it is just 'the *liós* of the cows', as Lisnagrow is 'the *liós* of the sheds' and Lisnagon, 'the *liós* of the hounds'. These names confirm the more domestic character of the *liós*.

The *dúns* were primarily fortresses, as the word in its verbal form means, even in modern spoken Irish, 'to close'. It is found in all the languages of Europe that were influenced by the Celts, and from it the modern English word 'town' is derived. A town is a closed-in place.

Another word for a strong place is *daingean*, and there are at least two important Daingeans in the kingdom of Meath: the Daingean of Offaly, and Dangan, near Summerhill, the scene of many battles in Tudor and Cromwellian times.

If a rambler in Meath comes upon a hill top of any kind, let him study its name and formation, but let him first climb to the top and look around him. If the day is bright he will be rewarded with a quite unexpected sight. The range of vision from our 'cairn-crowned hills' is extensive, and it has a delicate beauty of colour not to be found among rugged mountains.

Did Athcairne, Cormac and Laoire take time to look around on a fine morning at the same blue ring of earth and sky, and 'thank their gods for all the goods they gave'? Somehow I am sure they did. They built, on the sunny side of their own palaces, a special house for their ladies, which would go to show that they were not indifferent to the quality of their surroundings. The several Grennanstowns in Meath take their names from these sunhouses, and it may be more than coincidence that Aghanagrena, 'the field of the sun', is the Gaelic name of Goldsmith's Auburn – 'the love-liest village of the plain':

Where smiling spring its earliest visits paid,
And parting summer's lingering blooms delayed.'

THE ART OF MAKING A GLOSSARY
THE TRANSMUTATION OF LANGUAGE

Most of us have at some time or other been stirred to righteous indignation at the language put into the mouth of an Irishman by an English novelist or dramatist, 'Begob and begorra, and would you be after sindin' for the good praste to stretch his holy and blessed hand over the angashore.' You know the kind of thing. A language never spoken anywhere on land or sea. Even some of the expressions used by Anglo-Irish dramatists ring false to us in County Meath, of 'the mist that does be on the bog' variety.

Yet it is extremely interesting to notice the peculiarities of the language we speak. The difficulty is that we do not notice the peculiarities unless we have lived for a considerable time in some other part of the country, or out-side the country. If, for instance, you have never heard a boreen or a bonair called by any other name you hardly realise that these are not English words. If you have 'snigged' turnips or cut 'straws' you may not realise that your way of describing these operation is purely local.

Students of philology are in recent years showing a great interest in this matter of Anglo-Irish dialect, and glossaries have been published from vari-ous parts of the country. Two of particular interest to us are Liam Ua Broin's collection of about 500 words and phrases from south-west Dublin and a shorter glossary by Padraig O'Conchrubhair of Edenderry. From the former I take the following three words in sequence. In brackets after each is the note added by Prof. Hogan, who edited both glossaries:

Garron: An inferior horse, a nag. (Irish: *gearrán*)
Garrogues: Short drills in the corner of a field. (Irish: *gearróg*)
Gaubeen: A mopish, slow-witted person. [Perhaps this is the English dialect gawp].

Turning to the Edenderry collection we have under 'G', *gad*, *garrogues* and *gom*, all familiar to Meath readers, but a little further down is one new to me: 'haggard', as in the phrase 'like a haggard of sparrows' said of a crowd of chattering women.

Possibly some of my readers will ask what is the point of such collections, but a little reflection will show that the language in which people express their thoughts has a close connection with their history, national and social. The position of Meath on the flat eastern seaboard left it open to the first impact of every invasion, and every set of invaders left some permanent trace of themselves in language as well as in material ways. The early modifications of the Irish language are too difficult for ordinary students, but in a very gen-eral way we can follow the linguistic history of the past seven centuries.

When De Lacy and his marauders swept into Meath with their long bows and coats of mail, they spoke a dialect of French modified by a hun-dred years of marauding in England, and it would seem likely that their common soldiers spoke Welsh or Anglo-Saxon. When the Saxon workman killed a pig it appeared on the table of his Norman master under its French name 'pork'; the Saxon 'calf' was cooked as French 'veal', and the live sheep became dead 'mutton'. Something of the same kind happened when this mixed language came into contact with the native Irish language. In a couple of generations, of course, the Irish language triumphed, and men with Norman names knew neither a word of French nor English.

Later planters, however, were English speaking, for the native language of the conquered Anglo-Saxons had become the spoken language of England by the fourteenth century. This language gradually supplanted Irish in the Pale. In the centuries that followed, the English of England developed differently from the English of Ireland, so that today we use English words here that are only to be found in the Bible or Shakespeare. 'Fornint' for 'opposite' is the stock example. Others that come to mind are bespoke, bethought, unbeknownst, a-wanting and a-feared.

EASTERTIME AND MAY DAY TRADITIONS
COMMERCIALISM KILLED THE CLUDÓG

A Rathkenny man, writing to me a few weeks ago on Meath place names, says in a postscript that it is still the custom in North Meath to make an Easter *cludóg*, or collection of eggs. He asks if this is customary in other places. It certainly was customary all over Meath until fairly recent times, but I am afraid the chocolate Easter eggs are rather spoiling the ritual traditionally associated with the feast of the Resurrection, as commercialism has killed the old spirit of Christmas.

This is how Brian O'Higgins describes the Easters of his young days in Kilskyre:

Every housewife expected all the children of the neighbourhood to call on her, and to each one she gave an egg as a gift; eggs laid on Good Friday were marked with a cross, and every person, old and young, tried to get one of these to eat on Easter Sunday morning. That collection of eggs by the children was, and is to this day, called the *cludóg*, and *eating the cludog* was a very special feast carried out by the children themselves in the afternoon of Easter Sunday, no grown-up people being present ever.

The young people brought with their collection of eggs, bread and butter, salt and a saucepan, the makings of a good fire, and rugs, old blankets or clean sacks to sit on. They found a sheltered place at the back of a hedge, away from all hag-gards and thatched houses, and there lighted a fire over which they boiled the eggs. Then followed such a feast as a millionaire might envy. They would have tea later in their own homes, but eating the *cludóg* was a young people's communal banquet without which the day would not seem Easter Sunday at all.

I am afraid that old custom has gone, though there are some families in this parish who still mark the Good Friday eggs with a cross, and eat them on Easter Sunday morning. No longer are eggs such a treat that children boast of the number they eat – ten or even twelve was not beyond the capacity of the boys of forty years ago. Increased prosperity, as well as relaxation in the Lenten fast, no doubt, helped to bring about the change.

I have looked through several books of folklore from other parts of Ireland, and, strangely enough, none of them makes any reference at all to the *cludóg*. The word is not even in Dinneen's dictionary. Perhaps readers born in other counties will enlighten us on this point if there were any other Easter customs in your parish, please note them. For instance, is it considered wrong to draw blood on Good Friday? Or do children still believe that the sun dances on Easter Sunday morning?

I once heard an old Monaghan man say that when he was young, a hundred years ago now, little wooden spoons were made in every house at Easter for the egg-eating in the fields. He said they were called *smollachers*. Probably in those days the supply of cutlery in ordinary houses was limited.

Some authorities on folk customs say that our Easter eggs are the last survival of a pagan spring festival celebrating the new life of nature after the death of winter, and the miracle of renewed fertility, of which the egg was a symbol. A somewhat similar origin is attributed to May Day, the feast on which fires were lighted in honour of the god Baal – giving us the word *Bealtaine* – the modern Irish name for the month of May. Few days in the year are associated with so many superstitions as May Day. Of these the May bush is the best known, though I have met not-so-young people who thought it was put up in honour of the Mother of God.

In my young days we knew quite well that the purpose was to keep the fairies away from both people and cattle, as our grandparents put it. Only the very old really believed in the necessity for such protection, but the respect for custom was still strong, and I think most people felt that it was as well to be on the safe side. The May bush was always a hawthorn in my part of the country. The Mayflowers, which were thrown on it, were those yellow marsh flowers that look like buttercups but are bigger and glossier.

In South Meath, primroses and cowslips are used, and are made into chains or tied on with string. Miss Helen Roe, the well-known authority on high crosses, asked me about variations in types of Mayflowers last year, and I promised that I would try to make a survey, and let her know the result. Perhaps readers will let me have details of the exact May eve proceedings of the present day, and any customs now fallen into disuse which the old people still remember. Where and how was the bush erected? Who gathered the flowers? At what time of evening? Were flowers scattered at the doors of the house or thrown on the roofs of the cow stables? The May ritual was closely connected with cows. There were people who could charm the milk from them, or could take the butter off the churn. Stories are told of a hare being seen in the field early in the morning, and running off when the woman of the house came out to milk; and there being very little in the can that morning. Once a man fired a shot at the hare and wounded her in the leg, so that she was not able to run as fast as hares usually run. He followed her across the fields till she disappeared into a house and when he went after her he found, not a hare, but a woman, and she was bandaging up her bleeding leg.

I expect every reader has heard some variant of this story. In another case, where the cows were giving no milk, the owner went to a charm man for advice. He asked him if there was ever a stranger about at milking time. The farmer said there was a poor woman who used to sit on the stile by the roadside knitting in the summer morning sun, but she could hardly be responsible as she never had any vessel with her which would hold milk. 'Next time she is there,' said the charm-maker, 'go over to her and ask her what she is knitting. That will give you a chance to catch hold of the wool and break it.' The man did as he was told, and out from the broken thread gushed a stream of milk. In other versions of the story the milk was charmed into a long briar trailing round the gate of the milking field.

Sophisticated readers may think it a waste of time and paper to recall and record such *pishrogues* but serious students of ethnology find in them a valuable key to the minds and characters of a race. I, however, recommend them rather as stories which no Irish child should be deprived of. Tell them to the little ones, the four to ten year olds, instead of the ridiculous bedtime stories of bunny rabbits in waistcoats provided by ladies of leisure, whose cultural background is somewhat cosmopolitan. Such literature may satisfy children brought up in the artificial world of the modern city, but they are just not meaty enough for children of the land.

THE STORY OF AN OLD TOME
LOCAL INTEREST IN NAMES AND PLACES

Some time ago, when discussing famous Meath men who are in danger of being forgotten, I mentioned the name of James Martin, the poet of Millbrook. Soon afterwards, a reader sent me a very tattered old book in which, as he said in the accompanying letter, the name of Martin was mentioned. The first twenty-two pages were missing, and from page 23 to page 57 the left-hand pages were taken up with a long poem in Irish, of which a verse translation was given on the right-hand pages.

I thought the book so important that, though I was fairly certain of the authorship, I sent a description of it to Mr Alf MacLochlin of the National Library. Some time previously, I had got an introduction to Mr MacLochlin through the courtesy of Mrs McGurl, Meath County Librarian, who had already acquired photostat copies of Martin's works from him for Meath County Library.

Mr MacLochlin verified my conjecture that the book in question was *The Dirge of Ireland* a translation by Michael Clarke of a poem written in Irish by Bishop O'Connell of Kerry shortly after the Cromwellian war. The subject is the history of Ireland from the earliest times to the author's own day, with particular stress, as might be expected, on the defeat of the Irish chiefs, their exile, the confiscation of their estates, and the subsequent helplessness of the Catholic people. No one but God Himself can help them, but God seems to be forgetting:

> Dare we to ask you what you have in view,
> Whose nod alone whole broods of monsters slew;
> We think it time that you should look this way,
> Our sinking faith to strengthen from decay.

It was not thus that God acted in the time of St Patrick. And where is Mary 'that spotless virgin bride', and Michael, and Columba, and Kieran, etc. Some twenty Irish saints are invoked, with often a little biographical note like:

Most pious Finan, with his holy train,
And Finan grave, whose grot, was by Lough Lene;
Another Finan, replete with piety,
Who cured whole tribes from plague and malady.

Critics might not consider this first-class poetry. Its interest for us is not in its literary merit but that the author of the verse translation was a native of Whitewood, near Nobber. He lived on until 1847, though this work was published some twenty years earlier. From page 60 to page 177 there are notes on the poem, which are in effect a history of Ireland, with sources quoted. Pressure of space allows me only to make one quotation to show the quality:

> Our writers mention the flourishing state of religion and letters in this very age (the time of the Norman Invasion) in which no less than three of our prelates were canonised at Rome, namely, Celsus and Malachi, successors to the see of Armagh; and St. Laurence O'Toole, Archbishop of Dublin. They recite along with those a Christian, a Galesus, a Malchus and a Maurice, etc., prelates of the most exalted virtue and learning. It would have been better for the nation they could have mentioned a Brien, a Kennedy, a Callaghan, etc., etc., who with the sword would at once cut through the fascination, in their zeal for the honour of the Church!

It is one way of looking at it, certainly, but by far the most interesting part of the book occurs at the end. The author had to collect subscriptions to enable him to pay for the printing of his work, and it appears that, as a preliminary, he showed his translation to eminent people of his acquaintance, and published their letters of congratulation. There are three of these letters in the book, all in verse, and all rather long. They are from Mary Swallic, Kilbarry; James Martin, Millbrook, and — Moyle, Kilbarry. The dates are 1826 and 1827.

The first poem is chiefly advice as to the people he should avoid in soliciting subscriptions. Unfortunately for the curious historian, Miss Swallic does not mention names, but every reader of the time would have easily identified the people referred to:

The squire so puffed up with pride,
Can scarce reach his hand to his pocket,

Your wit and your verse he'll deride,
Though himself a most consummate blockhead.

The S– of the S– e 'tis true,
Translations or verse don't like any,
I deify the Nine Muses or you,
To squeeze from this creature a penny.

'Moyle' (it sounds like a pen-name) praises the poem at great length in this style:

How grand each wave, which thy rich fancy drew
How true thy meaning from each Irish phrase;
In English verse we now each passage view,
From your sweet pen in grand succession blaze.

He also refers to the worthless brood, the would-be wits, and the carping critics, so that we may conclude that in those days a poet's lot was not a happy one. Then he goes on:

I long to see great Martin's lofty lines
On your perfections in this work appear,
As Sol's bright gleam a twinkling star outshines,
So his will dim my strongest efforts here.

There follows Martin's poem; quite a different kind of composition, which I will talk about in a future article. Lastly, Clarke himself adds a rhymed account of his tour through Navan, Drogheda and Ardee in search of sub-scriptions. It is in humorous vein and would be of very great interest to people of the localities mentioned, for it is full of names and references that they should recognise. I will quote some passages later.

For the present I have only room to ask readers to reflect on the state of learning in this county a decade before the passing of the National Education Act. A large body of people who were able not only to read but to appreciate the points of a translation and to understand the classical and Irish historical references with which the work abounds. In addition to the men who rose to eminence in Church and State the hedge-schools pro-duced, they produced too these rustic Miltons.

JAMES MARTIN AND FRANK LEDWIDGE COMPARED
POETS OF THE ROYAL COUNTY

I have a large exercise book in front of me which is filled with stories and traditions written in the careful if rather stilted manner schoolchildren adopt when producing something for adult consumption. The note I am about to quote is from the pen of a girl from near Crossakiel, and it was written twenty years ago, when the teachers were trying to collect folklore all over Ireland:

> James Martin, the poet, was working as a miller in Oldcastle at Millbrook. One night when he was asleep he got a choice of any gift he would ask for. He chose to be a poet. At that time he had not much learning, but after that he could learn anything. He was highly respected by the clergy. He wrote a book called *The Fall of the Angels*. The Protestants called him names, such as One-eyed Crooked-toes. He had one eye from the time of his vision. One evening he had to cross a meadow, and the men tied about twelve traneens together on each side of the path. Every time he would fall he'd curse, and all the men began to laugh at him. Stories were made up about him.

This account may sound fantastic, and mildly amusing, but I would not feel justified in changing a word, though I will add my opinion on it, merely as an opinion. The reference to Protestants and the 'highly respected by the clergy' seems to suggest religious controversy and that may well have been so, as Martin was writing during the years of O'Connell's campaign for Catholic Emancipation.

On the other hand, it may mean rather that those who had got their education in the recently established free schools would have contempt for the learning of the hedge-schools. The former would, in general, be the Protestants. If Martin was respected by the clergy he was rather exceptional among poets who were traditionally partial to the wine-cup they sang so much about.

Getting the gift of poetry in a vision is like the common legend of the man who fell asleep near a fairy ring and awoke with the gift of music. Giving an eye as the price of the gift is an interesting and not so common addition to the story; try to remember and note tradition of this kind. They are an expression of the belief that genius has nothing to do with taking pains, but is a gift that may fall on the most unlikely person.

An Irish triad puts it very neatly:

Trí nithe nac feidir iad d'fhoghluim:
Guth, feile, agus filiocht.

(Three things that can't be learned:
Voice, hospitality and poetry.)

Here is a passage from Martin (he has been describing the Penal Laws):

Although we strive their horrors to forget,
Our vaunted country feels their evils yet.
For like some dove, when plundered of her young,
By anguish and maternal sorrow stung;
Sits injured Erin (reckless of our songs)
In mournful silence brooding o'er her wrongs!
The stern resentment in oblivion sleeps,
Yet sleepless memory o'er the picture weeps;
Although religion kindly intervenes,
To turn our eyes from those disgusting scenes –
There is not found in all the book, of crime,
(And search its annals from the birth of time)
A more disgusting, darker, bloodier page
Than that which shows the horrors of that age.

Note that the style is closer to English poetry than what was being written by contemporary English poets: Byron, Shelley and Keats. How different from Ledwidge, writing 'The Blackbirds' ninety years later on a similar theme, the execution of the poets of Easter Week:

I heard the Poor Old Woman say:
At break of day the fowler came,
And took my blackbirds from their songs
Who loved me well thro' shame and blame.

No more from lovely distances
Their songs shall bless me mile by mile,

Nor to white Ashbourne call me down
To wear my crown another while.

The similarity and the difference between the two passages is illustrative of the constant preoccupation of our poets with the sad beauty of our tragic history; the one is of the period when the language appeared to be dying, the other of the heroic revival. Ledwidge is nearer in spirit to the traditional '*Mise Eire, Sine me na an Cailleach Beara*', but poor Martin was wonderful considering the times he lived in. Get your children to learn these lines of his by heart; there is much in their schoolbooks that is less worthwhile.

In thirty years from now, Ledwidge will have been as long dead as Martin was when the little girl in Crossakeel recorded the information with which I began this article. Will the knowledge of his life, work and character be as meagre? It is up to us; to the people who know him as a child, a growing boy, a young man – he was still a young man when he was killed during the First World War – to keep his memory alive till some worthy Irish biographer is found to produce a definitive life. For, make no mistake about it, Ledwidge had that rare gift, the poetry that could not be learned, the vision which was believed to be vouchsafed only in the fairy ring. Are there enough lovers of Irish literature to ensure this biography for the fiftieth anniversary of the poet's death in 1967?

That Martin knew Irish is evidenced by this quotation from his tribute to Clarke's translation of *The Dirge of Ireland*:

And see, throughout, how closely you've adhered,
To th' Irish text, nor from the meaning veered,
You make the author's sense and beauty shine,
Without the addition, of a single line.

To the original you're still so true,
(Although so copious and expressive too)
That each true critic will your labours praise,
So do not dread what the dull Hyper says.

The Irish language was never completely lost in Meath, and that is something to remember when people exaggerate the difficulties of bringing it back as a spoken language.

What memories are there of other Meath poets, O'Neachtain, Tevlin, O'Brien, and the host of lesser-known ballad-makers? Are there any more old books and manuscripts lying around like the one from Kieran which has brought me to this subject?

MEATH POETRY

One of the first to realise the beauty of Irish folk songs was Charlotte Brooke, who was born near Mullagh, County Cavan, in 1740. She was of Protestant planter stock but, Irish being the spoken language of the district at the time, she soon grew to know and love the old songs and stories handed down from the days of the Schools of Poetry, and still familiar to the farmers and labourers around. There were even manuscripts to be had, and these she copied and eventually published with English translation in 1789 – the year of the French Revolution. It was titled *Reliques of Irish Poetry*.

Unfortunately, there were few of the upper classes like the Brookes. The majority looked upon everything native as inferior and so, while the romantics of Europe were collecting folklore and folk tales and folk songs, our rich herit-age was allowed to perish, or all but perish, with the native language. Only in our own time has an effort been made to gather the surviving fragments.

Local scholars who treasure and preserve what they can have always been there. Many were hedge-schoolmasters, and none was more remarkable than Peter Galligan, who died at Ballymacken, Nobber, in 1860. (The more correct name of the townland is, I think, Ballymacain, and it is in the parish of Moynalty.)

In his youth the hedge-schools provided education of a very high stand-ard, teaching Irish, English, mathematics and Latin enough to fit boys for ecclesiastical colleges; there is mention, too, of astronomy and the use of the globes. The Catholic catechism was also taught.

We have no evidence, however, that Galligan was a Latin scholar. His great love was Irish literature and he spent many years copying every manu-script he could lay his hands on.

The dozen or so that have survived are in various college libraries in Dublin, Edinburgh and Belfast, and a few are in private hands. Galligan signs off at the end of the Edinburgh manuscript's 722 pages, in extremely poetic Irish, that he finished his hard task on 10 February 1844, and:

Beannacht le na anam go Cathair na Gloire.
Oir b'ait leis go dearfa, dantai gus ceoltai.

Blessing with his soul to the City of Glory.
For joyful to him truly were song and music.

One of Galligan's manuscripts was still in Nobber in 1916 when the late Henry Morris got permission to copy it. The owner brought it to the local hotel every day until Morris finished the copying, rather than risk lending and losing it. He wanted it to stay in the area so that people would know that there was learning in Nobber once. I wonder where that manuscript is now.

THE ORIGIN OF FAMILY NAMES
TRACING THE DESCENT OF THE OLD STOCK

If we are to judge by poets and novelists of the period, it was the proudest boast of the Victorian gentry that their ancestors came over with William the Conqueror. Blue blood meant Norman blood, and names like Vere, de Vere and FitzRoy were the hallmark of nobility.

In Ireland, on the contrary, even the denationalised like to trace their descent from the Milesians, and value their O or *Mac*, while titles like The O'Toole, The O'Connor or The O'Lochlinn have a magic quality above modern knighthood or peerage. An old jingle which runs:

By Mac and O, you'll surely know
True Irishmen, they say;
But if they lack the O or Mac
No Irishmen are they.

The first half of the statement is true with certain exceptions; the second is completely misleading. Many Irish families had to drop their O and *Mac* at a time when Irish surnames were forbidden by law except to those 'loyal' subjects of Her Majesty Queen Elizabeth who were granted permission. Thus, in the O'Reilly country, there was the 'Queen's O'Reilly' in the castle, while the rest of the clan were Reillys. So if you have a name like Connell or Nulty, and know that there are the corresponding forms, O'Connell and MacNulty, then you may rest assured that you belong to an Irish family.

So much by way of introduction, for it is not always as simple as that. In primitive times there were no surnames. Everyone had a name given to him in childhood, and every name had a meaning. *Fionn* or *Finn*, meaning fair, is a simple example. *Fiac* (raven) and *Oisin* (little deer) are also obvious. Often in later life a name was added to or substituted for the original one, for the same sort of reason that gives rise to nick-names in our own day; *Caoch* (blind), *Trean-Fhear* (strong man), anglicised *Traynor*, and so on.

Many of these names are readily understood by Irish speakers of today; the meanings of others are lost in the mists of antiquity. Where there were two or more people of the same name they were distinguished by the addition of the father's name, as today we say in English John's Peter and Jim's Peter, or, following the Irish form, Peter John and Peter Jim. This custom is still quite common in the Gaelthacht. I know of Kerry men or Donegal men in Dublin known to their city acquaintances as Mr O'Sullivan or Mr Boyle, who, when they go home for Christmas, become once more Sean Phaddy Sheamais.

The generation before ours in Meath remembered this kind of name very well. I have myself heard of old people, dead perhaps seventy or eighty years, with three-generation names like Molly Paddy Pharaic, sad evidence of the turning away from the Irish language.

The usage I have just described is not peculiar to ancient Ireland. It is found in all countries before populations got too big, and every reader will be able to think of examples from the Bible. When Peter first came to Our Lord, He addressed him as Simon bar Jona (son of Jona) and added, 'Thou shalt be called Peter' (meaning 'rock,' the rock on which the Church was to be built).

In Ireland, as in Judea, the people were very conscious of the clan to which they belonged and, though named as I have described referred to themselves also as the Siol Cuinn (Seed of Conn) or the Ui Neil (grand-children or descendants of Niall). In the time of Brian Boru, about the year 1000, the practice of using surnames, as we understand the term, began, that is, the name of the father or grandfather was adopted as a permanent surname for all future generations of each family, for official use, though the ancient practice continued, and, as I have shown, still continues wherever the Irish language has survived. Those who took their father's name naturally had the prefix 'Mac'; those who felt that the grandfather or great-grandfather was a more famous man took big name with the prefix 'Ua', meaning grandson. The 'O' in the anglicised form of Irish surnames is the dative case of Ua, and in general the O families were the most important.

All this was before the Normans came, bringing a new type of surname, and for the moment we will pass over the Norman names, and see something of what happened to the Gaelic surnames in later centuries, when they were turned into some kind of English form. The law forbade the Irish O and *Mac*, and the remainder of the name was either written down more or less phonetically in English characters, or translated, more or less correctly, into an English word, or replaced by an English name of more or less similar sound. I may add that, in most cases, it was decidedly less. The officials who produced the English version did not worry about correctness. Some examples from common names will illustrate the way the system, or want of system, worked. Dubhan means a dark or black-haired person. It was a common surname all over Ireland, and when rendered into English spelling took various forms according to local pronunciation: Duane, Dwan, Duffney, Devane, and so on. Sometimes it was translated into Black, and Black occasionally changed to Blake, which is a different name, and not an Irish one at all. Dr Joyce tells of an amusing translation into Hook, because a similarly spelled Irish word means a fishhook!

Again, Iomhar was a common Irish name; following the sound it became Sever, and following the spelling, Ivor. With the Mac this gives MacEever, MaeEver, or MacIvor, and erroneously MacKeever. The Mac was sometimes translated into 'son', giving Ivorson, contracted to Ivors, or Eevers, and sometimes, even Keever's. That contraction is common in English and Scandinavian names – Nicholson to Nichols, Johnson to Johns, etc. The village of Ballivor takes its name from an Iomhar, or an Iomhar family, but I have never found out any details.

The Danes were here before the use of surnames became general, and their names became absorbed into the language, and their subsequent history is exactly the same as that of the native names. The Danish Olaf, for instance, is the Irish Amhlaoibh, a common Christian name in the south, anglicised to Humphrey – a transformation I won't attempt to explain – giving the surnames MacAuliffe and Humphreys.

The vagaries of the anglicising process make it difficult to be sure what was the original Irish of certain names. The kings of this part of Ireland, for instance, may, for all I know, be Quinns; the Quinns are, of course, descendants of Conn possibly the great Conn Cead Catha, Ard-Rí who reigned at Tara. In the absence of records, it is impossible to be sure, and few people have the time to consult the records that still exist. O'Growney wrote an essay on the Mul- and Gil- names, and as there are many of these in the county – Mulveys, Malones, Gilmores, etc. – I shall summarise it for readers before going on to Norman names.

SOME OF THE NAMES WE PROUDLY BEAR
OLDER THAT THE CRUSADE KNIGHTHOODS

In a world preoccupied with atomic weapons and interplanetary travel, we may be tempted to think that the slight, unexciting history of our parish is not worth recording. What is the good of looking back? What is there in Ireland's past in comparison with the great present and great future of the big nations whose way of life is dominates the world?

Yet Mr Van Yych Brooks, one of America's most distinguished writers, has written recently that the United States was dominated by English ideas until after the First World War, and only began 'to set, not follow, precedents … when a disillusioned generation went back to the soil in search of its roots'. In this, the Irish revival was an inspiration to some of the finest American thinkers. Mr Brooks mentions in particular Padraig and Mary Colum, W.B. Yeats and his brother, the painter Jack B. Yeats.

This cheering information I take from a recent and very able review by Francis MacManus of Brooks's book *Days of the Phoenix*. We are told that Yeats, urging his father to write the story of his life, said, 'It would tell people about those things that are not old enough to be in the history books or new enough to be in the reader's mind, and these things are always the things that are least known.' The book in question goes back, not to the things of the last century, but to just thirty years ago.

If such memories are important for a country like America, how much more so is it for us? Ireland is surely the land of the Phoenix, that mythical bird that can never be destroyed, but that always rises triumphantly from its ashes. This idea gave the name Phoenix Club to the society founded by O'Donovan Rossa, out of which the Fenian movement developed. If we value in the little things that make up our own civilisation we, too, will begin to set, and not to follow, precedents.

Fr O'Growney maintained that as our names are our most personal possession, the mangled and meaningless forms in which we use them in English is the main cause for our ignorance of our cultural heritage. He developed this theme in an article titled 'The Muls and the Gils' in the *Ecclesiastical Record* in 1898, the first sentence of which reads, 'At least one hundred thousand people of Irish birth or descent bear, in their everyday surnames, a record of the zeal for piety and learning which distinguished early Christian Ireland.'

It would appear that when the Irish were converted by St Patrick they did not adopt the custom of naming their children after the Apostles or other saints of the early Church. That would be presumptuous; instead they called themselves Servant of God, of Mary, of John, and of their own saints Patrick, Brigid, and the hosts of later men and women famous for holiness. *Mill* is a contracted form of *Mael* or *Maol*; *Gil* of *Giolla*, both of which may be freely translated as 'servant' or 'votary'. *Maol-Eoin* would be assumed as a name by persons devoted to St John the Baptist; *Giolla-Brighde* by followers of St Brigid.

When surnames were adopted in the tenth or eleventh century, the families of people so named called themselves *Mac* or *O Maoil-Eoin*, and *Mac* or *O Giolla-Brighde*. In English, these names appear as Malone or Maloney, and Gilbride or Kilbride. When Fr O'Growney was writing it is probable that not one in a thousand of his readers knew this simple fact. Everyone who has gone to school since 1922 has, of course, learned the spelling and meaning of his own name, so I will not labour the point, but pass to some examples common in our own county.

Maol-Mhuire, servant of Mary, has become *Mullery, Meyler,* and *Miles* or *Myles*. St Martin of Tours, the kinsman and tutor of St Patrick, was a favorite saint of the Irish, and those families deriving from his devotees are Gilmartins, Kilmartins, or Martins without any prefix. Martin is still a common Christian name in the west of Ireland, and a late revival elsewhere. The Gilpatricks have in places changed their names to FitzPatrick, which is quite wrong, as 'Fitz' is a French prefix meaning son like *Mac*, and is only found in Norman names like FitzGerald or FitzSimons. Servant of Colm was naturally common in Scotland, the adopted country of Colmckille, and has given the names Malcolm, Malcomson and MacColum.

Fr O'Growney adds, 'The rage for anglicisation has led to the fearsome form "Pidgeon"' used as a surname by some beknighted individuals.' The saint was called Colm (dove) from his gentleness, and love of the house of God. Who that has seen these gentle birds, symbols of the Holy Spirit, flying around the very Tabernacle, can have failed to see the appropriateness of the name, so frequent in the annals of the saints of Ireland?

St Finian of Clonard, whom the chronicles liken to Paul the Apostle, was the teacher of many great men, who adopted the names of *Maol-* or *Giolla Fionain.* There is a name, Gilfinnan, close to the original, but there are numerous corrupt forms: MacClennan, Lennon, Glennon, and the translated form, Leonard. In this connection, I think I remember an article by the late Mr Fenton on the Glennon family, written, at the time when Cardinal Glennon, a native of Meath, was visiting Ireland. Mr Fenton traced the name, not to St Finian, but to St Flannan. The fact that the name is locally pronounced Glannon, and often Flannon, would support this derivation, as far as Meath Glennons are concerned, but such a good scholar as Fr O'Growney must have had evidence for his statement. Is Lennon still pronounced Lannon?

St Erc, Bishop of Slane, gives the name Mullarkey. St Seachnall, who gives his name to Dunshaughlin, is hardly recognisable in the names Malachy, MacLoughlin, Claflin and Loughlin. St Alladh of Killala is the patron of those now called Mullally or Lally. St Senan's disciples are the Gilsenans, and local pronunciation here gives the proper sound to the 's', but some of the names, according to Fr O'Growney, translated themselves into 'Shannon'.

Where a saint was held in great affection it was usual to call him by a diminutive -*ín,* or *óg,* or to put *mo* before his name. We have not lost that custom, as witness our *Mairíns* and *Seainíns,* and even those who do not speak a word of Irish use the familiar, or alas! contemptuous forms *Mickeen, Jimeen,* and occasionally we hear the expression, 'There was my Rosie, or my Jimmie.' So the common name *Aedh,* now replaced by the completely different name of Hugh, is often found in the forms *Aedhan, Aedhog* or *M'Aedhog.* Servants of the saint with the name *Maol Maedhog* have often translated themselves into Molloy, but the Westmeath form, Leogue, is nearer in sound to the correct name.

Fr O'Growney says that the name was common in the Diocese of Ferns as a Christian name, written Mogue, but that some progressive people were changing to Moses! Boolavogue of '98 fame means 'the milking-field of M'Aedhog'. Clinton is 'Mac Giolla Fhionn-tain', the son or descendant of the servant of St Fintan. Muldoon and its variations come from 'Maol Domhnaigh', the servant of the Church.

The word *Mael* in ancient Irish meant 'a hero', and formed part of purely pagan or secular names like Maeldun (Muldoon), 'the hero of the fort'. In Christian times, a similar word, *maol*, signified a monk or cleric. *Maol* means bald, and it survives in the spoken language of Meath in 'meel', applied to 'a ditch or bank without bushes', or to a 'cow without horns'. The pronunciation is sometimes 'miley'. The tonsure, or shaving of the head, gave Maol the significance of tonsured cleric. The two words *mael* and *maol* became merged in personal names, and became synonymous with servant or follower. Naturally, clerics would assume such names in honour of their patron saints, as members of religious orders do to the present day. So, as in the case of Muldoon, some English versions are capable of more than one interpretation.

Giolla is not such an old word, and it came in time to mean 'a servant' in the menial sense, in which way it is still applied to boys who act as paid attendants to fishing or shooting parties, chiefly in the Scotch Gaeltacht. So *Giolla Rua* would simply mean 'the red fellow', and give MacElroy, Gilroy, etc., and *Giolla Buidhe* give MacIlwee or MacEvoy. By an Act of Edward III of England in 1465, it was decreed, ' that every Irish-man in the Counties of Dublin, Meath, Kildare, shall take to him an English surname of one town or colour, white, brown'.

Fr O'Growney believes that all the colour names in this part of Ireland are translations from *Giolla* names. He gives many instances of both forms surviving, e.g. *Glashan* and *Green*. A common one here is *Dunne*, translated Brown. However, as colour names were common in England, we cannot, without records, say whether a particular family of Browns or Blacks or Greys are Irish, or if they came in with the Planters. It matters little. The Irish nation absorbed the Normans and the Cromwellians, and we freely accord them the *Mac* or *O*, which is the title of an Irish citizenship older than the knighthoods of the Crusaders.

THE GEAROID IARLA TRADITION
GERALDINES IN SONG AND STORY

The legend of Garrett the Earl and his army, asleep in a cave under the hill awaiting the call to arise and free Ireland from her oppressors, originates from the same time as the dissolution of the monasteries. The Garrett in question is Garrett Fitzgerald, but when I first heard the story I thought his name was Garrett *Jeerla*, and it was long afterwards that I realised that this was the Irish *Gearoid Iarla* – Garrett the Earl. There is an ancient fort in Louth called Gearoid Iarla's Fort, and it is said that one night a man wandering in among the trees saw a sword hilt sticking out of the ground and a hunting horn hanging from a tree. He blew a blast on the horn and it echoed loudly through the fort. Stooping, he caught the sword hilt and was in the act of pulling it out of the ground when he saw all round him riders in armour rising out of the earth. In terror he released the sword which sprang back into the ground and with it the horsemen sank and disappeared. At the same time he heard a sad voice say, 'If you drew the sword as you blew the horn, you were the happiest man that ever was born.'

So runs the Louth version of the story. Here in south Meath the children say that the Earl and his horsemen are under the river called the Stoneyford, which joins the Boyne near Portlester. They are waiting till someone finds the silver shoe which the Earl's horse lost when crossing the river.

In Kildare the Earl is believed to ride round the Curragh once in seven years. William Rooney, the patriotic poet of the beginning of this century, tells the Kildare story in a ballad beginning:

Oh, quiet lies the cave amid the heather,
When Earl Fitzgerald dreams in slumber still,
Among his steeds and armoured knights together,
Amid the ferns and fraughans on the hill.

There must be a reason why a legend like this has persisted for four centuries while so many seemingly important events are completely forgotten. Who was Garrett the Earl? And why has he become a symbol of Irish freedom?

The Fitzgeralds (or Geraldines) were one of the great Norman families who came to Ireland in the time of Strongbow, They became extremely powerful, and if we include the two branches – Kildare and Desmond – their territory extended from south Meath to Kerry. They had castles on the coast as far north as County Down, and their fleets patrolled the seas. They were intermarried with the great houses in England and so were nearly related to various English kings. For a very long time the head of the family was the King's Viceroy in Ireland but ruled more as an independent sovereign than as a deputy.

So far there is no reason why they should be loved. But there is another side to their history. They intermarried with the great Gaelic families of Ireland, and to quote Seamus MacManus:

> When they tasted the pure milk of Gaelicism they never forgot its savour, so they became kindly Irish of the Irish, root and branch. The Geraldines afford the most numerous instances of mere men of blood, apostles of the sword, turning, under the influence of Gaeldom, into gentle sages and wise scholars.

Mrs Stopford Green, one of our finest historians, commenting on the Gaelic influence, writes, 'Nugents and Cusacks and Englishes and other foreign names were entered on the roll of Irish poets. But it is to the Geraldines we must look for the highest union of the culture of England and Ireland', and she goes on to describe how in the Geraldine houses there was welcome for the mighty and the needy, 'for every first-rate and free-hearted man that is refined and intelligent, affable and hilarious'.

Gearoid Óg, ninth Earl of Kildare, was even more Irish than his predecessors and, by his close marriage relationship with the MacCarthys in the south and the O'Neills in the north, was able to unite almost the whole of Ireland. He was believed to be in league with his cousin of Desmond to get French aid to drive the English out of Ireland. It was obvious that Henry VIII could not leave such a man at liberty and plans were hatched to wipe out the Geraldines, root and branch.

Gearoid the Earl was arrested and lodged in the Tower of London, and his son Silken Thomas was forced into a premature rising which, after some early successes, resulted in the defeat of all the Irish hopes and the ghastly murder of six of the Kildare family; all except a little boy, another Gearoid, who was smuggled to the continent.

Gearoid Óg himself died in the Tower, some say of grief, some that he was secretly murdered. In any case, the truth of his death was in doubt for a time, and it was natural that some should hold the wild hope that he had escaped and was preparing to return with an army to reverse the defeat.

The very name of Fitzgerald was a symbol of unity, and the boy on the continent, honoured and aided by the Pope and half the rulers of Europe, was the centre of all hope, though it was an O'Neill who was to be crowned at Tara. But changes in international policy, and the introduction of the 'great grey guns' for the defence of the Pale, put an end to the movement which seemed on the brink of success.

With the removal of the Geraldine menace, Henry VIII was able to turn his attention to the seizing of the monastic property. Few men are proof against the bribe of large estates, and so there were many willing to change their loyalties in return for an abbey or a convent with its demesne and woods, its granges and water mills, and its host of tenant farmers.

Many years afterwards, the one surviving Fitzgerald returned and made his submission to Queen Elizabeth. He was restored to part of his estates and his descendants were the Dukes of Leinster.

It was this lingering tradition that made Lord Edward Fitzgerald a symbol in the minds of the people when he joined the United Irishmen in 1798. It was as if Gearoid Iarla had come back. The fact that the legend survives around Portlester may have a special significance. The great house there had long been the seat of a branch of the FitzEustace family who had great possessions in Kildare. One of them was created Baron Portlestor in 1462 and was Lord Deputy of Ireland. His daughter married Gearoid Mór, the Earl of Kildare, and was mother of our Gearoid Iarla.

At the time of Silken Thomas's rebellion, the head of the house in Portlester was actively opposed to his young kinsman, and one of Thomas Fitzgerald's first acts was to seize Portlester Castle. FitzEustace mustered a force to assist the English side and, when the Fitzgeralds were defeated, he was well rewarded for his services with great estates in Meath and Kildare and almost half of County Wicklow. It may be remembered that soon after the monastery of St Peter at Trim was taken over, one part of the church, called the Cross church, was assigned to Francis Helbert ,'for repairing the king's manor at Portlester.'

A full account of the Eustace family of Portlester written by Major General Sir Eustace F. Tickell, is to be found in the 1905 *Journal of the Kildare Archaeological Society*. For an excellent account of the Geraldines see *The Story of the Irish Race* by Seamus MacManus, a book that merits a place on the bookshelves of every Irish home. It is written in language simple enough for any reader, but there is not a single statement in it which is not based on deep scholarship and backed by the authority of our greatest historians. The author is now a very old man, but young enough in heart to be interested in the proposed monument to Theresa Brayton of Cloncurry, who was the friend of his own poet wife, the lovely Eithne Carbery.

THE HUNGRY GRASS AND THE STRAY SOD
ORIGINS OF TWO OLD SUPERSTITIONS

Have you ever walked on the Hungry grass? Or stood on a stray sod? The superstitions attaching to both are still so well known, if not believed, that I would hardly have thought of mentioning them here but for a strange origin given to them in other parts of Ireland, which I came across recently.

'Hungry grass' is a translation of the Irish *fear gorta*, and it is by this latter name that it is known to everyone born east of the Shannon, even though they are two generations removed from Irish speech. How many native Meath people have heard the name? It is worth putting on record. Many are the stories of people returning from the town, walking for ease on the grass margin, who have been suddenly stricken with this unnatural hunger, and have had greatest difficulty in dragging themselves to the nearest house for the crumb of food to break the curse. They say that if the misfortune should happen far away in the lonely fields the victim might be got dead in the morning.

The stray sod admits of more rational explanation. Some fields, owing to their peculiar shape or to the lie of the land, are deceptive at night, and one may walk round and round all night and fail to find the familiar gap. The stray sod is usually called by Irish speakers *fód mearúil*, but when Irish was spoken here the term was *fód seachrán*, softened in pronunciation to sound like *fasharran*. I wonder how many in the district, besides myself, have heard it?

Now for the alleged origin. It is said that hungry grass grows wherever a dead body has been allowed to touch the ground, and that the stray sod is the grave of an unbaptised infant. From very early times it was customary, not just in Ireland, to put a cairn or heap of stones over graves, and the more important the person buried the bigger the cairn. With the coming of Christianity, however, the custom was abandoned in the case of common burials, and the dead were laid in consecrated earth.

The cairn henceforth was raised only over the suicide, the unbaptised, or the victim of war or fever who, for practical reasons, could not be brought to the churchyard. When a person died in the open, whether from accident, foul play or natural causes, and the corpse was removed for Christian burial, a cairn was raised on the spot, so that the ground polluted by the contact with death might be covered up, lest, after time, a living person might unwittingly walk upon it. No one would dare to touch the cairn; on the contrary, everyone who passed was expected to add a stone, with a prayer for the soul of the dead. Neglect of the double duty was believed to lead to some unlucky visitation. In some places a tree was planted, instead of or in addition to the heap of stones. In recent years, of course, both have been supplanted by the cross.

Though I have used the word cairn to designate these monuments, because it is familiar to everyone, it appears that the more usual term in modern Irish is *leacht*, and that where cairn appears in a place name the reference is to an ancient pagan burial site. We have, in this county, Carnaross, Rathcairn, Kilcairn and Cairnstown, to name but a few, and the famous structures on the Loughcrew Hills are officially known as cairns. I seem to remember hearing of a place in south Meath called the Hill of the Leachta, and I would be grateful to any reader who could place it for me. It may also occur in the form *lath*, *latha*, or, in north Meath, *let* or *letha*. But more frequently the word is translated into the English 'monument'. More than twenty years ago, a man from Cloneycavan (Ballivor) asked me why a spot on the roadside there should be called 'the monument', and I was completely at a loss till I read an article in *Béaloideas*, 1946, by Maire MacNeill, in which many similarly named places are noted in Leinster. I have since heard the name again near Killucan, and would be interested in any other examples readers may send me.

SOCIAL LIFE IN THE LAST CENTURY

Historians describe the decade following the famine as a period of apathy. The struggle for existence was too exhausting to leave any spare energy for political or national organisation. The attempt of the Tenant Right League to organise for some improvement in land laws was a disastrous failure. I may write on this in the future but for now I want to consider the everyday life of the people, their daily work, their customs and beliefs, their arts and crafts, and everything else that we understand by the term 'culture'.

Life has a way of going on in spite of the greatest calamities. Children will play in the rubble of their bombed-out homes, and even in the headlong flight of refugees, babies must be fed and the sick tended to. There will be an occasional laugh and a gleam of joy in the very presence of death. In the worst of times in Ireland there was still the May bush and Hallowe'en, the pattern and the wake.

OLD CHRISTMAS

Christmas then was the greatest feast of the year. The poorest tried to have some little extra in the way of food and drink. For many it was the only occasion when meat was bought: some landlords killed a beast and sold the meat cheaply to their tenants; in the towns there were butchers, though very much fewer than now.

I do not know if a Christmas pudding was made in every house, or if the custom came down gradually from the houses of the upper classes. The oldest people I remember never used the name 'plum pudding', which derives from an old English pudding actually made with plums. In rural Ireland it was just 'the pudding', the only one of the year. It was made on Christmas Eve, according to a strict ritual tradition. The kitchen was cleaned in the morning and the chimney swept with a furze bush. The pudding bag was made from a new piece of blay calico brought from the town the previous market day with the rest of the Christmas goods.

The bag was about the size of a rather narrow pillow case, and it was carefully back-stitched and then greased and well floured so that water would not get into the pudding during boiling. The mixture in those days consisted of flour, currant, raisins, sugar, spices and eggs mixed with new milk. I think there was also some melted lard, but neither breadcrumbs nor any of the other ingredients used nowadays.

While the mixing was in progress, the biggest pot in the house was half filled with water and put to boil hanging on the crook over a huge fire of turf. The pudding was made big enough to fill the bag a little more than half full, and the mouth of the bag was well tied with cord, leaving ends to be hung on the crook, so that the pudding was under water but did not touch the bottom of the pot. A drop of holy water was sprinkled on it with a prayer, for if all food was the gift of God the Christmas food was a special gift.

Even the animals and the fowl got a little extra to eat on Christmas Day. By nightfall the holly and ivy were up behind the holy picture and in between the plates on the dresser. The Christmas candle – not the ordinary homemade rush light but a mould candle, also part of the 'Christmas goods' – was lit. By this time the men of the house were in from their outside work, and from the kettle on the boil beside the fire (for adding to the pudding pot) a little drop was taken to make the punch for the assembled family. Though the door was open to welcome the Holy Family, the big fire and the unusually bright light gave an air of festivity.

POTEEN AND POLICE

It is likely that some of the Christmas punch in the last century was made from poteen. This is a matter on which we naturally have no statistics. The revenue officer, popularly known in each district as 'the gauger', was responsible for keeping an eye on illicit distilling, but he was only bound to act on information received. Naturally, the ordinary people did not inform; neither did the upper classes for they were glad to enjoy their keg of poteen and had no scruples whatever about defrauding the revenue. The police, the Royal Irish Constabulary, were the eyes and ears of Dublin Castle, but in matters of this kind it paid them to keep in with the local gentry, who were also the Magistrates and as such in a position to do them a good turn in the way of promotion or transfer.

The Irish police had been remodelled into an efficient uniformed force under central control by Drummond, a liberal-minded Under-Secretary, in the year 1836. He meant the force to be solely for the purpose of keeping the peace, and admitted Catholics to the rank and file. Afterwards a certain number of Catholics were admitted as officers, too, provided they were of the right kind from the point of view of Dublin Castle.

After Drummond's time in office the force was so organised that it became a weapon of oppression. Officers were trained to be loyal to the British Government; they were made to feel themselves masters of the people, they knew the ways of the people for they were themselves of the people. Yet they never fraternised more than was necessary to get information; they were frequently moved from station to station; each constable lived in fear that his colleague on duty would report him if he neglected what he had been taught to believe was his duty.

VISITORS' IMPRESSIONS

An English visitor, Alexander Somerville, writing in 1847, is quoted as follows in P.S. O'Hegarty's *Ireland Under the Union*:

One of the first things which attracts the eye of a stranger in Ireland and makes him halt in his steps and turn round and look is the police whom he meets in every part of the island, on every road, in every village, even on the farm land and on the seashore, and on the little islands that lie out in the sea … They are armed: this is what makes them remarkable – armed from the heel to the head. They have belts and pouches, ball cartridges in the pouches, short guns called carbines, and bayonets and pistols and swords. The only difference between them and the regular military is that the military do not always carry guns, and pistols primed and loaded, not always bayonets in their belts, not always swords sharpened. The Irish police never go on duty without some of these.

In the Phoenix Park at Dublin, a barrack of large size with drill ground is devoted to the training of these armed police, from which barrack they are drafted into the provinces as soon as they are trained to prime load and fire; to fix bayonets and charge; to march, countermarch and so forth; these to be distributed and shaken out upon the land in half-dozens or dozens.

Sixty years later a French visitor described 'The Force' in almost identical terms:

Is it a matter for astonishment to find Irishmen willing to adopt the trade of protectors of landlordism, the Castle and the whole English system in Ireland, in such numbers that the rank and file of the police (12,000 men) are in great part composed of the sons of Catholic and nationalist peasants?

And P.S. O'Hegarty adds, 'They were not alone England's eyes and ears in Ireland, but her right arm, and they held Ireland for England until Michael Collins broke them in 1920.'

The Christmas whiskey has led us into serious matters again. We will return to the traditions of poteen-making and dodging the gauger.

SUPERSTITIONS

Superstition is as old as mankind. Even in what we call 'these enlightened days' it is still very much alive. There are people who will not sit thirteen at table, who think a black cat is lucky, who turn coins when they see a new moon – in short who believe that things have a power which, according to reason and religion, they do not and could not possess. Some of these beliefs may be survivals from a more credulous age, some are newly invented: the fear of lighting three cigarettes with one match, for instance, cannot be older than the invention of cigarettes. It is all very silly and harmless enough, but there was a time when superstition was very sinister indeed, and people lived in fear of the evil powers which might bring misfortune on their crops and cattle or even on themselves or their children.

Such beliefs were not, of course, peculiar to Ireland: on the contrary we have very little record of witchcraft here in comparison with other countries of Western Europe where, during the Middle Ages, witch-hunting and trials by ordeal were quite common. It is less than 200 years since the last case of a witch being burned in England, while, as far as I know, there is only one much earlier record here of the formal trial and burning of a woman accused of witchcraft, and those concerned belonged to the English colony.

I am concerned here only with beliefs still surviving in Meath a century ago. Certain people were said to have the Black Art power from the devil to bring sickness or cure it, to foretell the future, and even to cause their victims to waste away and die. The practice of burying a sheaf is still remembered. If one wanted to bring about the death of an enemy, a sheaf of corn was taken into the house in the dead of night and pins were stuck into every joint of every ear. Then the sheaf was laid out and waked like a corpse, and carried out and buried with certain evil words instead of prayers. (One tradition is that the person officiating said the 'Our Father' backwards!) As the sheaf rolled in the ground the person it represented pined away and died. A woman not yet seventy told me that when she was a little girl she was a maid with an old woman, and assisted her in these mysterious rites. She did not know what it meant and does not know if the evil charm was effective. This would be, I think, an isolated instance; the practice is dead much longer than that.

In England there was a variant of the same idea, but instead of a sheaf, a wax figure was made to represent the victim, and each pin stuck into it was supposed to cause pain to the living person. The wax figure was finally melted away to bring death.

The belief in the power of the Evil Eye is not yet completely dead. Certain people, by the mere fact of coveting an animal which they cannot get by lawful means, are said to cause the animal to pine and die. So if a buyer is very insistent on having a particular cow or horse it is better let him have it lest he 'overlooks' it. The giving of a luck-penny is said to be a token that the owner is satisfied to give the purchase with a good will. Otherwise he might, by grudging the animal to the buyer, cause it not to thrive with him.

When one admires a child it is customary to add 'God bless it' as a sign that one has no evil intentions towards it. There are people still alive who are fully convinced that a child of theirs who died in infancy was over-looked. They remember the occasion when a certain neighbour remarked how big or how healthy looking the child was and did not say 'God bless it' and next day the child took ill and died. As a rule no one likes to tell the name of the possessor of the Evil Eye: some think it is a power of which the possessor is not even aware; others believe it is conscious malevolence.

CHARMS AND SPELLS

There were charm-women in most districts in the last century, and I have heard how people came from near and far to seek their aid. One man told me that as a boy in about the year 1860, he was sent with a bottle and a shilling to get a cure for a sick cow from a charm-woman three or four miles from his home. He met a companion and between them they spent the shilling and, not having much fear of evil consequences, filled their bottle from a stream and brought it back home with the kind of instructions they knew the charm-woman would have given: put a drop of the water in the cow's left ear and throw the rest behind the fire. There may have been further rites which I do not remember, but the story goes to show that at that time the younger generation no longer believed. The same man told me he remembered hearing the priest denounce this charm-woman and forbid people to go to her. The days of the Black Art were numbered.

I have never heard of 'spells' (the ritual words used to bring about super-natural effects) being written down in this part of the country. But the Folklore Commission gives actual words in Irish of *orthaí* (spells) found in manuscript books belonging to charm-makers in the south of Ireland. In the last generation these books were often destroyed by their owners as proof that they were giving up their evil ways, but a few came into the hands of collectors. I doubt if anyone now living knows any words of magic formerly in use here.

SPIRITUALITY OF OUR ANCESTORS

If the old people feared the possible ill-effects of curses, they had absolute faith in the power of prayer. They lived in the presence of God and asked His help in every difficulty of the day. They thanked Him for every blessing and bowed to His will in every calamity. So there were prayers for every occasion in the Irish language, and they were used in the original form long after English became the usual medium of conversation. An old priest has told me that in his student days, about the year 1890, he knew more than one old person in the Nobber district who did not know any prayers in English, but could repeat the whole Catechism in Irish. Unfortunately nobody recorded the traditional prayers in those days, and few now living can remember more than chance phrases, '*M'anam do Dhia 'gus Mhuire*' – My soul to God and Mary; '*Go soirbi Dia dhuit*' – God help you; and so on.

In translation, short prayers for all occasions are familiar to most of us, though they are rapidly being forgotten during the past forty or fifty years. On entering a house one said, 'God save all here'; the parting visitor was wished, 'God be with you', though if he had not been very welcome it might be, 'God speed you' when he was out of hearing. Work began, 'In the name of God' and ended with thanks to Him. The passerby said, 'God bless the work' and the workers answered, 'You, too.' No one mentioned any future plan without adding, 'With the help of God' or, 'If God spares me.'

PRAYERS FOR SPECIAL OCCASIONS

Such ejaculations are common in all Christendom but in Ireland the wording was particularly appropriate and often very poetic. On eating the first dinner of new potatoes one said '*Go mbeirimid beo ar an am so aris*', which defies translation. The English equivalent is, 'May we all live till this time next year.' If you threaded a needle for an old woman she said, 'God bless your eyesight'.

If you lifted a heavy weight the thanks was, 'That your strength may never fail.' If the job took some little time the prayer was, 'May you not be that long lying [ill] the year.' If you gave a drop of milk to a poor neighbour she said, 'God bless you and may you never be without milk or butter.' I heard an old woman say in return for some small service, 'May God rise up a friend for you, alannah, if ever you're in need.'

Putting out the light at bedtime, the old people said, 'Lord between us and darkness', and on lighting a candle they said, 'The light of heaven to our souls.' In mentioning any calamity, like a contagious disease, they said, 'Lord between us and all harm.' Children meeting a wicked dog said, 'The Cross of St Andrew between us and the dog.' I don't know why St Andrew was the object of this special appeal. There was a prayer in time of thunder and lightning, a prayer when crossing a river, and many others which are now to be found in Irish prayer books, but I have never heard Meath versions of them either in Irish or English.

ACKNOWLEDGEMENTS

Acknowledgements are due to Frances Tallon and Tom French of Leabharlann Contae na Mí (Meath County Library) for their work in the preparation of this text for publication; to Maighreád Uí Chonmhidhe's daughters Maire, Eithne, Meadhbh and Aoife, her sons Padraig, Sean, Loman and Ultan for their support to the project, and to her numerous nieces and nephews.